The
Forgotten
Child

The
Forgotten
Child

The powerful true story of a boy
abandoned as a baby and left to die

Richard Gallear

with Jacquie Buttriss

HarperElement
An imprint of HarperCollins*Publishers*
1 London Bridge Street
London SE1 9GF

www.harpercollins.co.uk

First published by HarperElement 2019

19 20 21 22 LSC 10 9 8 7 6 5 4 3 2

© Richard Gallear 2019

Richard Gallear asserts the moral right to
be identified as the author of this work

A catalogue record of this book is
available from the British Library

ISBN 978-0-00-832076-8

Printed and bound in the United States of America
by LSC Communications

For more information visit: www.harpercollins.co.uk/green

In memory of Joseph Lester, who saved my life

Contents

1971–85: THE ESCAPE

1986–2019: THE TRUTH

1954:
ABANDONED

CHAPTER 1

Left to Die

'What was that?' The whispered words faded to echoes in the dark mists of that frozen night, 17 November 1954.

Postman Joseph Lester had just finished his shift at Birmingham's sorting office and started out on his walk home along Gas Street, through the gap in the wall and down to the canal towpath at Gas Street Basin. It was nine o'clock; the temperature was two degrees below zero. Tired and shivering cold, he was keen to get back to his family in Ledsham Street and relax in front of a roaring fire. This was his usual shortcut home, so he knew his way through the fog that thickened the darkness and stayed well clear of the water's edge. There was nobody about – just the unseen lapping of water and the muffled, almost inaudible sounds of the city all around … until that faint something, a sort of whimper.

Joseph pointed his torch where he thought it came from, but he found it almost impossible to see anything. He retraced his steps and tried again, shining the beam to and fro over the water and straining his eyes to pick any form out of the darkness. As he moved his torch for one last sweep over the canal, the beam caught something pale. Was it his imagination? Had it moved?

There it was again. An eerie sound, was it a wounded animal? Surely even a rat wouldn't venture out on this wintry night. But rats aren't usually pale coloured. Could it be a kitten, or maybe the shape was just a piece of paper?

Joseph hesitated. It was probably nothing worth stopping for, but something niggled at him, making him turn back from his homeward path. He picked his way over the main bridge and round the basin to the other side, where he knew there was another low bridge, which was about where he thought the pale object must be. Sure enough, as he approached it from the back, he heard that sound again, fainter still. Whatever it was, he needed to find it soon. He clambered down and under the bridge, ducking to shine his torch through the profuse undergrowth.

'There it is!' he said out loud to himself, reaching what looked like a parcel wrapped in newspaper, only two or three inches from the water's edge. But this was no normal parcel. As he peeled back the paper, he found inside a scrawny newborn baby, white, cold and whimpering. Joseph was shocked beyond belief: he'd seen rats as big as cats down there, capable of attacking this baby or pushing him into the canal.

He wrapped him up again and placed him inside his coat, holding him close to try to warm him, and turned to go back up to the street, where he knew there was a phone box to dial 999. Police Constable Watson came to meet Joseph and took his name, then noted down his brief account of finding the baby.

'Well done, mate,' he told him. 'You might have saved a life tonight.'

Joseph smiled and went on his way, back to his wife and children. Meanwhile, the policeman hailed a squad car and took the baby straight to the Accident Hospital, where he was rushed through and seen straight away. A nurse gently opened up the two layers of newspaper and removed the thin, stained blanket beneath. She gasped when she saw the baby's roughly cut umbilical cord.

'Do you think the mother gave birth alone?' she asked.

'Yes, it looks like it,' said the doctor. 'And he looks under-weight, probably premature.' Clearly shocked, he examined the boy. 'He's only about two hours old, and his temperature is very low,' he said as he gently rubbed the baby's fragile skin in an attempt to warm him up. 'He's suffering from exposure. It's touch and go, I'm afraid.'

Another nurse arrived and weighed him before swaddling him in a soft, warm blanket.

'Call the night sister,' ordered the doctor. 'And see if you can find the Chaplain. This baby needs to be baptised, he may not survive the night.'

The night sister came and the Chaplain too.

'What name shall I give him?' he asked.

'Any ideas?' the night sister asked the nurses.

'He looks like a Richard,' suggested one of them, so that was the name he was given.

'We must transfer him to Dudley Road Maternity Hospital,' said the doctor. 'They can put him in an incubator to give him the best chance. Can you arrange that please, Sister?'

As they waited for the paperwork to be completed, the nurses gathered round baby Richard, who had by now regained a little colour and started to cry and kick his legs up. Everyone smiled to see him protesting.

'He's a determined little mite,' said the doctor. 'He might just make it.'

One of the nurses accompanied the baby in an ambulance to the Dudley Road Maternity Hospital, where they were better equipped to look after him.

On admission to Ward D6 and placed in an incubator, Richard rallied and his temperature normalised. Not only did he survive the night, he became the nurses' favourite.

Meanwhile, the next day's newspapers were full of articles about the abandoned 'canal-side baby'. The headlines read: 'BABY LEFT ON CANAL BANK', 'NEW-BORN BABY FOUND WRAPPED IN NEWSPAPER', 'CHILD FOUND UNDER BRIDGE', 'POLICE SEARCH FOR MOTHER'. In fact, the police used the newspapers to put out pleas for the mother to come forward, or for any information, but there was no response. It seemed the baby would have no parents named on his birth certificate.

Almost hour by hour, Richard's condition improved and he began to flourish. 'DAY-OLD BABY IMPROVING' was one of the second day's headlines.

Later that day, a woman was brought into Dudley Road Maternity Hospital and admitted for treatment, suffering complications after giving birth. She gave her name and address, but would say no more. However, with the press still badgering the hospital for news of the abandoned baby's progress, an astute nurse suspected a link. The police were alerted and sent round a constable to question the woman in her hospital bed. At first silent, her weakened state left her vulnerable. Within minutes, she broke down and admitted she was the woman they were looking for. However, she didn't give much away at that stage – just that she had given birth that evening at her lodgings (a story that would later prove to be untrue) and wandered round with the baby, tired and confused, before laying him down under the canal bridge.

While in hospital, it seems, she did not request to see the baby. However, had she asked, she would not have been permitted to visit him while the police were investigating the case.

The next morning's newspapers triumphantly carried the story on their front pages: 'CANAL-SIDE BABY: MOTHER TRACED' and other similar headlines.

Now the police charged her with abandonment and started to gather evidence from postman Joseph Lester, PC Watson, the first policeman on the scene, the doctor at the hospital where the baby was first admitted, and anyone else they could find.

On 22 December, Richard's birth mother was in the dock at Birmingham Magistrates' Court, where she had no alternative but to plead guilty to 'abandoning the child in a manner likely to cause it unnecessary suffering or injury'. The press reported the case in considerable detail.

The prosecution set out the evidence, explaining how the baby was found by the canal, very close to the water's edge, and the state he was in: 'The weather was bad. Exposure had endangered the baby's life and it was not likely the child would have lived, but for the keen observation of Mr Lester.'

The mother's counsel told the court that she was afraid of losing her lodgings and possibly her job too. 'And the fact that the baby was born prematurely, when she got home from work,' he explained, 'caused her to act in an unnatural manner.'

'I hope you realise the gravity of your offence,' the magistrate scolded her. All the available evidence, which was not very much, was heard. Finally, the magistrate looked straight at the mother and said: 'You might have faced a charge of infanticide, for what you did could have resulted in the child's death.'

Oblivious to all this, baby Richard was basking in the affection showered on him by the nurses in Ward D6 and only a day or two after his arrival was well enough to thrive outside the incubator. He fed hungrily and was soon ready to be discharged from hospital. On 28 November, just 11 days after his birth, the duty doctor wrote a letter to Birmingham Children's Officer:

THE BIRMINGHAM (DUDLEY ROAD)
GROUP OF HOSPITALS

DUDLEY ROAD HOSPITAL,
BIRMINGHAM 18.

Your Ref.
Our Ref.

Tel. NORthern 3801
Ext.

28.11.52

Dear Sir,
Re Baby "Richard" Cunningham

This baby has remained well and free from infection since admission. He is gaining weight satisfactorily and is now as far as we can tell perfectly fit and well

Yours faithfully

[signature] M.B. CHB
(HP. to Dr Doney)

The following day, a form was filled in at Birmingham Children's Department to take over responsibility for him.

P19804   Ch. 12

CITY OF BIRMINGHAM

CHILDREN'S DEPARTMENT, 102, EDMUND STREET, BIRMINGHAM 3.

ADM. No. *1802*

To: *Mr Watson, Field House Nursery*

Please admit :

NAME	DATE OF BIRTH
CUNNINGHAM Richard	*17-11-54*

Religious Denomination *?*

Address from which admitted *Dudley Road Hospital Ward D.6.*

Name and address of parents, or nearest known relative or friend :
Mother Mrs Lucy Cunningham ? Address

School last attended :

Reason for admission (under Children Act, 1948 / Children and Young Persons Act, 1933)

Baby had been found abandoned was admitted Dudley Rd Hospital now fit for discharge. ? length of stay.

Order given at *11-30* o'clock *a.m.* on the *29th* day of *Nov.* 19 *54*

                          ERNEST J. HOLMES,
               from D.Rd. Hosp.   Children's Officer.

Sent herewith :
(1) N.R. Identity Card —   (4) Medical Certificate ✓   (6) Immunisation Card —
(2) Ration Book —   (5) Medical Consent —   (7) Weight and Feeding *from*
(3) Medical Card —   Instructions
                                  6 lb-5½ ozs Hosp.

That afternoon, the nurses gathered to wave off baby Richard as he was handed over to a woman from the Children's Department, who took him to Field House Nursery – the place that would become his first real home.

1954–59: THE EARLY YEARS

Field House © Annette Randle

CHAPTER 2

Field House

December 1954 (1 month old) – Appears a normal child for age. Plump and round.

September 1955 (10 months old) – A happy, fair child. Can sit and crawl. Goes after toys and is responsive and friendly.

August 1956 (nearly 2) – Growing taller. Jealous of baby in his 'family'. Happy and jolly in between times.

Field House progress report

Friends are often amazed at how vivid my early childhood memories are. My earliest recollection is from the age of about two and a half to three. I was running around the huge lawn in front of Field House, enjoying the freedom of space in the sunshine, when I was excited to find a metal watering can lying on the grass. I must have seen the gardener watering plants, because I knew what to do with it. With some difficulty, because it was quite big and heavy for me, even though it was nearly empty, I picked it up. Inside, I saw a little water at the bottom, so I half-carried, half-dragged it across the grass to a flower bed – I suppose I thought the flowers needed watering and I remember trying to lift the spout to pour water over them. I was thrilled when a trickle came out and wetted the earth around one of the plants. That memory has always stayed with me and I've loved gardens and gardening ever since.

I know it's a cliché, but the sun always seemed to shine at Field House and I was a happy child. That's what I remember most – being happy, whether playing with the other children or exploring on my own. Those memories have comforted me ever since.

As a child, I was always hungry. I don't know why because at mealtimes we had a lot of food and the staff encouraged us to eat as much as we wanted. Every now and then I would run through the grand front door (which was always open) and across the hall to the kitchen to see what I could find.

As I approached the kitchen one day I could smell the steak pie they were cooking for our lunch – my favourite. When I peeked in, round the kitchen door, I saw a trolley with several loaves of sliced bread, all wrapped in waxed paper. One was already open, with half taken out. I reached for it and looked inside to see if it had any burnt crusts – I always loved the burnt loaves best. This one looked just right, so I turned around with it, and as I carried it out, I saw one of the cooks smiling and winking at me. They were all so kind – I think I amused them with my cheeky ways. I ran outside again, across the lawn and found my favourite tree, whose branches swept the ground. After clambering up on one of those branches, I ate the crusts from each piece of bread. I was in Heaven! It seems strange now, but nobody ever told me off for taking the bread – or for climbing the tree for that matter.

I often sat in that tree and gazed at the beautiful house, with its tall windows arranged in a pattern on each grand facade.

At that stage, as far as I knew, I hadn't seen any other build-ings at all, so I didn't realise how lucky we were to live in such an elegant mansion, with its mown lawns, ancient cedar trees and wonderful views of the Clent Hills. Every day, I watched Matron drive in or out in her little car, a pale green Austin A30, which she parked on the gravel to one side of the house.

When I wasn't running around or climbing trees, I used to take myself off for a walk around the outside of the building. We were all friends at Field House, but from a very early age, I enjoyed being on my own as well. I loved to see what was happening in the large, walled vegetable garden behind the house. All our vegetables were grown there and I enjoyed watching them day by day as they came up out of the ground and revealed their produce. To me, the whole process seemed like magic! We grew our own fruits too. Often in the summer we'd have raspberries and strawberries and in the autumn the cooks made us delicious apple crumbles. Blackberries grew abundantly in the hedgerows lining our drive, so we would each be given a little basket to pick some – under supervision, of course. I remember eating most of mine, but some must have been taken back to the kitchen because they were often added to the crumbles.

All the year round, the kitchen's delicious smells lured me in, again and again. Often the best times were when the cooks were baking cakes. I have to admit that every now and then, when I thought they weren't looking, I would pop in and pinch an iced bun or a slice of Victoria sandwich from a plate – I loved that. The cooks never seemed to mind. The head cook was a large and jolly woman. In fact, all the staff seemed jolly to me. Whoever appointed the people to work at Field House, with children from all different backgrounds and circumstances, they chose very well. If any of us had a problem, from a scraped knee to a crisis of confidence or a terrifying nightmare, there was always somebody on hand to comfort us.

There were several housemothers and I think we each had one special one who would take particular care of us and encourage us to do the right things and to play well with each other. I can remember my housemother as if I saw her yesterday – very slim, with straight dark hair and a kind, smiley face. She was very bubbly and I loved her for that. I only wish I could remember her name. I suppose each housemother must have had responsibility for two or three children at a time and sometimes, especially when the new babies came in, I think I may have been a little jealous of the attention she paid them. However, as far as I can remember, I was quite an easy-going child and always happy to make my own amusements.

Sometimes, at night, I remember waking up to find I had wet the bed. This wasn't unusual at Field House, but it did upset me and I couldn't help crying. I don't know how they knew, but my housemother, or one of the others, would always come and change the sheets and calm me down with soothing whispers and a cuddle until I fell asleep again.

The matron was different. We all had to call her 'Matron' and so did all the staff – it wasn't Joan, or Mrs Smith, or anything like that, it always had to be 'Matron'. A tall woman, she was quite thin and stern. I remember she did sometimes have a kindly face, but most of the time she was strict and everyone was a little afraid of her. She was that old-fashioned sort of matron they used to have on hospital wards to make sure that everything was clean and tidy. Nothing got past our matron! We were all wary of her – nobody ever said 'boo' to

Matron. I think the staff were all wary of her too – they were constantly cleaning. As soon as that little green car came up the drive, crunching the gravel, and drew up outside, I noticed the great flurry as everybody started doing things!

While all the housemothers were kind to us, they sometimes had to be quite strict as well, to make sure we did the right things and followed the routines as much as possible. If we were asked to line up on the front lawn, that's what we did. And if it was time for lunch or an afternoon lemonade, we had to stop what we were doing and come straight away. I don't remember a bell – the staff just came out and found us around the grounds and gathered us in.

Although the house was big, we only really used the ground floor. In all, there were about 20 to 25 children, plus the babies, who were in a separate part of the house. There were at least as many staff as there were children. I can still remember the uniforms the housemothers wore: striped dresses with belts round their waists and pure white tabards slipped over the top.

Although the doctor usually came to do vaccinations and check-ups on our progress, writing down his findings on special forms, there were other times when he was called out to someone who was ill. We all had the usual illnesses, being together so much and passing them on to each other. I know from my medical records that I had whooping cough when I was two and I remember the doctor coming to see me when I had measles, aged three and a half. But the worst thing I ever had was salmonella food poisoning when I was about three, because I had to be taken to Hagley Green Hospital in the doctor's car. I must have been very ill with it as I was kept in for about five weeks.

Throughout the summer, the staff would sometimes organise games for us, like taking turns hitting the ball. But I never joined in those games for very long as I lost interest in balls and bats. Instead, I would go off to a little den I'd made and study the insects that hid under the logs.

I wasn't really interested in group games. For me the biggest entertainment was the gardens, the beautiful place we lived and the countryside around it – I just loved playing there. I looked at the buttercups and how they were made; I watched the butterflies flitting about and settling, so that I could study the patterns on their wings.

One day, my housemother came over and sat on the grass with me, watching the bees buzzing over a clump of lavender. 'I like bees,' she said. 'They are good for the flowers, taking pollen from one to another and back to their hives, where they make honey.'

'Really?' I asked in wonder. 'Do the bees make our honey that we sometimes have at teatime?'

'Yes, that's right,' she nodded with a smile.

'But they sting, don't they?' I continued. 'David had a bee sting.'

'Not usually, only if they feel threatened. David was trying to hit them with his bat. Bees only sting if they think we are trying to hurt them, but wasps are the ones you want to look out for. They can give you a nasty sting, so best to stay clear of them.'

'How do I know if it's a wasp?'

As my housemother explained the differences, I took it all in and never forgot it. From an early age I was fascinated by nature and loved to learn about it.

As well as organised games and a large amount of space to

build dens and trees to climb, we had swings and small climbing frames, which we took turns on.

I don't remember having any best friends at Field House because we were all friends together – I liked everybody and none of them were horrible or selfish, so we just got on. We missed the older ones when they had to leave, but new children came in to replace them and it was all part of the pattern of our lives. We were all different ages under five, so it was like a big family. Yes, that's exactly the right word: it was the ethos of the place, we all felt loved and looked after. We took it for granted, cocooned as we were from the outside world, not knowing that children's homes could be any different.

Of course, children were occasionally naughty and they would have their legs slapped. If they were very naughty, they would have to go and see Matron. That induced the fear, oh yes! Just the thought of it put them off doing anything naughty again.

I wasn't immune. Sometimes I did get into minor trouble, possibly for over-eating – I did a lot of that! Or maybe I didn't come when I was called. I have to admit that there were occasions when I ignored the call because I wanted a bit of extra time – I suppose all children do that. It was usually when I was in the garden. I used to love it so much that I was often in a dream, but when they called us, we had to toe the line, we had to go in. If they wanted to wash me down, there was no messing about: it was soap and water time and that was that.

As I approached four, I became more aware of the beauty of Field House, both inside and out. It was a classical design – Georgian, I think. Through the elegant porch and the huge front door was a beautiful hallway that stretched so far ahead, it seemed to me to go on for ever. There was oak panelling along the left-hand side and an old oak sideboard. A huge chandelier reflected the light in the centre of the hall and to the right was a grand oak staircase with beautiful carved banisters and turned finials, polished to a high sheen. In fact, it was the sweet smell of beeswax polish that pervaded the whole house. When I stood at the bottom of the stairs and craned my neck, I could see all the way up the staircase as it curved round and round the squares of space, through each floor, creating a pyramid effect, at the top of which was a beautiful painted ceiling. Every landing was surrounded by huge oak doors and the only light flooded down from skylights at the very top.

'You must never go up those stairs,' I remember Matron telling us one day. It was an order. But, on one occasion, looking upwards, I began to wonder what was on the upper floors. It was just curiosity, but almost involuntarily, I found myself climbing up the first flight of stairs. Halfway up, I realised what I had done and looked over the banisters, but there was nobody in sight, just distant sounds from the kitchens. Everybody else seemed to be outside, so I tiptoed on up the polished treads to the first landing. There were doors everywhere, all of them closed. I was desperate to go and see what was inside one of the rooms, but I didn't dare – somebody might be lurking behind, ready to pounce on me. I dreaded to think what my punishment would be. I turned to go back down, but it was too late.

One of the doors opened and Matron herself came out.

'What are you doing here?' she asked in her sternest voice as she towered over me.

I could barely get the words out. 'S-s-sorry Matron …'

'You know you're not supposed to be up here?'

'Yes, Matron.' I hung my head, expecting the worst.

'Well, go straight back down those stairs and never come up here again. Do you understand?'

'Y-y-yes Matron. I'm sorry.'

She was pointing at the stairs, so I began to clamber down them as quickly as I dared, until my housemother arrived and took my hand to help me down the rest and sent me out to play with the others on the grass.

Later, at bedtime, she kindly reinforced the message, as Matron had probably asked her to do. But she said it with a tolerant smile.

'I'm sure you were just curious,' she said.

'Yes, I only wanted to see ...'

'There's nothing much up there,' she explained. 'Just offices, staff bedrooms and lots of cupboards, where we keep the clothes and sheets and things.'

I nodded. I couldn't help being inquisitive and adventurous, which did lead me into other tricky situations from time to time, but I never ventured up the stairs again.

The sleeping arrangements at Field House were very straightforward. Being such a grand house, all the downstairs rooms were very large, with high ceilings and long sash windows, letting in generous beams of light. The babies were all in a room beyond the staircase, in their cots.

The first door to the left of the front door led into the girls' dormitory, which I never saw inside. The boys' dormitory was the same but opposite, to the right of the front door and looking out over the front lawns. There were usually about 10 to 12 of us in there, our little metal-framed beds placed at intervals around the walls of the room, with tables and chairs in the centre for us to play at if the weather was bad, though in my memories it hardly ever was. The room itself had been stripped bare of its grandeur and painted white, but it still had its wooden floors and the ceiling's decorative cornices. There were full-length curtains at every window.

My bed was by the window at the far side of the room, so I had a remarkable view in the daylight, but there were no lights outside, which made it so dark at night that it seemed almost haunted. I was glad then that I wasn't alone.

Although most of the staff slept on the upper floors, they were always alert for any problems with the children – I suppose some of them might have been on night duty. I know they were there for us because one night the rain was pouring down in torrents, beating against the windows so hard that it kept us all awake for a while. Finally, I must have dozed off, perhaps for an hour or two. Suddenly I awoke to a great flash of lightning, followed immediately by loud thunder cracks that must have struck very close by. At first, I feared it had broken our windows, but they were still intact. I grabbed hold of my scruffy old second-hand teddy bear, Jeffrey, and hugged him tight. The lightning lit up the room again and again with crashing roars, which terrified us all. I hid myself and Jeffrey under the covers. Only moments after this crescendo, my housemother and two of the others rushed into our room and straight away, comforted us all, gathering us together in little groups and calming us down.

Sometimes, on more peaceful nights, I would hear the sounds of animals outside, such as badgers or foxes making their way round to the back of the building, where the hens were kept, but I don't remember them ever catching any, though the staff probably wouldn't have told us if they had. Often, I used to wake early and peep out to watch the stately deer or the rabbits and hares scampering across the lawns.

Any toys or games we had were donated by well-wishers, so they had often been well used. As well as Jeffrey, I also had two toy cars. I used to play with them a lot, pushing and spinning them round while making the noise of a car, and I would park them under my bed every night.

When the weather was bad, we played in our dormitories, the girls in theirs and we boys in ours. We had a big bag of little blocks of wood and I used to piece them together to make shapes and patterns. Sometimes we built towers. I remember going upwards as far as I could before they all crashed to the floor.

We also had colouring books and crayons, which we enjoyed. On Sundays we set out all the little Formica-topped tables and chairs in the middle of the room and were given watercolour paints in little tins, one each. We had to get the water to wet the paints with our brushes to colour in the pictures or make our own. I loved that. The staff would come round and say things like: 'Oh, that's very good', or 'What colour are you going to paint this?'

I used to love our painting on Sundays – I'm sure that's what started my love of art growing up.

As you have probably guessed by now, mealtimes were always my favourite time of the day. We sometimes ate breakfasts and teas in our dormitories, but we always had our lunch in the big dining room at the back of the house, all seated at long refectory tables – the boys at one and the girls at the other, with a housemother at each end. We had to say Grace at the beginning of every meal:

'*For what we are about to receive, may the Lord make us truly thankful. Amen.*'

We were encouraged to eat everything on our plates, but I didn't need much encouragement – the food was so good, I don't think I ever left anything! We were allowed second helpings if there were any and I always had them.

Next to our dormitory there was a bathroom, with a black and white tiled floor. I remember there was one bath in it – a big white iron affair. That was on one side and along the opposite wall was a row of wash basins. We would line up and wash our hands before every meal, then at bedtime we would brush our teeth, wash our faces and hands. The house-mothers watched us to make sure we did this thoroughly before we got into bed. As there was only the one bath, we had to take turns every two or three days.

We each had a small cupboard next to our bed for our clothes – it was a tiny cupboard with a drawer above it, where I kept my treasures. We didn't have many clothes but if we needed something else, there was a store of second- or third-hand clothes upstairs, so one of the housemothers would go and get it for us. In fact, none of them were our own clothes. One of the other boys might wear a pair of shorts one day and I would be wearing them the next, but none of us minded.

In the winters, although the building was so large, it was hardly ever cold as we had huge iron radiators, probably Victorian, and they kept us snug. At night, we all had hot water bottles, just to make sure. If ever we still felt cold at night, we only had to say and someone would bring us an extra blanket.

Field House was good in so many ways. One of these was the way we were taught to mix and play with any disabled children we had with us. Whatever their disability, we always included them in our games and talked with them. Nobody ever made fun of them or left them out. Sometimes, their disability might have been the reason why they were put in care, but we all played together. There was one boy who couldn't eat properly or use his hands and he used to dribble, but nobody said anything, he was just part of the group. If he couldn't join in a game, one of us would always sit out with him to keep him company – it was the normal thing to do.

Every night, one of the housemothers would sit on my bed and read me a short story. It was a lovely part of bedtime. Some of them were very short stories, like *Jack and the Beanstalk* or *Rumpelstiltskin*, but often I wouldn't hear the end of it because I had already fallen asleep. I suppose that was the idea! It certainly worked.

CHAPTER 3

The Monkey Man

September 1958 (nearly 4) – Grown into a fine boy – sturdy,
adventurous and agile. There has been a very marked
improvement in this child. Much happier. Laughs and plays
and sings. Speech quite fluent. Has a lot of imagination.
Co-operative and gets on well with other children. Plays very
well by himself.

Field House progress report

There was always so much to do in the gardens of Field
House that often we didn't have any extra entertainments
organised, though I do remember one occasion when a big
van arrived and out jumped a man in multicolour clothes. He
built a sort of booth out of wood and striped fabric on the
lawn. We all gathered round and the housemothers organised
us into rows on the grass.

'We're going to see a puppet show,' one of them announced.
'It's called Punch and Judy.'

None of us knew what a puppet show was, but as soon as it
got under way we were all laughing and shouting out at the
puppets' antics. We had a wonderful time and talked about it
for days afterwards.

26

'I liked the policeman best,' said the boy next to me in my dormitory as we were getting ready for bed that evening.

'I liked it when they threw the string of sausages,' I replied.

I often took myself for walks around the gardens or to the vegetable gardens at the back of the house. One very still day, sitting in the cedar tree to the left of the house, I could hear the sound of trickling water. When I craned my head in that direction, I couldn't see much, except for an ornamental gate in a wall, which hid what lay beyond. I had never been down that side of the house, so I clambered down and set off to find out what it was. A few days earlier, my housemother had read me a story about an explorer. I had asked her what an explorer was and she explained, 'An explorer is someone who goes to new places and finds out what animals live there and what flowers grow there.'

'Could I do that?' I asked.

'You could, if you want to, when you grow up.'

Well, I knew I wasn't grown up yet, but now I felt just like an explorer, walking alone into an unknown place to see what might be there. I was so excited at the thought that I didn't even consider whether I was allowed to go there.

When I reached the gate, it was closed, but I gave it a little push and, much to my surprise, it swung open, revealing a magical place, a beautiful garden so different from everywhere else. I walked in and looked around. It was a fascinating place. Everywhere I looked there was something new and different – things I'd never seen before. I could hardly believe it.

'I went to a beautiful garden today,' I told my housemother at bedtime that evening.

'Did you really?' she said with a smile, as if she wasn't sure whether I was just imagining it.

'Yes, I went through the gate in the wall and saw such beautiful things.'

She put her head on one side. 'Tell me what you saw.'

'I saw red trees and places where water was running and jumping up in the air. I saw strange flowers and lots of butterflies.'

'Ah, that must have been the Japanese garden,' she explained. 'The red trees are called acers and the jumping water was a fountain. I think there are quite a few pools and small fountains in the Japanese garden.'

'What does Japanese mean?' I asked her.

'It means from Japan. We live in a country called England, but right the way across the other side of the world there is a country called Japan.'

I don't suppose I really understood what the world was, let alone places so far away, but the next day she brought me a round thing she called a globe to look at and she showed me where England was on the globe, and then she turned it and pointed at Japan.

'You are allowed to go in the Japanese garden as long as you're careful,' she told me.

In the days and weeks that followed, I returned to the garden repeatedly. I walked around its carefully raked paths, between the ornamental cherry blossom trees, and watched the little waterfalls and fountains. I noticed different butterflies and caterpillars and several types of insects there too.

Against the background of trickling water, I heard the familiar buzzing of bees and a strange new sound. I followed where it came from and found a very peculiar-looking creature. I had never seen frogs before, let alone a toad, so I watched it closely, as it sat and watched me, like a staring match. This now became my favourite place. I suppose I could have brought some of the other children to see it, but I liked having it to myself for a little while.

Many years later, I found out that this was a very special Japanese water garden, designed by a famous woman called Gertrude Jekyll, so I suppose we were very honoured as small children to have that as part of our playground.

In the autumn at Field House there was a special treat – conker trees, as we called them. I loved running out in the mornings to inspect the newly fallen conkers from the chest-nut trees. I would pick up the most beautiful ones I could find and polish them with my shirt or my woolly jumper, before putting them into my pocket. The housemothers made holes in some of the chestnuts for us and threaded lengths of string through them, so that we could play conkers.

'Be careful,' one of them warned. 'Don't swing them around or you might hurt each other.' The housemothers showed us how to use them: 'Take turns to try to hit the other person's conker, like this.' They stayed out with us to make sure we did it the right way.

I liked playing conkers with all the others, but what I liked best of all was polishing the ones in my pocket and taking them out at night to put in the little drawer in my bedside cupboard as additions to my collection. I was just learning to count, so the conkers were ideal and I counted them every night before I got into bed, like a miser counting his gold sovereigns.

* * *

From my earliest memories, I loved looking from the lawn, across the fields and up to the Clent Hills, so it was a great excitement every summer, for those of us who could walk far enough – a four-mile round trip – to have regular outings to those very hills. Sadly, my friend with the callipers couldn't come on those days, but I know he had special treats at Field House while we were out and he was always as excited to tell us about his day as we were to tell him about ours.

On sunny days, almost every week, the kitchen staff would pack up sandwiches and drinks for us and put them in bags, which the housemothers carried. Straight after breakfast, we were lined up and counted, before setting off in a line down the long drive, past the lodge at the bottom, through the gate and out onto the country lane.

We must have looked a strange sight, a long crocodile of small children, walking two by two, dressed in a motley collection of hand-me-downs. Years later, when I saw *The Sound of Music*, with Maria making curtains into clothes for the children, it reminded me of our 'make-do-and-mend' outfits. But we were young and we knew no different, so it didn't matter.

As we walked, the housemothers started us off singing jolly songs, like 'Old MacDonald Had a Farm', 'The Grand Old Duke of York' and Ten Green Bottles'. We learnt a lot of songs on those walks. Sometimes we crossed fields and the grown-ups told us what crops the farmer was growing and how to look after the countryside, by walking round the edges and making sure we shut the gates behind us. In some of the fields the crops were taller than we were! As we walked along the lanes, they told us about the hedgerows, the wild flowers and the birds.

THE MONKEY MAN

Every time we approached Clent village, the excitement rose and, sure enough, there leaning on his gate was an old gentleman with long grey hair and a weathered look, smoking a wonderful, ivory-coloured pipe carved into a man's face. I now know that it must have been a Meerschaum pipe. There was something about the smell of that pipe – even out in the fresh air, it had an alluring, aromatic scent. But it wasn't just the man that fascinated me, it was the monkey sitting on his shoulder. I think this gentleman must have lived on his own in his little old cottage with just the monkey for company. He always seemed to wear the same scruffy clothes, with holes in his shirt – he even made us look smart!

Small and brown with darting eyes, the monkey sat on the man's shoulder, its arms round his neck, its eyes following us as we passed by. We weren't allowed to touch the monkey, but we could stop and watch it if it was moving about, which it often did, coming alive and showing off when it saw us approaching. It would twitch its fingers as if playing an instrument, then clamber around, doing somersaults. Sometimes it made a chattering sound, as if saying hello to us. This monkey was one of the highlights of our outings. Perhaps we were also a highlight of the monkey's day, watching this straggly troupe of small children walk past, waving and calling out jolly greetings as we went by.

Finally, we climbed the lane to the top of the hills and there we could run free and play for hours, punctuated by sandwich breaks. The adults organised ball games for us to join in, but we didn't have to, so I used to wander round looking for insects and rabbit holes.

At the end of the day, we packed everything up and set off on the long walk back to Field House, where we could look forward to a hot meal on our return, before a quick wash-down. We were so tired those evenings that we'd go straight to bed and lights out, then followed the deep sleep of exhaustion after a long, happy day.

The only other trip we ever went on while I was at Field House was quite a surprise. I must have been about four and a half when my housemother told me one morning to dress quickly because we were going on a special outing.

'It's just for the older ones,' she explained. 'We're taking you to Hagley railway station to see a steam train coming through.'

'What's a steam train?' I asked. I had heard of trains, but didn't know what steam had to do with it and I was quite excited to find out.

There were just a few of us on this trip and we set off straight after breakfast, walking along the lanes to the station. As we approached, the road widened and we saw cars and other vehicles passing by. I had always loved playing with my little toy cars, so this was a fascination for me. Soon I started to recognise some of them from the models I and my friends played with. We saw a bus too – it was bigger than I expected and had a lovely chugging sort of sound.

Looking back, I suppose that was the purpose of the day for us, to experience noisier, busier surroundings, as the staff knew that one day soon, most of us would live in more urban surroundings and we would almost certainly need to take buses and trains and learn how to cross roads. Indeed, we were all lined up along the edge of the pavement and told to look right, left, right. Most of us had problems with that, so the staff came along and patted us all on our right shoulders. Then we had to practise crossing the road.

We walked through the station building and were introduced to the station master, who took us all out onto the platform.

'Stand back,' he said. 'It's very important, don't go any nearer than this.'

So, we spread out in a line along the back of the platform and waited. I don't think any of us children knew what was going to happen, so there was a lot of nervous anticipation. We listened to the announcement the station master made with his megaphone. That fascinated me in itself – the way it made his voice louder.

'Look,' said my housemother, pointing along the track into the distance. 'Can you see the steam?'

'Oh yes,' I said, peering in that direction and seeing the white and grey cloud that seemed to be moving towards us. I was mystified that I couldn't see the train itself, but that soon changed as it drew closer. Small at first, it grew bigger and bigger, turning into a roaring, snorting monster. The giant engine emerged from its steamy shroud as it pulled into the station with a squeal of brakes. I stood back with a gaping mouth, in awe of the noise, the steam and the pungent smell of burning coal in its fiery furnace. I remember being frightened of it – fascinated, but fearful. The whole station seemed to shake.

Once the train had stopped and people started to get out, I was able to see that it was painted in a dark green colour, very shiny with gold writing on it. From where I was standing, I was lucky enough to be able to see into the driver's cab, where the train driver operated some shiny brass knobs and levers, while another man shovelled coal into the hungry furnace. I must have taken a step forward to get a better look, but my housemother immediately yet gently pulled me back.

New passengers boarded the train and settled into their carriages while the guard walked up and down, closing doors. Then he waved his flag, the engine fired up and the train began to move away, creeping slowly along the track, snorting bursts of steam as it went. The driver and his assistant leaned out of their cab and waved cheerily at us, followed by some of the passengers as their carriages moved past us. Of course, we all waved back like mad, which was great fun, waving and waving until the train had disappeared round a bend up the track.

That was an incredible day and I can still almost taste the coal dust, but I was glad at last to get back to the peace and quiet of Field House.

A day or two later, one of the housemothers brought in some second-hand model trains for us to play with and a book about steam trains that we gathered round to look at. Now we had not just the humming of car engines to make, but also the steam and roar, the squealing brakes and clanking noises of that amazing train as we shunted our new toy steam engines across the floor of our dormitory. It didn't stop there either: for days afterwards, the lawn became our station and we became the trains.

Christmas was always a special occasion to brighten the winter months at Field House. None of us had families to spend Christmas with, so the housemothers did all they could to make it special for us, although they must have had their own families too.

There was no build-up like there is today. The first we

knew of it being anything different was on Christmas Eve, when fir trees were brought in from somewhere in the grounds. One was placed in the girls' dormitory, another in the boys' and one in the dining room too. The tree in our room was almost up to the high ceiling and wide all around. I remember the lovely scent of the fir needles that pervaded the dormitory. The staff came in and decorated it for us while we watched them, our excitement mounting as they adorned the branches with glittery silver and red tinsel, gold-foil wrapped chocolate coins and, right at the top, a large silver star.

'Tomorrow is Christmas Day,' explained my housemother as she put me to bed that evening. 'If you are all good boys, there will be some presents under the tree when you wake up in the morning and a chocolate coin for each of you. We will come in and give them out.'

This was such an exciting prospect that it was hard to get to sleep that evening, but finally, we all did, and sure enough, when we awoke it was Christmas Day and there were presents all around the bottom of the tree. We leapt out of our beds with squeals of delight, but three of the housemothers were already there too, so nobody had the chance to touch the presents until it was time.

'You can all sit on the ends of your beds and look at the presents. There are enough for everybody and you can all choose one each, but no squabbling. I am sure you will share them with each other,' said one of the housemothers.

I could hardly contain my excitement. The presents were all sorts of toys and games and cuddly things – none of them wrapped – so I remember casting my eyes across all this bounty to see if anything particularly appealed. We had been so well brought up to share and take turns that none of us were selfish enough to grab something that someone else wanted. If I chose something that another boy had his eyes on, he might say, 'I would like that', and I would give it to him.

'Here you are,' I would say. 'I'll choose something else.' And the housemothers would smile at me and make sure I kept my next choice.

I remember the Christmas after my fourth birthday, how excited I was when I spotted something straight away that I would ask for as my choice. It was a round metal thing with coloured circles painted round it, a push-down button at the top and a sort of spike underneath. Having never seen one before, I wanted to know how it worked and what it did. I waited as patiently as I could until it was my turn, hoping desperately that nobody else would choose it first. Fortunately, it was still there, so I went and pointed at it.

'That's a spinning top,' said one of the staff. 'I'll show you how it works, if you like.'

'Yes, please!' I exclaimed.

She came over and pressed down the button on the top, which sent the top spinning on its spike, so that the coloured circles made patterns. When it went fast they seemed to disappear, but when it slowed down it was wobbling about all over the place, which made me laugh. I loved that spinning top. It was the best toy ever and I played with it a lot, but I let the others have goes with it, too, just as I did with my two toy cars.

One of the other boys would say: 'Please can I play with your red car?'

'Yes, you can,' I would reply.

He would play with it for a while, then he would bring it back and park it under my bed alongside my other car. It was the same if I asked to borrow anyone else's toy. We were all very good at that, we all shared everything.

What I remember best about our wonderful Christmases at Field House was the food. To start with, the smell of roasting turkey wafted through the house. It was so enticing that I found it very hard to have to wait until lunchtime.

Finally, it was time to go into the dining room, where there was another tall Christmas tree, with tinsel and various other decorations hanging on it, including crackers. We jumped up and down to see the tables specially decorated with red table-cloths and strewn down the middle with more crackers. We were so excited to pull those, but we had to wait till after we'd finished eating. It was a lovely, heart-warming occasion and we had a delicious meal, piled up high. Even I felt full after just one plateful!

Later that afternoon, we all stood together and sang carols round the dining-room Christmas tree, with its lights twinkling. It was a magical time. Most of the housemothers were there, including mine, joining in with us as we sang 'Away in a Manger', 'Once in Royal David's City', 'Jingle Bells'and other well-known festive songs.

We all loved the whole, very special Christmas experience, but it didn't last long. On Boxing Day the trees came down and everything went back to normal again, except we still had our presents to play with. And I loved my top – I enjoyed setting it off and watching it spin, round and round. I soon discovered that I could make it spin faster and longer if I wanted and after that I spent hours with it, perfecting the way I spun it.

* * *

Birthdays were celebrated in a low-key way. The staff would tell us 'This is Richard's birthday' or 'This is David's birthday' and at teatime there would be a cake with a single candle in it, whatever the age. The birthday child would blow out the candle and then we all sang 'Happy Birthday' and that was all – no presents. What I hadn't yet grasped was that with every birthday, the time when I would have to leave drew nearer. None of the children could stay at Field House beyond their fifth birthdays, so I was now perilously close to that time.

CHAPTER 4

Chosen

November 1958 (aged 4) – Physically very fit. Sturdy.
Speech fluent. Making much better progress. Is imaginative
in play. Likes to play alone. Still has an occasional temper
tantrum.

Field House progress report

Every now and then, we older children had to line up along
the lawn. Now four and a half years old, I was aware that,
after these line-ups, children sometimes left Field House, so I
didn't want to be in the line, but if I tried to hide, one of the
staff would be sure to come and find me.

'Come along, Richard. There are people coming to see you
today,' explained the housemother. 'And they could become
your mother and father. If they decide they would like you to
be part of their family, they'll be able to take you to live with
them in their home. Wouldn't that be lovely?'

I must have shrugged or shown my indifference in some
way. I know she wanted me to be excited, and I should have
been, shouldn't I? Some children were, but not me. I didn't
want anything to change, I wanted to stay at Field House for
ever.

But the housemother had to get me into the line, so she took a different approach.

'It won't take long, then you can go and play again.'

'Oh, all right,' I reluctantly agreed.

So, she encouraged me to change, and dressed in my 'Sunday best', mainly charity clothes, I joined the line-up on the lawn outside Field House, my eyes staring at the ground and my insides trembling lest someone should pick me.

Couples arrived and joined one of the housemothers to walk along the line, looking at each of us and whispering to each other as they went by. Occasionally, they would stop and talk to a child, then they might ask to take that child for a walk around the grounds. It was all rather unnerving and I was always highly relieved when nobody picked me and I could indeed run off and play.

On one of these line-up days, a couple did stop and talk to me. I think they just asked me my name, how old I was and what I liked doing best. They seemed happy with my answers and turned to the housemother.

'Can we take him for a walk and get to know him better?' asked the woman.

So off we went. I told them I liked cars, so they took me to see their big green car, parked in the drive. It looked a funny shape, like a shiny green bell. The man opened the bonnet and showed me the engine, which was quite exciting.

'Where else shall we go?' asked the woman. 'Is there anything you would like to show us?'

My first idea was the Japanese garden, but I thought they might like that too much and take me away.

'We could go round the lawn,' I suggested.

The woman took my hand and I led them to my favourite parts of the garden.

'This is my tree,' I explained when we reached the tall cedar tree with its low branches. 'I like to sit in this tree and eat burnt crusts.'

They exchanged glances.

'Then I took them down the drive.

'Sometimes we go for walks down to the lane,' I said. 'And up to the hills.'

'That must be fun,' said the woman.

'Yes, we sing songs and eat sandwiches and see a man with a monkey.'

'A monkey?' asked the man. 'A real monkey?'

'Yes, he sits on the man's shoulder when we walk past.'

There was a pause as we came to the bramble hedge.

'This is where we pick blackberries,' I told them. 'We have little baskets and pick the fruit to put in a crumble.'

'That sounds nice,' the woman said. 'What's your favourite food?'

'Steak pie and gravy,' I said, licking my lips.

They kept on asking me questions, and I tried to be polite, but I wished they would go away and I could get back to playing. Finally, I think they gave up on me.

I was so happy that I ran three times round the lawn before going in for tea.

Although I didn't want to be picked in these regular line-ups, sometimes, if they didn't pick me, I would wonder, *Why haven't they chosen me? What's wrong with me?*

I knew that I was getting older and would soon be too old to stay at Field House, but I didn't want to think about that – I couldn't quite believe it.

My lovely, kind housemother sat me down one day.

'Let's have a talk,' she said.

'Have I done something wrong?'

'No, not at all,' she reassured me with a smile. 'But you will soon be five, so it's nearly time for you to leave Field House and move on,' she explained. 'If you don't have a new mummy and daddy to take you out of the line next week, you will have to move to another house, maybe a house with lots of children, all much bigger and older than you.'

I didn't like the sound of that.

'Will you come with me?' I asked.

'No, I'm afraid that wouldn't be allowed,' she said in her gentle voice.

I thought about that a lot over the coming days and nights, but I couldn't quite accept it. *This was my home, the only home I had ever known. Why couldn't I stay here?* Finally, on the next line-up day, my housemother gave me some nearly-new clothes to put on.

'Try and keep clean and tidy,' she said, grinning. 'No climbing trees today!'

The Matron herself spoke to me after breakfast: 'Hello, Richard. I'm glad you are looking so smart today. I'm sure you will be glad to know that we have a couple coming to see you this afternoon, so we won't have to put you in the line for long. They will come and choose you and then I want you to be a good boy and be polite to them and get to know them while you show them round the gardens. Will you be able to do that?' She waited expectantly with a half-smile. I'd never seen her smiling even the smallest bit before, so I tried to be brave and smile back.

'Yes, all right,' I agreed.

So, we all lined up as usual and I was placed near the beginning this time. My housemother came out of the front door with a couple and they walked straight in my direction. This seemed very strange. They ignored all the other children and homed in on me. I suppose it must have been to do with my age and the fact that the staff wanted me to go to a family home, rather than a larger children's home, so they thought they were doing this for the right reasons. I thought so too, as I was frightened of the idea of all the big boys there might be at the children's home.

The couple walked over and stopped in front of me, just as Matron had said.

'This is Richard,' said the housemother. 'He's a happy boy and likes playing in the garden.' She turned to me and introduced them. 'This is Mr and Mrs Gallear,' she told me. 'Will you take them for a walk and show them round our gardens? They want to know all about you and the things you like.'

'All right,' I nodded uncertainly.

The woman was very short and she had a big smile. She seemed really pleased to be there and to see me. But the man wasn't smiling. He stood back, towering over her.

'Come on,' she said in a friendly voice, taking my hand in hers. 'My name is Pearl and Mr Gallear is called Arnold. Now, where will you take us first?'

As I walked out of the line, I looked back over my shoulder at all my friends, who watched me go away from them, across the lawn with these visitors – still strangers to me.

'Would you like to see the vegetable garden?' I asked them. 'I love watching things grow in the garden.'

'Yes, that would be lovely,' Mrs Gallear said in a bright voice. 'Wouldn't it, Arnold?'

He grunted, with a slight nod and followed as I led his wife to the path.

'That's the boys' dormitory.' I pointed through the long window as we passed by. 'I sleep next to this window.'

'That's nice,' said Mrs Gallear. 'How many of you are there?'

'Ten of us,' I replied. 'All boys.'

When we reached the vegetable garden, I picked up a small can and watered a row of newly planted seeds. 'These will be lettuces,' I said proudly. 'I helped the gardener sow the seeds.'

'Well done,' said Mrs Gallear with a beaming smile. 'We have a garden at home. Maybe you could come and grow some lettuces in our garden too?'

'Maybe,' I agreed, looking sideways at Mr Gallear, unsure whether he wanted me doing anything in his garden.

As we wandered among the rows of vegetables, I looked at each of the visitors in turn. Pearl Gallear was small and slight, with short, dark grey, curly hair, though I don't think she was very old. She wore glasses, a flowery dress and a long coat over the top. The thing I liked best about her was her smile. Thinking back now, it was a warm, genuine smile – I felt she really liked me.

Arnold Gallear had a serious face. He wore black-framed glasses and looked awfully tall to me, well-built but not much hair. It was only later, when he bent over to pick up a coin and put it in his pocket, that I saw the funny thing he'd done with his hair: he had a big bald spot and he'd combed thin strands of his light brown hair over the bald part. I longed for it to be windy and blow it all away.

'Do you like vegetables?' asked Pearl.

'Yes, we have lovely vegetables every day with our lunch.'

'Lucky you!' she said with a tinkling laugh. 'What other foods do you like?'

'Steak pie,' I said. 'And puddings and gravy … and cakes and burnt bread crusts …'

'Well,' she laughed again, 'I'm glad you enjoy your food!'

Pearl chatted to me all the time and made a very good impression on me. She was quiet, gentle and very kind – I really liked her.

I saw Arnold taking a sideways look at me. He didn't smile, but he didn't frown either. I felt unsure of him, because he wasn't friendly and warm like Pearl. But I was pleased somebody was taking an interest in me – and Pearl certainly was.

'Where else shall we go?' she asked.

'Come and see the Japanese garden,' I suggested, leading them round to the side of the house and through the gate in the wall.

'Ooh! Isn't this beautiful?' She seemed quite excited.

I took them round to look at the little waterfalls and showed them where the toad sometimes sat, but he wasn't there that day. I told her what I had learnt about the plants and the animals that lived there.

'Oh, you are a clever boy!' said Pearl with an admiring look. 'Isn't he, Arnold?'

But Arnold grunted and turned his head away without saying anything. It might have been a 'yes' sort of grunt, but maybe not.

45

Finally, we went a little way down the drive and I told them about our summer outings to the Clent Hills.

'This seems like a lovely place,' said Pearl as we walked back towards the house.

'Yes, I love it here,' I grinned.

'We've enjoyed talking to you,' she said, which I thought was rather odd as Arnold hadn't said a word. 'But I'm afraid it's time for us to go now. Perhaps we might be able to come and see you again. Would that be all right?'

'Yes,' I agreed readily. Pearl seemed to be a lovely woman – I thought I'd definitely prefer to be with her than with a lot of big boys in a home full of strangers. So, off they went and I ran in, just in time to wash my hands and join my friends for tea.

That night in the dormitory, getting into bed and falling asleep to another bedtime story that I didn't hear the end of, I didn't give the visitors another thought. The next day, I remembered they'd been and I wondered whether I would ever see them again. I would have liked to see Pearl, but wasn't so sure about Arnold. And I didn't want to hasten leaving my idyllic life with my friends and all the kind staff, so when nobody told me anything, I didn't ask.

It must have been a few days later, maybe a week, when my housemother sat me down and told me: 'Tomorrow, your new mother and father are going to come and collect you.'

I was shocked. 'What do you mean?'

'Do you remember Mr and Mrs Gallear, the nice couple who came to see you last week?'

'Yes, but nobody said anything, so I thought they didn't like me.'

'Well, they *did* like you and they want to take you home.'

'Are they my real mother and father?' I asked. Children in books always seemed to have mothers and fathers, so I assumed I must have too.

'Not your birth mother and father, no, but they want to be your foster parents.'

'I liked her, she was nice.'

'Good. Well, they will be your foster parents – your foster mother and foster father. You will call them Mummy and Daddy.'

'Oh.'

'Won't that be nice?'

'Tomorrow?' I asked, suddenly welling up with tears. 'Does it have to be tomorrow?'

'Yes,' she said gently, giving me a cuddle when she saw how upset I was. 'Don't worry, they are looking forward to taking you back with them to their house, which will become your new home. They will look after you. You're going to have your own bedroom and you will have a lovely time making lots of new friends where they live.'

I couldn't speak for crying. My stomach went all wobbly and I just couldn't take all this in. I suppose I didn't want to and it all seemed so sudden – I had no time at all.

'Can I take my cars and my spinning top?'

'Yes, of course you can. We'll put them in your case to take with you. I expect you will have some more toys to play with at their house, and maybe some new clothes of your own too.' She gave me another hug.

'Can't I stay here a bit longer?'

'No, little soldier, I'm afraid you can't, but they're not coming till after lunch tomorrow, so you can enjoy all this afternoon and tomorrow morning in the garden. Have a good run round, play with your friends and sit in your favourite tree, whatever you like. I'll come and find you out there when I've gathered all your things to pack, then we can talk some more. Would you like that?'

I nodded, as more tears trickled down my cheeks.

'Here, take my hankie.'

It was a fine summer's day and I walked around all my favourite places, ending up on a branch of the cedar tree. How could this happen to me? I knew others had gone to foster homes before me, but I couldn't talk to any of them to find out if they were happy there.

At bedtime I was tearful and my housemother soothed my fears as best she could.

'What if I don't like it there?' I asked her.

'You *will* like it,' she reassured me. 'It may take you a little time to settle and get used to belonging to a proper family, getting to know them better, and all their routines. You'll soon forget all about us. You will make new friends and I expect you'll be starting school soon. You'll love school, you can learn all sorts of new things at school.'

She did her best to inspire me with confidence, but it didn't really work. For once, I didn't fall asleep before the bedtime story finished – I don't think I was even listening. As I lay in my bed with the lights out, a shaft of waning daylight shining across my bed from a crack in the curtains, I hoped against hope that when I woke up in the morning it would all be a dream and I wouldn't have to leave after all.

1959–71: THE CRUEL YEARS

Richard at school, aged 8

CHAPTER 5

Goodbye to Happiness

July 1959 (4 years, 8 months) – Fine healthy boy. Much more stable and happier. Full of imagination, conversation, knowledge of everyday things.

Richard's last progress report before leaving Field House

30 August 1959 was a beautiful sunny day, but it didn't feel sunny to me. It was the day my cosy world fell apart. That afternoon I would have to leave the only home I'd ever known – a happy home of fun and laughter with my friends, a secure place where every adult loved us and cared for us. I knew nothing of my beginnings, but I did know I didn't want to leave Field House. I didn't want to go and live anywhere else, I wanted to stay there for ever.

It was my last morning so I went to all my favourite places. First, to the vegetable garden, where I had 'helped' so often. Everything was growing well, including 'my' lettuces, poking up through the soil, and the runner beans I'd planted and watched growing up their canes.

'I'm leaving today,' I told the kindly gardener, trying to put on a brave face.

'Are you now?' he said. 'We'll miss you.' He paused. 'Have you got time to pick a few of these beans for the kitchen before you go? Then you can eat them for lunch.'

'Yes, please,' I said, perking up at the thought.

Next, I visited the Japanese garden and said goodbye to my friend the toad, who sat and croaked as if he understood.

The rest of the morning went far too quickly and when I went in for lunch, I was overjoyed that it was steak pie, mash and gravy with 'my' beans. It was all delicious, so I had another helping.

The housemother at our table told the other boys that I was leaving and they all came up to say goodbye to me as we left the dining room. I didn't like them saying goodbye – I didn't want to say goodbye, I didn't want to go.

Finally, I went to my dormitory, where my housemother was packing my few belongings into a little, scuffed leather suitcase and ticking them off on a list.

'I've packed some spare clothes for you,' she explained in her kindest voice. I didn't realise it at the time, but perhaps she didn't want me to go either. 'I've put in your favourite toys too.'

'My cars?' I asked.

'Yes, both your cars and your spinning top.'

I pulled open the drawer by my bed: it was empty.

'Where are my conkers?' I asked, my anxiety rising.

'In your case.'

I tried desperately to think what else I might need. Then I realised …

'Where's Jeffrey?' I wailed. 'My teddy!' I felt under my bedcovers for him. 'He's not in my bed, I can't go without him.' I was panicking now.

'It's all right,' she tried to soothe me. 'Jeffrey is in the case too – I knew you wouldn't want to go without him. I had to squash him in, but I think he'll recover all right. I expect he's a bit worried about going to a new home too.'

'Oh, really?' I hadn't thought of that.

'I'm sure we have packed everything now,' she reassured me. 'Let me give you a big hug.' She put her arms round me and for those last few moments I felt secure. Would I feel like this with my new foster mother, in my new home? I had to hope so. I held on for as long as I could, then she gently pulled away.

'Come on, it's time to go.'

At two o'clock that afternoon, we stood on the drive, my housemother holding my hand and carrying my case in her other hand. This was a terrible moment – the phrase 'gut-wrenching' comes to mind when I think back to the forlorn little boy I was, standing, waiting.

'They'll be here in a minute or two,' she said. 'Now, I want you to be a good boy and be happy in your new home.'

I couldn't say anything, so I just nodded.

'You will have a good life and a good future with your foster parents.'

But I hardly knew them. I screwed up my eyes and hoped to vanish, but when I opened them again, I was still there.

The crunch of the gravel heralded the approach of a vehicle, which suddenly came into view and parked beside the house. I recognised it because one of the other boys had a toy version that looked the same. A small Ford van, it was hand-painted in two shades of blue. My housemother squeezed my hand and we walked across together. It wasn't far and yet it seemed like a huge gulf of despair to me. I knew I had to try and be very brave.

Mr and Mrs Gallear both got out of the van and Pearl gave me a lovely smile and a wave. I immediately felt all right with her. If only Arnold looked happier to see me, I might have felt a bit better, but he wore the same stern, distant expression that he'd had the first time they came. I felt instinctively that he didn't like me, which made me feel very uncomfortable. At that moment, young as I was, I knew it was Pearl who wanted me, not her husband.

'Wave back to your foster mother,' coaxed my housemother.

I did a little wave to her, but I felt too sad to smile.

As we walked towards them, Pearl came to meet us, wearing another flowery summer dress. She looked lovely, walking with footsteps as dainty as a dancer and beaming her happy smile at me. But standing by the van, like a dark shadow in the background, was Arnold, who was not even looking at me. Though I tried my best not to cry, I was sobbing inside. I clung to my housemother, but she gently released my grip and knelt down, with Pearl standing next to her, looking anxious.

'Be a brave boy,' said my housemother. 'I won't forget you and we will all be thinking of you, but these are your new parents and this is your new life.' She stood again and passed my hand over to Pearl, who grasped it warmly, along with my little case.

'There's a list of Richard's things in the top of the case, together with his medical notes for you to give to his new doctor.'

'Thank you,' said Pearl.

'Off you go now,' said my housemother. 'You will be fine.'

I gave her a little wave and walked with Pearl to their van. In fact, I was focusing on it. From the little toy van one of my friends had, I knew there were only two front seats. *Where would I sit?* For a moment I hoped they would not have room for me and would leave me behind, but not so. *Did Arnold know what I was thinking?* As he walked round to the back and opened out the two rear doors my heart sank.

'We've been looking forward to taking you home with us today,' Pearl said with a smile and a squeeze of my hand. 'We've put some carpet in the back of the van for you and a cushion to sit on,' she explained. 'To make you more comfortable.'

She gave him my case and he tossed it in the back. Now that my things were in there, I had to resign myself to going. I trusted Pearl, but I was wary of Arnold. At the time I didn't know the word 'vulnerable', but that's how I felt. I was reticent to clamber in, so Arnold lifted me up roughly and into the van, closing the doors behind me. Inside, I sat on the cushion with my legs stuck out in front. The only windows were at the front and little squares of glass in the rear doors, so I couldn't see much either way.

Although I was fascinated by vehicles and knew that this was a Ford Thames van, I had never actually been inside any vehicle so this was all a new experience for me. Normally, I would have been excited, but not today. Arnold and Pearl got in and closed their doors. He started the engine and we were off. I had to put my hands out behind me so as not to fall off my cushion, going over the bumps.

As we went down the drive, I turned around to look through the back windows and saw Field House for the last time, receding and getting smaller as we went. Desperate to keep it in view, the tears running down my face, I craned my neck to see the building, my dormitory, the lawn, my friends and everyone I loved all disappearing for ever. Through the gates we went, round the bend and off down the drive towards the lane that led to the outside world. I was miserable – I had left behind everything I knew and loved and had no idea where they were taking me.

It was a very warm day and soon it became uncomfortably hot and airless in the back of the van. I struggled to keep my balance as we moved along the twisting country lanes. Before we had even reached the main road, my tummy started to feel like collywobbles inside and I began to feel ill – I think it must have been the upset and uncertainty.

Suddenly I was sick. I vomited all down the front of my clothes and my legs, onto the cushion, the carpet – everywhere. I started to cry in earnest now, as Arnold rammed on the brakes and Pearl turned around with a sympathetic glance.

'I'm sorry,' I said as Arnold pulled into the side of the road, muttering loudly. 'Sorry,' I repeated, 'I didn't mean to do it.'

But that was only the start of my troubles. As Pearl whispered soothing words, Arnold yelled, 'You stupid child!'

He flung his door open and stomped round to the back of the van. As bad-tempered as he might be, I still thought he was going to clean me up and sort things out.

But I was wrong.

He yanked the doors open and with an angry face and staring eyes, dragged me out, down onto the ground. Then, right there on the gravel at the side of the road, he laid into me, fists flailing, blow after blow, shouting at me all the while.

'How dare you make a mess like that, pouring out your

filthy insides all over my van! You little brat!' he shouted. 'Haven't they taught you how to behave?'

'I didn't m-m-mean it,' I stammered. But he hit me all the harder.

I could understand why he was cross. I knew I shouldn't have done that, but I couldn't stop myself. Again and again he hit me, as I instinctively curled myself into a ball.

'Sorry,' I whimpered, again and again. 'Sorry, I didn't mean it.'

There I was, a little boy, not yet five, and he was a big strong man, raining punches on me. He was out of control. I didn't understand most of the words he said, but I heard Pearl's protests. The tears were pouring down my face and I could tell from her voice that she was crying too.

'Stop it, Arnold! Stop hitting him!' she pleaded. 'That's enough. Please stop, you're hurting the poor child. He's only little, and he couldn't help it – he was car sick.'

I was crying, she was crying, and still he hit me a few more times until he'd finally sated his rage. He stood back and Pearl leant down and gently helped me up, dabbing at my tears and washing the worst of the sick off me with some water and a hankie.

'There, there,' she tried to soothe me. 'You must be hurting. We'll sort you out properly and put some cream on your bruises when we get home.'

'Stop feeding the brat that drivel,' ordered Arnold, 'we've got a long journey to do!' He tore me away from her, frog-marched me round to the back of the van and this time he more or less threw me in and slammed the doors shut.

I was in shock, whimpering as quietly as I could, unable to believe or understand what had happened to me. No adult had ever hurt me in any way before, let alone hit me. I had never known fear of anyone. At Field House, I had always been treated with love and care by the wonderful staff, even when I was naughty. Already I missed them so much – I wanted to ask Pearl and Arnold to take me back there, but I didn't dare.

Was this how my life would be from now on? Were all mums and dads like this? As we set off again, I nursed my bruised and battered body, but I couldn't stop crying, even when he shouted at me to shut up. He clearly didn't want me, yet they had chosen me.

The journey from Field House to the Gallears' home in Birmingham was probably only about an hour and a half, but it seemed like for ever to me, in my misery and sickness, which didn't stop. I was very nearly sick again, but somehow managed to prevent it, fearful of another beating. Worse still, I was trembling with the shock, the pain and humiliation. I did not understand: how could the lovely matron and house-mothers let me go away with this evil man? Why did nobody protect me? I was sure they would have stopped him if they'd realised what he was like. If only I could tell them, I knew they would come and rescue me – but how could I let them know?

From the back of the van, I couldn't see much of the changing landscape, from rural to urban as we went through the city, though I glimpsed enough to know this was like nothing I'd ever seen before – an alien landscape. The one thing I did notice, as we drove along, towering over everything else, were the huge black windowless buildings in the mid-distance, which I later found out were gas tanks. Finally, we seemed to leave the city behind and travelled down side roads lined with little brick boxes with windows, some of them joined together in rows.

'Here we are,' announced Pearl as the van slowed down, turned and came to a halt in what seemed to be a dead end (in fact, it was a driveway). 'Welcome to your new home.'

From the back of the van, all I could see was a brick wall, so I didn't reply. But I was highly relieved that the van had stopped and I hoped I wouldn't feel sick any more. Arnold came round and threw open the back doors. Fresh air at last! But he stood there with a threatening scowl. Highly aware of the awful stench of vomit that covered me and the floor of the van, I desperately wanted to get away from it, to be outside, but I was reluctant to get out with that man standing by the open doors like a predator waiting to clutch his prey.

'Hurry up and get out,' he barked, 'and bring your stinking things!'

I had no choice, so I jumped down in front of him into the afternoon sunshine. It felt as if my stomach leapt after me – I was so afraid. I remember that once I had steadied myself, I was glad of the breeze to waft away some of the smell. Arnold towered over me in a menacing way, the sun glinting sharp rays off his glasses. Pearl was unlocking the front door of a tiny house – well, it seemed tiny to me, attached to another house just the same.

Having spent all my life so far in Field House, with its huge rooms and wide windows, surrounded by acres of its own land, this was a strange sight.

'Get inside!' ordered Arnold. 'You smell disgusting, get those stinking clothes off!' he sneered.

I was surprised to see that Pearl looked almost as frightened of him as I was.

'Don't worry,' she said, 'I'll take him in and sort him out.'

Arnold went off and she came to help me out.

'You poor boy,' she said in her soothing voice. 'You must feel awful in those smelly clothes, we'll soon clean you up and sort you out.' She picked up my case and took me by the hand. 'This is our house,' she added. 'It's your house too now.'

I suppose I should have said something nice, instead I looked down at the ground and all I could see was concrete. I didn't know that word, but it seemed to me that this hard stuff was everywhere – the driveway, the road surface, even on some of the houses. I had never seen anything like it. And the houses themselves were like toy houses.

I would soon come to realise this was a normal suburban road – a cul-de-sac – but I couldn't see any wide green spaces or trees or distant hills, only a few small flowers in gardens down the road. Worse still, I could hear a continuous rumbling sound in the background, which I later found out was traffic. At Field House there had always been peace and quiet, except for the birdsong in the trees, so this was all a huge shock to me.

'Let's go inside,' suggested Pearl, leading me in through the front door.

CHAPTER 6

The House of Dangers

Stepping into a small gloomy hallway, the first thing I noticed was the strong smell. I recognised it as a clean smell, similar to our bathroom at Field House. It was the smell of bleach. How strange that it should be in the hall of this house instead of beeswax polish. I suppose I thought everybody lived as we did, so now I would have to learn different ways.

Standing in the hallway with Pearl, I was wary of Arnold, standing behind us. She must have known.

'Let's go up to the bathroom first and clean you up properly,' she said. She led the way up the stairs and straight into a clean white bathroom. 'Take off all your clothes,' she said, opening my case and getting out my change of summer clothes. She ran warm water into the basin and used soap and a flannel to wash me down, then dried me with a fluffy towel – much nicer than the scratchy old ones I'd been used to.

'Can I go to the toilet?' I asked, desperate by now.

'Yes, of course, it's just next door to the bathroom.' She opened the door for me.

Meanwhile, she must have put my case in one of the bedrooms.

'That's better, isn't it?' she said. 'You're all clean and smell nice again. Let's go downstairs and I'll show you round the house.'

We walked down the thin, red cord carpet running down the middle of the stairs. At the bottom the hall floor was covered in lino, with a flowery pattern. There were three doors from the hall, one of which was closed.

'That's the front room,' explained Pearl, opening the door just wide enough for me to see a dark, formal room with old-fashioned furniture and quite a musty smell. 'You're not allowed to go in there on your own, only when one of us is with you.' She quickly closed the door again.

'This is the kitchen,' she said, taking me through an open doorway to the back of the house. It seemed very clean and sparse. Again, there was a lino floor, with a different flowery pattern and a flowery mat in front of the sink. Almost everything in this house seemed to be floral!

'This leads to the garage,' she said, opening a door at the side of the kitchen. 'You can play in there if you want to, when the weather is bad.' She opened another, narrower door at the back. 'And this is the pantry. We keep all of our food nice and cool in here.' She opened that door to show me the shelves, stacked high with tins and packets of all shapes and sizes.

Being a boy who loved his food, I was relieved to see that they had so much of it stored away, but I was puzzled there were no cooking or baking smells in here. I was quite hungry by now, having not eaten since lunch, but I knew I would probably have to wait until it was a meal time.

'We bought this house when it was newly built,' said Pearl, 'so we could choose to have a nice modern kitchen.'

I suppose it was very modern for its time, with a stainless-steel sink, cupboards and a small work surface, plus a Formica and tubular steel table and four matching chairs – all very neat and tidy.

'This is our sitting room,' she said, taking me back through the hall and opening the third door, which led into a lighter, airier room. 'Arnold and I come and sit in here in the evenings.' She indicated the sofa and two armchairs. Then I noticed the strange wooden cupboard thing in the corner, with a small piece of glass in the front.

'What's that?' I asked, pointing at it.

'That's our television.'

'What's a television?'

'You switch it on and it shows moving pictures of things, like in the cinema.'

'What's a cinema?' This was all new to me and my curious mind.

Pearl explained in more detail about films and television programmes, which intrigued me.

'Does it have programmes for children?' I asked.

'Yes,' she replied, lowering her voice. 'But Arnold might not let you watch those.' She didn't explain why. 'We don't watch it much,' she continued in a whisper. 'Arnold doesn't like most of the programmes they show.'

'What do you like?' I asked Pearl, innocently, too young to interpret her reticence.

She looked a bit uncomfortable. 'I don't know,' she eventually answered. 'Arnold doesn't like me watching it when he isn't here – he likes to decide what we watch.' She paused. 'He likes *Dixon of Dock Green*, so we watch that.'

Just then there was a metallic noise. 'What's that?' I asked, turning towards the corner of the room where it came from. That's when I saw the cage and its yellow and green occupant. 'You've got a budgie!' I exclaimed. It was the first time I had smiled since I came into this house.

'Yes, that's Joey,' she said.

'We had a budgie at Field House,' I told her. Then I turned to the bird and said, 'Hello, Joey.' He didn't reply, but he cocked his head to one side as if interested in what I was saying. 'Hello,' I repeated.

'He doesn't talk,' explained Pearl, 'but I think he likes you.'

I was pleased because I could look forward to getting to know Joey and maybe teach him to say 'hello' – I would enjoy that.

Also at that end of the room was an oak gate-leg table and four chairs.

'This is where we eat our Sunday lunch,' explained Pearl. 'The rest of the time we eat in the kitchen.'

There were two windows and a French door to the back garden. I looked outside to see if there was a lovely big lawn to run around and trees to climb, but I was disappointed. There was a concrete raised area and some steps down to a patch of grass, but it was very small and being a new house, there was nothing much growing there yet.

'Now, let's go back upstairs and I'll show you where your bedroom is,' suggested Pearl. 'We can unpack your case.'

At the top of the stairs was a landing, a bathroom and three bedrooms. I'd already seen the bathroom, which was very small, but it had everything it needed. Pearl showed me where my toothbrush and face flannel could go and she'd bought a new pale blue towel.

'It will be your towel,' said Pearl. 'Just for you.'

I was rather pleased with that as I'd never had a fluffy new towel of my own before.

'This is our bedroom, Arnold's and mine,' she said, pointing to a closed door. 'It's at the front of the house. And there is the spare room.' She pointed to another door.

'Now, this is your bedroom,' said Pearl, pushing the door open and ushering me in to a tiny room – everything seemed so small here.

While Pearl busied herself opening my case and checking all the things on the list were there, I looked round the room. The first thing I noticed was the lino on the floor – a plain, light grey colour, with a dark brown coconut mat next to the bed – not soft like a furry rug, this mat looked hard and scratchy. There were thin brown and white, flowery nylon curtains at the front window. They were see-through – the sort that stick to you every time you brush past them.

The furniture, a dark wooden bed, matching chest of drawers and wardrobe, took up most of the room.

'Would you like to see what's in your case now?' asked Pearl. 'You can unpack it, if you like, while I go downstairs and put the kettle on and we can have a nice cup of tea. Come down and join me in the kitchen when you're ready.'

After she left the room, I lifted the lid of my little case and took everything out.

First, the few clothes, all of them washed and ironed, but, as usual, none of them new. I put them away in my drawers, along with a dressing gown, coat and shoes. My housemother had thought of everything. When I opened the bottom drawer, I saw several brand-new items of clothing, which Pearl must have bought specially for me. They were really smart and I looked forward to wearing those.

THE FORGOTTEN CHILD

Ch. 47

CITY OF BIRMINGHAM CHILDREN'S DEPARTMENT

Name of Child _Richard Cunningham_ D/B _17-11-54_

CLOTHING AND OTHER PERSONAL EFFECTS IN POSSESSION OF CHILD

on transfer from _Field House Nursery_

to _Mr + Mrs Gallear_ on _30·8·59_

NOTE : List should include any clothing child is wearing. If own property indicate by entering letter " O " on left of article.

Article	No.	Condition	Article	No.	Condition
CLOTHING, etc.			Underskirts		
Overcoat	1	(bahendine)	Brassieres		
Raincoat	1	mackintosh + hat	Bodices	2	
Suit			Suspender Belt		
Sportscoat/Blazer	1	Good	Knickers		
Trousers			Vests	2	
Pullover	4	2 sleeveless (good) 2 long sleeves (")	Underpants	3	
Cardigan			Pyjamas	2	
Dresses			Overalls		
Blouses			Hat, Cap or Beret		
Skirts			Gloves		
Shorts	5	2 corduroy 3 khaki	Handkerchiefs		
Gym. Slip			Towels		
Boots			Flannel		
Shoes	2	1 new 1 good	Toothbrush	1	
Sandals	1	good	Brush and Comb	1	
Slippers			Suitcase		
Socks	3	good	Bible		
Stockings			dressing gown	1	
Ties	2	"			
Shirts	4	2 aertex (New) 2 flannel (")			
Braces	2	1 good 1 fair			
Belts					
Jerseys (Jumpers)					

PERSONAL EFFECTS (stating amount of cash, or bank book balance) :—

few Toys

DOCUMENTS	Case History		Medical Records	
	Insurance Card (No.)		Medical Card	✓

Date _29·8·59_ Above items received by ....

Compiled by _K.M. Green_

Recipient to retain second copy and return original to : _R.E. Gallear_

4,000 3/56

66

Finally, I went back to look in the bottom of my case, where I found Jeffrey and tucked him into my bed. There were my two little cars with their opening doors and metal wheels that used to send sparks flying when I raced them on the flagstones in Field House. I parked those under my bed, just as I'd always done. Then I got out my precious spinning top, which I put on the floor of my wardrobe. Right at the bottom of my case, some kind soul, probably my housemother, had put in a colouring book and some crayons. I was so pleased about that because it showed kindness and I would enjoy colouring in the pages every now and then.

Down the stairs I went, as quietly as I could, so as not to disturb Arnold, wherever he was. I went into the kitchen and Pearl pulled out a chair for me to sit on. She poured out two cups of tea and we sat there companionably, sipping and chatting. I liked that: I liked the tea – I've loved tea ever since – and I liked Pearl's almost musical voice and her warm smile.

'Did you finish unpacking?' she asked. 'And did you find the nice new clothes I bought you?'

'Yes, thank you. Can I wear them tomorrow?'

'Of course you can,' she replied. 'Would you like a biscuit?'

'Ooh, yes please!' It was a long time since I had eaten and now that my tummy had calmed down, I felt quite hungry.

'Do you think you will like having your own bedroom?' she asked me.

'Yes,' I said, nodding, though I really didn't think I would like that, but I couldn't say so. Ever since I was a baby, I had slept in a dormitory with my friends at Field House – I was a little afraid of how I would feel, being on my own so much here.

Suddenly I heard heavy footsteps. In an instant the cosy atmosphere changed as Arnold strode into the kitchen.

'What's he doing here?' he asked, but didn't wait for the answer. 'Take him up to bed!'

'Yes, Arnold.' Pearl nodded nervously and turned to me. 'Come along, I'll take your cup of tea up for you.'

So off we went, up the stairs and into my room, where she put the cup down.

'I must go and get Arnold's tea ready,' she explained. 'I'll come back up and put you to bed as soon as I can.'

I sat on the edge of my bed and watched her leave, closing the door behind her. Perhaps she would bring me something to eat too when she came back. Though I couldn't tell the time yet, I knew from my tummy that it must be time for a good meal. After I had finished sipping what was left in my cup, I went over to the window. I gazed out at the view and discovered that my room was at the front of the house, though I could see nothing but brick and concrete houses along concrete streets, with rows of red rooftops, all looking the same. There was not a tree or hedge and hardly a blade of grass in sight. I'd never seen a view like this before: where could I run and play?

I went back to sit on my bed. The room was bare, with nothing to look at – no pictures on the walls, no picture-books anywhere either. I closed my eyes, wishing with all my heart that I was having a nightmare and I could wake up and be back where I belonged, in our big, light, cheerful bedroom in Field House with all my friends. I hardly dared open my eyes again, but when I did, I was still a stranger in a cold little space.

After that cup of tea I wanted to go to the toilet again, but I was apprehensive to go out of my room. What if Arnold saw me? So I sat and waited until I could wait no longer. I opened my door a crack. Downstairs I could hear them both talking – Arnold's voice curt and loud against Pearl's softer tones. I tiptoed out onto the landing. But where was the toilet? I'd forgotten already. All the doors were closed and I didn't know what to do.

Just then I heard footsteps coming up the stairs and dashed back into my room, fearing the worse. But it was all right: it was Pearl who came in. I was so relieved that I blurted out: 'Can I go to the toilet?'

'Yes, of course you can,' she smiled. 'Go whenever you need to.'

'I can't remember which door!' I explained, in an anguished state.

She showed me and I came back to find her getting out the hand-me-down pyjamas from a drawer

'Time for a bath and bed,' she said. 'You've had a long day. I thought you might feel more comfortable in your familiar things the first night.'

I was grateful for her thoughtfulness. It had indeed been a long and difficult day.

Pearl took me through to the bathroom and turned on the bath taps, then helped me to undress. As she tested the water, I noticed the red patches with bluish tinges beginning to show on my arms and legs. I'm sure there must have been some on my back too, because that was sore all over, but there was no mirror to check. I climbed into the lovely warm bath that immediately started to soothe my tired, battered body. Pearl passed me a large sponge and some soap. At Field House I had been used to splashing about and having fun in the bath, with the other boys coming in and out to wash and clean their teeth, chatting and laughing in the background, while one of the housemothers washed me all over. But now, here, it was dead quiet and I had a sudden urge to make some noise, so I slapped my hand down into the water and made a big splash.

Immediately, Pearl flinched. 'We have to be quiet,' she explained. 'Arnold doesn't like noise.'

So, no more splashing. I sat still while she soaped the sponge and washed my face first, then my body.

'Poor boy,' she said in her soft voice as she lightly washed over my tender skin. 'Don't worry, I don't think those bruises will show when you have your clothes on tomorrow. You'll be able to go out and meet the other children, make friends and play with them if you want. That will be nice, won't it? But first, a good night's sleep will do you a lot of good.'

'Thank you,' I whispered as she helped me out of the bath and wrapped me up in my big bath towel, then gently rubbed me dry.

I put on the Field House pyjamas and we went back to my bedroom, where she tucked me into bed and put out the light. No story to lull me to sleep, no other children to keep me company ...

'Sleep well,' she said and left me alone in the dark – hungry, hurting and in a state of high anxiety. It was only now that I realised I had never been in a room on my own before and I didn't like it. At not yet five years old, I remember feeling overwhelmed. I was still shocked and confused by Arnold's cruel beating when I was sick that afternoon – I didn't understand. Worst still, after my bath I could feel more strongly the tender bruises all over my body, especially my back. Arnold's attack and the long, car-sick journey had made me very tired. My tummy still cried out for food, but it didn't look as if I would have any tonight. I tossed and turned on the lumpy mattress to try and find a comfortable position. I was miserable but, despite it all, I soon fell into a fitful sleep, full of nightmares. It must have been one of those that woke me.

Immediately, I was upset still to be here, alone and bereft. I must have been disoriented in a strange room, the pale glow of the street lamp through my flimsy curtains casting eerie shadows, distorting everything around me. Though scared of the shadows, I was even more afraid of Arnold. He had become the ogre of my nightmares, but now that I was awake, I realised afresh that he was real, terribly real.

At that moment, I wet the bed. I couldn't stop myself.

Oh no!

At Field House, one of our lovely housemothers would have come in and comforted me with loving care, but not here. I cried in panic, trying desperately not to make any noise, but I couldn't stop myself sobbing.

I heard a creak on the landing. The door burst open and Arnold stormed in, towering over me, shouting and swearing. I can't remember most of what he said that night, especially the swear words, which I'd never heard before, but one or two things stood out, though I didn't understand them.

'You little bastard!' he shouted at me as he pulled all my covers off. 'Look what you've done! You don't deserve our kindness in taking you in. Your parents didn't want you, nobody wants you. You're a bastard child, even God doesn't want you!'

I cowered and sobbed more loudly.

Taking hold of my pyjamas in one hand and my ear in the other, he pulled me right out of bed and threw me onto the floor. As he yelled all the insults he could think of, I curled myself up in a ball on the coconut mat, while he rained slaps and punches on me and kicked me again and again, as hard as he could with his bare feet.

He was in a frenzy. Instinctively, I put my hands round my head to protect myself, but my body hurt with every blow. At one point I think I soiled myself too, but I couldn't help it – if only he would stop. I heard myself scream out for help, but that angered the monster even more. However, my scream must have woken Pearl as the door opened and in she came, with an anguished expression and tears streaming down her face.

'Stop! Please stop!' she wailed at Arnold. 'You've done enough,' she pleaded. 'If you go back to bed, I'll sort Richard out and clean everything up.'

Arnold still had hold of me in one hand, his other fist ready to punch me again, but suddenly he dropped me, stormed out and slammed the door behind him.

'There, there,' soothed Pearl. 'He's gone now, so let's clean you up and make you comfortable again.'

She led me into the bathroom, carefully took off my wet, soiled pyjamas, gave me a good wash down and put the big towel round me to go back in the bedroom and keep warm while she got out the new pyjamas she had bought me. After unfolding them, she passed them to me to put on, while she stripped the bed and turned the mattress: new sheets and pillowcases made it all smell nice and fresh again.

She tucked me in and said goodnight with a sorrowful smile. I gave her a weak smile back, but I was still sobbing inside. My whole body ached and throbbed from the tyrant's attack. She turned off the light and closed the door, leaving me crying quietly to myself, under the covers. I was so tired, but was it safe to sleep? Would he come back for another attack? It was only my first night here – would every night be the same? Sore all over, I curled up in my bed and cried myself silently to sleep.

CHAPTER 7

One Day at a Time

When I woke up the next morning – my first morning away from Field House – everything seemed calm, but I was wary. Stiff and aching, I sat up in bed and listened. All I could hear was the distant clinking of cups or plates, which seemed to come from downstairs in the kitchen, but no voices. *Should I get up?* No, I decided it might be safer to wait and see, but I didn't have to wait long.

'Richard?' called Pearl's voice up the stairs. 'Arnold has gone to work. Are you awake?'

'Yes. Shall I get dressed?'

'I'll come up.'

I heard her running lightly up the stairs and my door opened.

'You can wear some of the new clothes I bought you, if you like,' she said with a warm smile, getting them out for me to look at. 'You choose.'

This was a first for me. I picked a pale blue short-sleeved shirt and some red shorts and she helped me put them on.

'Are you hungry?' she asked.

'Yes,' I replied, politely. In fact, I was more than hungry – I hadn't eaten since yesterday lunchtime, except for the one biscuit Pearl had given me. I imagined a big breakfast all laid out for me to choose from, with porridge or cereals, toast and fruit, so I gladly followed her downstairs. But the kitchen table was bare.

'I'll just put the kettle on,' she said. 'We'll have a cup of tea and I'll butter you a slice of toast.'

So that was it – one slice of toast for my breakfast that first morning.

It was a great relief to me that Arnold had gone to work. Pearl seemed more relaxed too, as she chatted away to me at the kitchen table.

'We have some nice neighbours,' she told me. 'And there are quite a few children living in our road, some of them are about your age. They often play together outside, so you must try and make friends with them if you can.'

'Are there some boys?' I asked.

'Yes, and they play together very well. I'm sure you will enjoy that.' Pearl poured us both a second cup of tea. 'You'll soon be ready to start school,' she added. 'The infants' school is only just round the corner, behind our garden, so we'll be able to walk there. The teachers are very nice. They'll teach you to read and write and you'll be able to learn all sorts of things.' She paused to sip her tea. 'What would you like to learn about?'

'Cars,' I said straight away. 'And I love animals, so I'd like to learn more about them – especially insects. We had a lot of insects in the Japanese garden at Field House.'

Thinking of that, my bottom lip suddenly started to quiver. I think she must have noticed.

'Well, when we go to the shops, maybe we could go to the library, register you for a library ticket and find you a book about insects. Would you like that?'

Pearl was being very kind to me that first morning and I did appreciate it, after all that had happened in the previous 24 hours. I was still wary, listening out in case I could hear a car in the drive, or footsteps in the hall, as I didn't know that when people worked, it was usually all day. But I felt safe enough when it was just Pearl and me, and I was quite keen to meet the other children and make some new friends. Although I'd always liked playing on my own, I did miss the company and the fun of sharing my bedroom with other children, eating our meals together and running around the gardens with them.

That whole morning Pearl said nothing about Arnold. I wanted to ask her why he hit me, but I didn't dare. She acted as if nothing had happened and I didn't want to upset her, but I couldn't get it out of my head and every now and then, the bruises reminded me it was real.

We cleared away the breakfast things and she gave me a tea towel to dry the washing-up. I felt quite proud to be trusted with that job and dried everything carefully.

'Thank you,' she said when we'd finished. 'Up you go to brush your teeth,' she prompted me.

Back in my bedroom, I looked out of the window, but there were no children outside yet, so I went down to the sitting room to say hello to Joey the budgie. He seemed a little surprised, but again cocked his head to one side, as if listening intently, though I just kept repeating the same thing: 'Hello, Joey.' He sidled up to the bars and I put my little stubby fingers through to touch his feathers. I was very gentle and he didn't seem to mind.

I walked across the room to look out of the glazed door and get a better look at what the garden was like. I craned my neck to see if there was more space beyond this disappointing patch of brownish-green lawn, but no, there wasn't even space to run more than four or five of my little strides. Not at all impressed, I had a wobbly moment, with a few tears, as I stood there and tried to imagine myself back at the lawns of Field House.

'You can go out to the garden if you like,' suggested Pearl with a smile, as she came to see what I was doing.

'Can I get my toy cars and play with them in the garden?'

'Yes, of course.'

So that's what I did. Once outside, it seemed very strange. I could hear a whole mixture of sounds. There was a sort of rumble, which I didn't recognise, but must have been the traffic sounds from the main road. There were some sharp and scraping metal sounds, which I later learned were from nearby workshops, and of course the joyous sounds of children playing at the infants' school behind us. It made me want to go and join in. But I couldn't hear any birdsong. I just sat alone on the raised concrete area, racing my cars to and fro, crashing them and trying to raise sparks.

I didn't feel I belonged here. I didn't fit in, and I knew I wasn't wanted by Arnold. If only I could let my housemother know, she would surely come and fetch me. But I knew it was no good.

Just then, Pearl stuck her head out of the door: 'Would you like a cup of tea and a biscuit?'

'Yes, please,' I replied enthusiastically. I quite enjoyed our companionable tea breaks, chats and, of course, the biscuits. Perhaps she would let me have an extra one this time.

'You'll be with the little ones when you start school,' Pearl explained to me as we sat together at the kitchen table. 'In the first class. They will all be the same age as you and there will be lots of lovely things for you to do.'

'I heard the children playing,' I said. 'Do they have any lawns to play on?'

'They have a big field.' She nodded. 'I expect you'll love that – I think it's even bigger than the lawns you showed us at Field House.'

I grinned.

'When can I start school?'

'As soon as you're five. So that's in November, but you have to wait till the start of the next term after that, which means you will start in January.'

'When's January?' I asked her.

'After Christmas.'

I had no idea how long away that was, but at least I now had something to look forward to: school sounded like the best place to be.

After our mid-morning tea break – it was never coffee, always tea – Pearl opened the front door and took me out onto the little piece of concrete she called their drive. Sure enough, there were two girls sitting on the adjoining piece of concrete, outside their house, which was on the other corner at our end of the avenue.

'Go and tell them your name,' suggested Pearl.

So, I walked across.

'I'm Richard and I've come to live here.'

'Oh, that's nice,' said the older of the two. 'My name is Jacqueline,' she added with a friendly smile. 'And this is my little sister, Susan. You can come and sit down with us, if you like. Susan can't go very far, so we usually just sit out here and play with things.'

We were soon chatting away. I discovered that Jacqueline was about a year older than me and Susan a year younger. Susan had an unusual look about her face, but I didn't take any notice really. We had several children at Field House who had disabilities and we had been taught to just be normal with them and include them as much as possible in our games, so I did the same with Susan. She seemed a happy child, always smiling and friendly. Jacqueline was marvellous with her – protective, but also encouraging her to do new things.

'It's nearly the end of the holidays and I'll be going back to school soon,' said Jacqueline. 'But Susan will still be at home, so maybe you could sit with her sometimes when I'm not here?'

'Yes, of course,' I replied, smiling at Susan, who didn't say anything, but I could tell she seemed pleased.

Jacqueline told me about some of the other children who lived down the road.

'I'm not sure how much I can play today,' I said, 'because I only arrived yesterday, so I'm just getting to know everything, but I hope I'll be let out to play here most days.'

'Oh, that's good,' said Jacqueline. 'If I see any of the other boys, I'll tell them you're new here and they might come and call for you to come out and play with them.'

'Thank you, that would be nice.'

Pearl opened the front door and called me in for lunch, so I didn't dawdle. I just said goodbye to the girls and went straight in.

'Wash your hands,' she said.

'We used to wash our hands before lunch at Field House too,' I said.

'Good! Then we can sit down together to eat.'

I was a bit puzzled. There was no mouth-watering smell of steak pie, or apple crumble, as there would have been at Field House. In fact, I couldn't really smell anything, other than bleach. So, what were we having for lunch? It was always a big cooked meal there, the main meal of the day. But here it was sandwiches, either cheese or ham or occasionally both, if I was lucky. What a disappointment! Almost starving hungry by now, I knew I just had to accept what I was given. Maybe there would be a cooked meal for me tonight – I could only hope.

We finished lunch with a cup of tea.

'I know you liked your gardens at Field House and you helped with sowing and collecting the vegetables,' said Pearl. 'I'm afraid we have only a little garden here and we haven't done anything with it so far.' She paused. 'Would you like to have part of our garden to grow things in? You could grow some flowers and maybe some vegetables and fruits too. What do you think?'

'Oh, yes, please,' I said, quite excited at the thought. 'But I might need some help.'

'Well, I could help you,' offered Pearl, with an enthusiastic smile. 'I'd really like to have a pretty garden and also to grow things to eat. We could go and buy some tools and various seeds and plants for you to put in. How does that sound?'

'Good,' I replied, though I suppose I realised we couldn't do it all at once.

That afternoon, the sun shone, so Pearl let me go outside again to see if any of the other children were playing in the road.

'You mustn't go any further than halfway down the avenue,' she said.

I sat on the kerb near our house and played with my two

cars. Then a boy walked along and came to sit next to me on the kerb. I offered him one of my cars and we played together with them for a couple of minutes.

'Are you new?' he asked.

'Yes, my name is Richard. I have just come to live with the people in this house, here. What's your name?'

'Johnny,' he said with a grin. 'I'm nearly five.'

'So am I. Are you at school yet?'

'No, my mum says I will start after Christmas.'

'That's the same as me!'

We became firm friends that afternoon. He had some glass marbles in his pocket, which he got out and showed me. I hadn't seen marbles before – they felt so smooth in my hand and I loved the coloured wavy bits inside each one. We played with them for a while, then he suggested I come down to his house and play in his garden.

'I don't know,' I said. 'I only got here yesterday, so I'll have to ask my foster mother whether I can come.'

'What's a foster mother?' he asked.

'Well, she's not my mother – I haven't got one – but she's like a mother.'

'But I thought everyone had a mother,' he said. 'How can you not have a mother?'

'I don't know. I was in Field House Nursery Home since I was born, so I've never had a mother, only a housemother, and now a foster mother.' I paused. 'I don't really understand it either.'

I went inside to the sound of Pearl singing a happy song while she swept the kitchen.

'Can I go and play with Johnny in his garden?' I asked. 'Just for a little while. Please may I go?'

'Which house is it?'

I had to turn to Johnny and he told Pearl which number it was.

'Oh yes, I think I've met your mother,' she said. 'Will she be happy to have Richard there as well?'

'Oh yes, she always says she loves it when I bring my friends to play in our garden.'

So, Pearl agreed and off we went.

'I think we'll make a tent today,' said Johnny, as we walked up his path.

'How can we do that?' I asked, not altogether sure what a tent was.

'You'll see,' he replied. 'Mum will help us.'

I do remember that Johnny's mum was lovely. She gave me a very warm welcome and brought us both orangeade drinks and delicious chocolate biscuits. Then we went out into their garden and she brought out a wooden clothes horse and a big sheet, which Johnny showed me how to make into a tent.

'Right,' he said. 'Now the tent is our camp and we can play cowboys and Indians.'

I didn't like to say that I had no idea what cowboys and Indians were. I didn't know, of course, because I had never watched television, where they showed so many cowboy and Indian films and programmes in those days. But I don't think Johnny minded that he had to show me how to use one of his toy guns. I soon got the hang of how to shoot it and to make the sounds of shooting a gun and bullets whistling through the air, so we started our game.

'I don't have any bows and arrows,' he explained, 'so we can't be Indians. We are both cowboys and we have to stop the Indians attacking our camp.'

'Watch out, they're attacking from the ridge over there!' he shouted, pointing at his back fence, and we both got busy shooting at them. 'Well done, Richard,' he said after a while, 'we got them all. Phew, that was a close one!'

It was great fun – I loved playing with Johnny as he was so bubbly and imaginative. I soon discovered he had lots of good ideas for games we could play the next time.

After another drink and a biscuit, I began to worry that I might get into trouble if I was late going back, especially if Arnold got home before me, so I thanked his mother.

'It was lovely to have you here,' she said with a beaming smile. 'Come again soon.'

I walked back up to Arnold and Pearl's house and found that the door was unlocked, so I could go straight in.

'Did you have a good time?' asked Pearl as soon as I came into the kitchen. She was peeling some potatoes. 'I'm just preparing Arnold's cooked tea,' she said. Then she sat down at the kitchen table and beckoned me to do the same. 'Now, tell me all about it.'

So, I did.

'It was great fun,' I said at the end. 'Can I play with Johnny again tomorrow?'

'We'll see,' she replied, then seeing the disappointed look on my face, she gave in. 'Yes, I expect so. I'm glad you have made some new friends already, Richard. Well done! Now, go and wash your hands – they must be grubby after playing in Johnny's garden – then I'll make you some tea.'

Well, that was good news, so I dashed upstairs, rinsed my hands quickly and dashed down again, desperate for a good meal at last. But when I came down, there was nothing cooking, no tempting smells and only a little plate on the table.

'Sit down,' said Pearl. 'What would you prefer, Marmite on toast or baked beans on toast?'

I tried hard to hide my disappointment. 'I don't mind,' I replied, as I didn't know what either of those things were – we had only eaten fresh foods at Field House, apart from the occasional helping of delicious Carnation milk with our jelly.

After I'd finished this meagre feast, we both had a cup of tea and a biscuit, which felt quite cosy … until I heard the sound of the key being turned in the front-door lock.

'Quick!' said Pearl. 'Run up to your bedroom before Arnold sees you.'

I just made it across the hall and onto the first step.

'What is that brat doing down here when I come home?' he snarled.

'I'm sorry, Arnold,' said Pearl in a quavery voice.

At that moment, I think I realised she was frightened of him. He was certainly in a bad mood, so I ran as fast as I could up the stairs, into my bedroom and shut the door. I sat on the bed and listened to their voices – his loud and angry, hers quiet and anxious.

What had I come into? I wondered. *Were all homes like this one? Did Johnny's parents behave this way?* I knew I had to be quiet and keep out of sight, so I stayed in my barren bedroom. I don't know how long it was before I suddenly thought, *My cars, what have I done with my cars?* I felt in the pocket of my new shorts. Phew! There they both were, so I parked them under my bed, got out the colouring book and crayons I had found in my little case the day before and chose a picture to colour. It was late afternoon and the sun was still shining outside, so it was a long time before I could go to bed. As I coloured in the picture of a flower garden, I began to detect the delicious cooking smells wafting up the stairs. It smelt a bit like the steak pie smell that I loved so much. *Would I be allowed to go downstairs and have some too?* But no, I finished off the picture and still nobody came.

Eventually, though it was still strong daylight, I thought I might as well get ready for bed, so I opened my door, tiptoed across to the toilet, pulled the chain and then crept into the bathroom next door to brush my teeth.

At that moment, in came Pearl.

'Oh, good boy, Richard,' she said in a pleased sort of voice. 'I came up to help you get ready for bed, but I see you've already started. Now, I don't have long this evening, because Arnold needs me downstairs, so just have a quick wash and we'll get you into bed.'

As we went back into my bedroom and she turned down the covers, I saw that Jeffrey had a new friend: lying in the bed next to my beloved scruffy bear was a black-and-white spotted dog. Pearl smiled when she saw my happy face as I reached to pick him up and give him a cuddle.

'Do you like him?' she asked.

'Yes, I love him,' I replied, genuinely delighted that Jeffrey had a friend at last, just like I'd found Johnny that afternoon. 'I love him! But where did he come from?'

'He's a handsome fellow, isn't he? I bought him for you after we chose you that day we first met you.' She paused, watching me hug my new cuddly toy. 'What will you call him?'

I looked at him and thought for a moment.

'Billy,' I said. 'I have no idea why!'

'An excellent name,' she smiled. 'Now, into bed with you and you can all three snuggle down together.'

She tucked me in, paused at the door, then closed it and left me. So that was the end of my first full day at Arnold and Pearl's house. As I thought through all the things that had happened that day, the children in the avenue, Johnny and the games we played, I smiled to think I already had some friends but it was all tinged with a nagging fear: apprehension. *What if Arnold came into my room?* I dreaded to think what would happen, yet I must have been tired as, eventually, I drifted off to sleep.

In the still of the night, I awoke to feel as if someone or something was strangling me. I don't know whether I might perhaps have cried out before realising that I had just made a muddle of my bedclothes. My sheet and blankets were all jumbled up. I must have been tossing and turning in my anxiety not to make a sound … and that's when I heard the creak on the landing.

I froze. The door handle turned and the door itself flew open. Screwing up my eyes, I pretended desperately to be asleep, but I could hear him approaching the bed. I could smell him as he stood hovering over me, ready to pounce. It could only have been a few seconds, but each second seemed to last an agonising hour.

I wanted to scream for Pearl, but I already knew that would only make things worse. I was breathing heavily now, just waiting for him to grab me, almost wishing he would get on with it. Then it happened. He pulled away the bedclothes, saw that I had wet the bed again, which I think must have been while I was waiting, and grasped my arm to pull me out onto the floor.

'You're a useless little bastard!' he yelled as he laid into me, hitting and punching and kicking me, all the while shouting insults I didn't understand. He ranted and raved with every punch, but I stopped listening – I just focused on trying to protect myself from his heavy blows on my helpless body.

Pearl must have heard the commotion and came running in, just as she had the night before.

'Please stop, Arnold. You're hurting him,' she wailed, tears streaming down her face. 'Please, please stop hitting the poor boy,' she begged him. 'Arnold, I'm pleading with you to stop.'

But still he kept up his onslaught on my poor back and shoulders as I lay curled up on the coconut mat. A few hits more, as if he didn't want to give in to her, and finally, abruptly, he stopped, stormed out of the room and left Pearl to pick me up, soothe me and sort out the mess.

I hurt all over, but again just bruises – somehow he managed not to break any of my bones, but I was almost too sore to move. Pearl changed the sheets, turned the mattress, gave me a quick wash-down, changed my pyjamas and put me back to bed again, staying just long enough to make me as comfortable as possible and soothe me a little more before leaving.

'There, there,' she said, stroking my cheek. 'You poor boy! Now, off you go to sleep.'

I could feel every bruise, the old and the new. I ached all over and my tummy was in turmoil. But worse still was the fear that it would happen again tomorrow night … *every* night.

What had I done to deserve this? Why me? How could I cope?

CHAPTER 8

Poor Joey

My housemother at Field House had told me I must call my foster parents Mum and Dad. 'Because they are your mother and father,' she had said.

It probably worked for most children, who were fostered in happy homes where everyone was loving and caring, but it was difficult for me. I didn't really know what a family was until I met Johnny and some of the other children in the avenue and went to their houses, where I could see how lovely their families were and how they had conversations together. Their dads showed their children as much love as their mothers did. They also played with them, talked to them, had fun with them and took an interest in everything their children did.

In our house, Pearl and Arnold's life excluded me. They had conversations, but only between them. I would have liked to have a conversation or a discussion with him, but no. Arnold never smiled at me, never talked to me, except in anger. I couldn't understand why he was so different to all the other dads.

Arnold and Pearl probably talked about me, but not in front of me. I didn't seem to be a part of their lives. Looking back, I suppose I was always on the sidelines yet I wanted to be involved despite Arnold's rages and beatings. I didn't want him to hate me. I would have liked to be part of the family, rather than … well, I don't know what they saw me as.

Pearl was kind to me and seemed to like having me around, when Arnold was at work, but when he was home she was different – subdued and nervous, subservient to him. Arnold himself made it clear in so many ways that he didn't want me there; he didn't even want to see or hear me in the house. I was happy to call Pearl 'Mum', but I just couldn't bring myself to call Arnold 'Dad'. Fortunately, he didn't want me to speak to him anyway, so I don't suppose he noticed. As an adult, I have never been comfortable about referring to them as 'Mum' and 'Dad', so I have always used their first names instead.

The first few days passed by, shopping with Pearl, making new friends and playing games with them in the avenue, going to their houses and meeting their parents. On one of these days, Johnny's mother noticed some bruising on my arm.

'Did you fall down the stairs?' she asked, with a look of concern.

I hesitated for only a moment.

'Yes.'

It seemed easier to pretend – I don't know why I didn't explain, but something made me feel I shouldn't.

Johnny showed me his new tricycle and let me have a go on it, so the moment passed and nothing more was said. I was so glad to have made good friends like Johnny and the other children and we had such fun together. Maybe it wasn't so bad being here after all – if only I could put Arnold out of my mind – but I knew it could not be for long.

As well as playing in my new friends' gardens, Pearl sometimes let them come to play in my garden, as long as they left before Arnold came home. Most of my friends' gardens had swings and ball games and one had a sandpit. To begin with, I was rather ashamed of our garden, but Pearl remembered what she had said.

'Shall we go and buy you some seeds to plant in the garden?'

'Ooh, yes, please!'

'I've got some food shopping to do too, so we can get what we need in the little hardware shop on the parade.'

Pearl held my hand as we walked to the local shopping centre and that made me feel good. There were no supermarkets in those days, just several little shops, and all the shopkeepers were friendly and welcoming. We went into George Mason's and walked across to the counter. This was the grocer's and all the shop assistants wore smart brown overalls and big smiles. The whole shop smelt of cheese and meat and bread.

'Half a pound of butter please,' said Pearl. 'And two slices of your lovely ham.'

'Hello, young man,' said the assistant as he wrapped up Pearl's purchases. 'You're new round here.'

'Hello,' I replied with a shy smile.

'This is Richard,' explained Pearl. 'He's come to live with us.'

Next, we went to the baker's for bread and finally, to the hardware store.

'We've come to buy a few little tools and some seeds for Richard.'

She pointed at me.

'Oh yes?'

'He's going to have his own patch in our garden, so what do you have?'

'Well,' said the storeman, 'it's nearly autumn now, so you could plant a few winter pansies and some bulbs for next spring.'

'What do you think, Richard?' asked Pearl.

I was pleased to be asked my opinion.

'Yes, please,' I said with a nod. 'And can I grow some vegetables too?'

'Of course,' agreed Pearl with her tinkly laugh. 'But they'll have to be small vegetables because it's only a small garden.'

'Yes.' I nodded. 'I want to keep some grass too.'

So, the storeman packed up some bulbs and seeds for us.

'Would you like a little fork and trowel?' he asked. 'And a little dibber to make holes with?'

'Yes, please.' I turned to Pearl. 'And please can I have a watering can as well?'

'Yes, of course,' she said. 'I remember you watering the vegetables when you took us round the gardens at Field House so definitely a watering can.'

As soon as we arrived back at our house in Greystoke Avenue, I was impatient to get outside and make a start. Once Pearl had put all the food away in the pantry, we took our gardening purchases outside. We spent the rest of the morning clearing away the weeds before planting the pansies and the bulbs.

'Phew!' she said, clutching her back. 'That was hard work.'

'Yes,' I agreed, holding my back in just the same way. It was a lovely warm feeling, doing something like that together.

'Time for lunch?' she asked me, knowing already what my answer would be. 'Let's go in and make ourselves some sandwiches.'

After lunch, we went back out and sowed the vegetable seeds in short, neat rows.

'Now it's up to you,' she said with a smile. 'You must be sure to water your garden every day.'

While Pearl went in to iron some of Arnold's shirts, I went out in the road and invited two of the boys to come round and look at what we'd done.

'The flowers are called pansies,' I explained with pride. 'And we've put in some daffodil bulbs for next spring. Over here,' I pointed, 'we've sown some seeds for vegetables as well.'

'That's very good,' said Johnny. 'I wonder if I'd be allowed to do that too? I'm going to ask my mum and dad.'

I had worked up quite an appetite that day, so I was glad when it was nearly teatime. Surely today, after all our work, she would cook me something more substantial? But, no. The most Pearl ever made for me was chips and baked beans or chips and a fried egg. Today, for a treat, it would be chips and one sausage. Her chips were surprisingly tasty, but how I yearned for a Field House steak pie.

'Don't go near the chip pan,' she warned as it bubbled on the stove. It was strange how it was liquid when it was hot and solid when it was cold – Pearl called it dripping.

'What is dripping made of?' I once asked her.

'It's a mixture of oil and fat, like the fat from the meat I cook for Arnold's supper. That's why it looks white.'

Finally, the weekend came and on Sunday I sat with them at the wooden table in the sitting room and had a roast lunch, with fresh vegetables and gravy. I was so excited! I wasn't allowed second helpings, but at least it was a proper meal. Of course, the situation at that lunch table was fraught – I was not allowed to speak and I tried to eat as quietly as I could, all the time looking down so that Arnold could not accuse me of looking at him.

While the daytimes were happy, when Arnold was out, the nights were full of fear and frequent torments, though thankfully not every night. The apprehension often resulted in my wetting the bed, but sometimes I got away with it, soggy and miserable, but unmolested. And Pearl never told me off. Other nights were horrific.

On one such occasion, I woke in the darkness, when even the street light had gone out, to find I had wet the bed. I lay there in my little bedroom on the other side of the house to the neighbours, fearing his visit, wondering how I could dry the sheets. Then I had an idea: when we had raced our toy cars on the flagstones at Field House, one of my cars had some friction underneath and often produced sparks which looked almost like fire. And fire meant heat – heat was good for drying things. So, I sneaked out of bed as stealthily as I could and picked up the car from its parking place underneath, then turned back the sheets and rolled my car back and forth to try and raise some sparks. But it didn't work on the soft material. Even worse, I had forgotten that it made a slight whining sound. This must have woken Arnold. I heard the creak on the landing and my heart beat faster as I scrambled back into bed and pretended to be asleep. But it was too late …

He stormed straight into my room, flailing his belt.

'You bastard!' he shouted, wrapping one end of the belt round his hand, while yanking me out with the other. 'You're nothing but trouble, always in the way – a useless bag of shit!'

I didn't know the words, but I did know he was angry, *very* angry, and he was going to take it out on me. He lashed me with the belt and punched me with his other fist by turns, drawing blood this time across my back, then kicked my legs repeatedly.

'Your mother didn't want you, your father didn't want you and nor do I!' he shouted, just as Pearl came running in.

'Stop it, Arnold!' she shrieked, seeing the blood. 'Please stop. You've wounded him, he can't take any more!'

As usual, he finally stopped and left Pearl to clear up. She took me to the bathroom and gently washed the blood from the belt cuts on my back, before changing me and the bedclothes.

'Into bed with you,' she said with a gentle smile. At last I was dry and clean again, in new sheets, as I silently sobbed myself to sleep.

'You'd better wear trousers today,' said Pearl, helping me to dress in the morning. 'We must hide those bruises on your legs, or your friends will wonder what happened to you ...' She paused. 'And you mustn't tell them.' She gave me a frightened look and I knew I couldn't let her down.

'I promise,' I reassured her, glad now that I had said nothing to Johnny's mother.

Every day, I made new friends in the avenue and for a while the other boys made me leader of the gang, perhaps because I was the new boy and I had some different ideas for games that we used to play at Field House. Their temporary admiration did wonders for my self-esteem in contrast to the way Arnold demeaned me with all the hurtful, nasty names he called me.

My friends' experiences of course were all new to me. They had real mums and dads and had always lived with them. Everyone was well-looked after and they all seemed very happy. I don't know whether any of them noticed how different things were for me. I would have loved to ask them questions and tell them about what was happening to me, but I didn't understand it myself, so how could I explain? In any case, I didn't dare – besides, I'd promised Pearl – so at nearly five years old, I had to keep my bitter secrets to myself.

Most of the children had tricycles or homemade 'trolleys', built of wooden planks or boards on top of old pram wheels. We all joined in and had goes on them. I was a bit ashamed – I suppose that I didn't have anything like that – but nobody seemed to notice and they gladly shared what they had with me. However, one Saturday morning, I had an unexpected surprise when Arnold, who had been making something in his shed, brought it round to the front of the house and, in an off-hand sort of way, placed it in front of me.

'I made this for you,' he said, without looking directly at me.

I was so astonished that I didn't know what to say at first.

'Go on, take it down the avenue and show your friends,' he urged.

'Thank you, Dad,' I said with a gulp. I could hardly believe that this was the brute who attacked me so furiously most nights, who had never before paid me any other kind of attention, yet here he was making me a toy so that I could be like my friends. I still find it strange that he did that – I suppose it was the only way he could show his better side, but of course, I knew it wouldn't last.

Proud to have a trolley of my own, I trundled along, pretending it was a bus. I invited Johnny and Martin, the other boy my age, to come on board, then made a 'ting-ting' sound like the conductor did when he gave the tickets out on the bus that Pearl had taken me on one day.

One day, Martin asked me: 'Do you want to come and look at my dad's new car? It's brand new.'

'Ooh, yes, please!' I replied, grinning with excitement. I had always loved cars. 'What is it?'

'It's a red Renault Dauphine,' said Martin as we walked down to his house. 'I'll get my dad to unlock it so we can have a look.'

It was a very distinctive car – a strange shape, with the engine at the back.

'Sit in the driver's seat,' suggested Martin. 'Isn't it good?'

'It's so different, I love it!'

From then on, I was fascinated by anything to do with cars. One day, when we were having our tea and biscuits, I told Pearl about Martin's dad's car and how keen I was on cars.

'Wait there a minute,' she said, going off to the back room. She came straight back, holding a sort of paper book. 'Here's something for you to look at.'

'What is it?'

'It's Arnold's car album,' she explained. 'There's a picture card in every packet of his cigarettes, so when it was car pictures, he sent off for an album and stuck them all in.'

She put it down on the table in front of me and opened the first page.

'Wow, this is amazing!' I said, quickly turning more pages to see if it was all about cars, and it was.

'You can take it up to your bedroom, if you like,' she suggested. 'You could look through it all properly before bedtime.'

'But what about Arnold?' I asked. 'Won't he be cross?'

'Don't worry about that. He probably won't notice and I don't think he'd mind. But if he does, I'll tell him I gave it to you to look at, so he won't blame you.'

So, I took the album straight upstairs and studied every single car picture – I only wished I could read. I was so engrossed, I didn't even hear when Arnold got home. By the time I'd finished looking, it was getting quite late so I assumed I wasn't having anything more to eat that night and put myself to bed. I tossed and turned quite a bit, probably because I had only eaten a biscuit since lunchtime, but I tried to think of all the cars I'd seen and that sent me off to sleep.

It must have been the middle of the night when I woke, ravenously hungry. At Field House hunger had always been my downfall, but the staff were so tolerant that I always got away with taking food from the kitchen.

There was no sound from Pearl and Arnold's bedroom, no creak on the landing, but I could almost hear my tummy rumbling. I had no food in my bedroom, so I decided to tiptoe down the stairs and see what I could find.

I'd seen Pearl open tins of Carnation milk to have with jelly, so I knew where the tin opener was and how to use it. I hoped my hands would be big enough to work it. My thoughts coming down the stairs were entirely focused on food. In my bare feet I crossed the kitchen and opened the pantry door – and there it was, a tin of Carnation milk right there in the middle of a shelf, just within my reach.

Oh, I was so pleased with myself as I got it out and took it to the table that I forgot about everything else. I drank the lot, straight from the tin – it was delicious, the most wonderful thing! But when I looked at the empty tin and the empty space on the shelf that was when I realised someone would be sure to find out.

I'm going to be in real trouble, I thought.

There was only one thing I could do: I pushed the lid back down on top of the tin and placed in back on the pantry shelf. Now I would be fine.

Then, as I was about to close the pantry door, I saw a packet of ginger biscuits.

I'll have one of those, I decided, reaching the packet down.

They were my favourites, so I took my time and enjoyed that biscuit, then another and another. It was at this point that I wondered if maybe Joey might get hungry in the middle of the night too, so I tiptoed across the hall, into the back room and over to his cage.

'Would you like a biscuit?' I asked him.

He gave me a look and I thought he nodded his head, so I took another biscuit out for him and wedged it between the bars of his cage. He cocked his head on one side, as usual. Perhaps he was saying thank you.

Oh dear, I thought, *perhaps I'd better go back to bed now. Nobody knows about this, but I think I've got away with it.*

I crept back up the stairs as lightly as I could. I didn't seem to have woken Arnold, which I thought was amazing. My stomach full, I felt quite triumphant as I climbed back into bed and fell fast asleep.

In the mornings, I often woke when it was light because of the thin curtains, but I always stayed in bed until I heard Arnold slam the front door on his way out to work.

That morning, however, he didn't leave straight away. I heard raised voices and then Arnold shouting up the stairs at me.

'Come down here at once, you little bastard!'

Of course, I knew straight away.

I leapt out of bed and ran down the stairs, dreading what was to come, yet knowing that if I dared dawdle, it would be all the worse for me.

Arnold stood in the middle of the hall and his face said it all. I knew what I'd done and I began to tremble. He frog-marched me roughly into the kitchen, where Pearl was standing sadly, staring at the empty tin of Carnation milk that stood on the table.

'Look what you've done!' he snarled.

'Did you have that during the night and go back to bed?' asked Pearl, her voice wavering, while Arnold stared from her to me.

'Yes, I did,' I owned up in a little voice.

'Oh,' she replied. 'Don't worry about that for a moment.'

I thought that was odd.

She turned to Arnold, as if they'd decided he would speak next.

'Did you give Joey a ginger biscuit?' he asked.

'Yes,' I admitted. 'And ...' I added bravely, 'I had one myself.'

'Well,' he began, with a cruel smirk on his face, 'you've killed him. He's dead!'

'No, I haven't!' I remember my shock and my tears of indignation. 'He can't be,' I protested. 'I just thought he was hungry, so I gave him something to eat.'

Arnold took hold of me, still in my pyjamas, and propelled me through to the sitting room and next to the cage.

'See for yourself!'

He made me look and there was Joey, lying on his side at the bottom of his cage. I looked where I had put the biscuit and there was half of it left, still between the bars.

'I didn't kill him,' I said.

'Yes, you did. It's all your fault he's dead.' I could see Arnold's face contorting with anger. 'How dare you come downstairs and steal food and kill our budgie in the middle of the night! You're a thief and a murderer!' he seethed, taking his glasses off and putting them down on the table.

I knew what was coming. He swiped me hard with the back of his hand, which sent me reeling to the floor, where he punched and kicked me again and again.

'You're a murdering bastard!' he shouted. 'You belong in the gutter! You should be in prison, like your father!'

'I'm sorry, I'm sorry!' I cried. 'I know I've done wrong.'

But he took no notice. Red in the face, his eyes were full of rage. I knew I deserved it, but I was surprised to see that he looked excited to be punishing me.

While he taunted me with Joey's death and all my supposed shortcomings, all I could think about was that poor little bird: I loved him, I didn't want to hurt him. Surely it couldn't be my fault that he'd died – or could it? I felt guilty that it must have been me and I knew I had to take the punishment for my bad behaviour.

Pearl must have heard Arnold swearing and hitting me from the kitchen and ran in to try and stop him.

'Leave him alone,' she pleaded. 'He knows he's done wrong, he won't do it again.'

A few more punches and then he stopped and stalked off to work, leaving Pearl to pick me up and sort me out, as usual. But this time I was so upset about Joey that I hardly felt my bruises.

'Poor old Joey,' I murmured. 'I'm sorry – I just thought he was hungry, like me. I didn't mean to kill him.'

'Come on, wipe your tears,' she said, dabbing at my face with her hankie and helping me up off the floor. 'Let's go and get you dressed and then we'll have a nice cup of tea.'

As we sat at the kitchen table, half an hour later, Pearl was very sympathetic. 'I know you didn't mean to hurt poor Joey,' she said in her soothing voice, 'but don't come down to take food from the pantry again or you'll make Arnold angry again and we don't want that, do we?' She gave me a nervous smile.

We sat in companionable silence for a minute or two, until I felt I had to ask her about something that Arnold had shouted at me in his fury, something I didn't understand.

'Why did Arnold say I should be in prison, like my father?'

'Oh, you don't want to worry about that,' she said gently. 'He doesn't know what he's saying when he's in a temper. Take no notice.'

'But I haven't got a father, have I?'

'No,' she agreed. 'We're your mother and father now.'

That night in bed, trying to get to sleep, I thought back over all the horrid things Arnold had shouted at me. Was I really all the things he called me? Did I have a mother and a father? Could it be true they didn't want me? And why did he always tell me that nobody wanted me? I think Pearl did. And what was that about prison? I was convinced that could not be true. Was he making it up?

This was all so distressing for a not-quite-five-year-old boy. Looking back, I can see now that it gave me a terrible feeling, as if he'd robbed me of my identity. At Field House I had been loved and everyone was kind to me. I was sometimes a little cheeky, or jealous, or even naughty, but I was mostly a good child. But, if this brute Arnold kept shouting these awful words at me, perhaps he was right – could it be true that I was a bad person? And now that I'd killed poor Joey, was that the proof? Yet, I'm sure Pearl understood and my new friends seemed to like me, or were they just pretending?

Oh dear! I was so confused. My head hurt from thinking about it, but finally, I fell into a fitful sleep. Like every night, I slept and woke by turns through the night, waking in case he should come in, and if he did, I'd wet myself waiting for him to grab me and start attacking me all over again.

'And you needn't think you can tell anyone about this,' he'd say. 'Because nobody would believe you.'

In those days, the late-1950s, he may have been right.

CHAPTER 9

Christmas Capers

At Field House Christmas had been a festive time – a lovely day of wonderful food and lights and carol-singing. Here, it was different because Pearl and Arnold were both in the Salvation Army, so in the days leading up to Christmas we visited different places, singing carols, including 'Away in a Manger' and some of the others I remembered from earlier Christmases. Every night, it seemed, we'd go and meet up with the Salvation Army band in a shopping centre or street somewhere nearby. At each place, the brass band, with their big shiny instruments, started playing and a uniformed Arnold went round the gathering crowd and collected money in a special tin.

Because I was so young, Pearl held my hand while we stood and listened to the music, or joined in the singing, then walked along with the band every time they moved, still playing, to a new place. Always dark and cold and damp, it even snowed one night, but I didn't mind when the band was playing – I loved the sounds they made. I hoped the jolly singing and successful money-collecting would put Arnold in a good mood, so that he wouldn't feel the need to come and beat me those nights. Mostly it did.

Finally, it was Christmas Eve and, being a Thursday, Arnold was out at work. I came down for breakfast as usual and passed a couple of old boxes in the hall before joining Pearl, humming a tune at the table.

'It's Christmas Day tomorrow,' she said. 'So would you like to help me decorate our Christmas tree today?'

'Ooh, yes, please!' I replied with excitement. But I was somewhat puzzled. 'Where is the tree?'

'It's in one of those boxes in the hall.'

'It must be a tiny tree,' I said. 'Our trees at Field House were huge, they reached all the way up to the high ceilings.'

'Well, they must have been real trees,' she said, clearly amused.

'Yes, but trees are always real, aren't they?'

She laughed, then apologised. 'I'm not laughing at you,' she explained. 'It's just that we have a pretend Christmas tree that comes in pieces in a box and we have to put it together on its base.'

'Oh, I see,' I said, though I didn't see at all – I couldn't imagine how a whole tree could come in such a tiny box.

'Come and look …' She took my hand and we went out to the hall, where she untied the string and lifted up the flaps of the battered box and there it was. 'See? It's made of dark green plastic and we have to take the pieces and slot them together. I'll do it and then we'll decorate it together.'

Pearl carried the tree box. 'You take that one,' she said, indicating another. 'It's much lighter.'

In the sitting room, Pearl moved the easy chairs up nearer the sofa to make a space in the corner of the room and then she unpacked her box, matching up all the pieces. Finally, while I sat on the floor and watched in awe, she 'built' the tree. It looked quite good, if you didn't look too closely.

Next, we opened my box. There was a lot of silver tinsel, a set of big lights, several glass baubles and some little ornaments, including a snowman, a man with a white beard dressed in red with a funny hat on and a large star. I decorated the lower part of the tree and Pearl did the higher branches, then finally fixed the star on the top.

'We had a star on top of the Christmas tree at Field House,' I said. 'What is the star for?'

'It's to help us remember the baby Jesus,' she explained. 'When he was born, he was such a special baby that there was a big star in the sky above the stable where he was born.'

Now that we had finished decorating the tree, we stood back to admire it with its lights turned on. I felt very proud to have helped decorate it, even though my snowman was a bit wonky.

We spent the rest of that morning at the kitchen table, cutting and gluing strips of coloured paper to make paper chains. Finally, Pearl got the step ladder from the garage and festooned them around the walls of each room. They all looked wonderfully festive by the time we had finished.

'Next,' she said, 'we're going to have lunch and then we'll make some mince pies.'

I had no idea at all what those were, but I was glad she was letting me help. We made the pastry, then rolled it and cut wavy circles out of it. My final job was to put in the spoonfuls of mincemeat before she put the tops on and baked them in the oven.

They smelt delicious when they were ready.

'Why don't you try one?' she suggested, when they'd cooled a bit. 'Just to make sure they are good to eat.' She laughed while I greedily wolfed down the warm mince pie.

'Mmmm!'

It was delicious – I was really getting into the spirit of Christmas now.

'Let's have a cup of tea,' she said. 'And a biscuit, of course. Or would you prefer another mince pie? It is Christmas, after all. I'll have one, too.'

'Yes, please!'

I'm in heaven now, I thought. *Just Pearl and me – all the fun we'd had today, and now* two *mince pies*. As I munched the still-warm second mince pie, she began to tell me what was going to happen over Christmas.

'Your dad's mother and brother are coming to spend Christmas Day with us, so I'll be doing a lot of cooking in the morning.'

'Are they nice?' I asked, hoping his brother wouldn't be horrid like Arnold.

'Yes, very nice,' said Pearl, reassuring me. 'I'm sure you will like them.'

I remembered that at Field House I always had a present at Christmas.

'Will I have a present?' I asked.

'Yes, you will. Father Christmas gives out the presents to all girls and boys who have been good during the year.'

'Have I been good?' I asked.

'Yes, you have,' laughed Pearl. 'Most of the time.'

'Who is Father Christmas?' I asked, puzzled I'd never heard of him before.

'He's a jolly man with a white beard and a red hooded jacket.'

'Like the little man I hung on the Christmas tree?'

'Yes, that's a model of him. He loves children and spends all year with his elves, making or collecting presents ready to deliver them on Christmas Eve.' She paused. 'It's Christmas Eve tonight, so he will come and land his reindeer on the roof and climb down our chimney, then he will tiptoe up to your bedroom and leave some presents for you.'

I liked the sound of some presents, not just one. But at the same time, I remember feeling fearful about this man coming into my room and I went quiet – I associated a man in my room with pain. *If he comes into my room, he will hurt me*, I thought. I didn't want that to happen.

'Oh, I don't mind if Father Christmas doesn't come,' I said. 'That will be fine.'

Pearl seemed to sense what I meant.

'No, no!' she said. 'He won't hurt you. He'll come in and leave you some little things in one of Dad's socks and maybe a Christmas box, as long as you're quiet and good.'

'He won't hurt me?'

'No, I promise he won't hurt you.' She smiled reassuringly and I believed her – I trusted her. 'Maybe,' she continued, 'we could leave him a mince pie to eat and some sugar lumps for his reindeer?'

'Ooh, yes!' I replied, distracted by having something to give this special visitor.

Suddenly there was the sound of the key in the lock and heavy footsteps across the hall. Arnold burst into the kitchen.

'Get that piece of shit upstairs and out of my sight!' he shouted at Pearl. 'I've been at work all day and I don't want any noise.'

'Come on, Richard,' she said, picking up a mince pie, some sugar lumps and a saucer. 'I'll take you upstairs and get you ready for bed.'

After I'd had a wash and brushed my teeth, she set out the mince pie and the sugar lumps on the saucer near my bedroom door, put Arnold's longest sock at the end of my bed, helped me into my pyjamas and tucked me in.

'Now remember, be very quiet and don't make Dad angry.' She turned to go, then stopped and turned at the door. 'And don't worry about Father Christmas. He will come in and out so quietly, you won't even hear him and I promise he won't hurt you.'

And it came true! On Christmas morning I woke to find a bulging sock at the end of my bed and a large box wrapped in Christmas paper, right next to it. I looked across at the saucer and that was empty, apart from a few small crumbs. I could hardly believe it. Reaching for the sock first, I delved into it, pulling out an apple, an orange, a bar of soap, a tin of toffees with a picture of cowboys and Indians on the top and a little picture book about cars. I opened the tin and popped a toffee in my mouth. Mmm!

Next, I leapt out of bed and sat on the floor to open the box. Inside, I found the most amazing thing. It was like a small red and creamy-coloured suitcase. I undid the latches and lifted the lid to find it was very strange inside – I'd never seen anything like it. There was a big round, flat circular thing and a long bar, with a pin sticking out underneath it at the end, sitting in some sort of rest. I could pick up this bar and swing it round over the circle, but I didn't know what it should do. Then I noticed that it had a cable and an electric plug, so I lifted it out from the box and took it to the wall to plug it in. That was when I saw that underneath where the case thing had been there was a square paper pocket with a shiny, hard, round black circle inside it. There was a hole in the middle and some writing round the hole, but I couldn't read yet, so I didn't know what it said.

I was just trying to puzzle all this out when the door opened and Pearl came in.

'Has Father Christmas been?' she asked.

'Ooh, yes, and he brought me lots of presents!'

'Good! I saw some soot downstairs from the chimney, so I thought that must have been him.'

Pearl sat on my bed while I showed her all my presents. Finally, she looked across at the red and cream suitcase thing, with its lid up.

'Ooh, what's that?' she asked.

'I don't know.'

'It's a record player,' she explained, coming to sit with me on the floor. 'A portable record player and this is a record. It's Max Bygraves, singing "Tulips from Amsterdam". Shall we plug it in and see how it works?'

'Yes, please.'

So, she plugged it in and showed me what to do, then we sat and listened to the music on its quietest setting. It seemed like magic to me. I'd never heard anyone singing like that and I couldn't understand how this thin black record could sing like a man. I was going to ask her, but just then we heard Arnold's harsh voice calling up the stairs.

'Pearl, come down here!' he shouted.

'Coming!' She stood up and went to the door. 'Now you'd better not play that again because Dad is soon going to fetch his mother and brother, so he won't want any noise when they come back.'

While she went off to see what Arnold wanted, I got dressed in the new things Pearl had bought me to wear on Christmas Day. Then I had one more peek proudly at my new record player and closed its lid. This was the best present I'd ever had. And for the first time since I came here, the delicious cooking smells wafting up from Pearl's kitchen reminded me of the kitchen at Field House.

I crept down quietly to see if I could have some breakfast. Pearl was very busy in the kitchen, but I saw some bread and butter laid out for me on the table, so I sat down to eat that and then she made us both a cup of tea. I just sat and watched her as she checked things in the oven and stirred the pans on the stove. She looked more flustered than usual. I could hear Arnold too, making noises in the sitting room.

'He's just opening out the gateleg with an extra chair and laying the table for me before he gets in the car to fetch his family,' Pearl explained. 'They only live a few streets away.'

I just hung around, watching Pearl, curious to see what food we were having, but at the same time trying to keep out of her way. When Arnold left, she took a box into the back room and I followed her to watch. She opened the box and took out some exciting, colourful crackers and set them in front of everyone's place on the table.

'What have they got inside them?' I asked.

'There's usually a hat inside, with a little gift and a joke.'

'What's a joke?'

'Jokes are funny. You'll have to ask Uncle John – he's always telling jokes.'

She went back to the kitchen and I lingered to admire our handiwork on the Christmas tree. I noticed afresh the ornament of the man in a red outfit with a white beard that I'd hung on a low branch. Now I knew who he was.

'Hello, Father Christmas,' I whispered to him. 'Thank you for my lovely presents.'

It wasn't long before I heard a car pulling into our drive and voices as our visitors came to the door. Pearl must have heard it too as she took off her apron, tidied her hair in the hall mirror and opened the front door to welcome them in.

'Happy Christmas, Mother,' she said to the elderly lady, who smiled and returned the greeting to Pearl.

'Happy Christmas to you too. And this must be the little man you've taken in.' She gave me a warm smile.

'Yes, this is Richard,' said Pearl, turning back to welcome in Arnold's brother.

'Happy Christmas, John. Come in and meet Richard.'

'Hello, Richard,' he said with a big grin. 'Merry Christmas. Did Father Christmas come and see you last night?'

'Yes,' I replied, trying to be polite. 'He brought me lots of presents and a record player.'

'Oh, that sounds wonderful! Perhaps you could show me later?'

Before I could reply, Arnold cut in.

'Don't pander to the boy, he'll only get big-headed. Children should be seen and not heard.'

'Oh, surely, Arnold, it's Christmas,' said the woman I had been told to call 'Grandma'. In her long black velvet dress and lots of jewellery she looked austere, but she had a twinkle in her eyes as she smiled at me.

He just shrugged, and showed them into the front room.

This was the room I'd seen only briefly from the doorway, but had never been in before. I was quite surprised – the rest of Arnold and Pearl's house was quite modern, but this was the exact opposite. It was quite a large room, filled with Victorian furniture, plush velour curtains, comfortable armchairs, carpet and a beautiful old grandfather clock. It reminded me of the visitors' room at Field House.

Pearl went off to the kitchen and brought me back some lemonade, while Arnold took some bottles out of the polished sideboard and poured drinks for his guests. I remember feeling a bit awkward at first, but Uncle John soon put me at my ease.

'I was very sorry to hear about old Joey,' he said. 'I'm sure he must have been on his last legs.' I appreciated this as I still felt bad about Joey. 'I love budgies,' he continued. 'I've got one in our lounge – his name is Omo.'

'That's a funny name. Why did you call him Omo?' I asked, curious as ever.

'There's an advert on the television for a washing powder called Omo, showing white sheets hanging on the line. When I bought Omo he was white as well, so that's why I called him Omo. You'll have to come and see him sometime.'

'Yes, please!'

I liked Uncle John, right from the start. It was strange because he was Arnold's brother, but nothing like him. Uncle John told me some of the things he had taught Omo to say. He seemed so relaxed talking to me, while Arnold talked with his mother and Pearl carried on with the cooking.

'Are there any other children nearby for you to play with?'

'Yes, lots of children – two of the boys are the same age as me. They're called Johnny and Martin.'

'What sort of games do you play?'

'Oh, mostly with our trolleys and some of them have tricycles, or we play marbles and sometimes we go to Johnny's garden and play cowboys and Indians.'

'That sounds fun. Do you ever play armies? I used to be a soldier in the Army.'

'Dad is a soldier in the Salvation Army.'

'No, that's not a real army.'

I shot a glance at Arnold, but he was deep in conversation with his mother and didn't seem to have heard. Phew!

'Do you know any jokes?' asked Uncle John.

'No, do you?'

'Oh yes, I know a lot of jokes! What do you get if you cross Father Christmas with a duck?'

'I don't know.'

'A Christmas quacker!'

It took me a few seconds to understand, but when I did, I laughed and laughed.

'That is very funny.' I don't think anyone had ever told me a joke before. 'Tell me another one!'

'All right, here's another one about ducks. What side of a duck has the most feathers?'

I'd never seen a duck close up, but I thought it should be the same both sides.

'I don't know,' I said.

'The outside!'

'That's clever, I never thought of that!' I giggled.

'Here's another animal joke: what do you call a donkey with three legs?'

This time I laughed before hearing the answer. 'I've never seen a donkey with three legs,' I said. 'What do you call it?'

'A wonky!'

This was fun. I wanted to hear more jokes, but I could tell Arnold was getting annoyed by my laughter and was relieved when Pearl came in to tell us lunch was ready, so we all went through to the dining table in the back room.

'Now, doesn't that look beautiful?' said Grandma. 'What a lot of work you have done, Pearl.'

'It wasn't just me. Arnold laid the table and Richard helped me decorate the room and the Christmas tree yesterday.'

'A waste of space if you ask me!' sneered Arnold.

I wasn't sure if he meant the tree or me, but his mother came to the rescue.

'Stop being so bad-tempered, Arnold. Everyone has to have a tree at Christmas, but not everyone has such a beautifully decorated one as this.' She turned to me and gave me a big smile. 'Well done, Richard! Thank you for helping Pearl – she had a lot to do, getting everything ready for us to enjoy today.'

She made me feel happy and proud that day. Both Pearl and Uncle John looked pleased too. I'd never seen anyone tell Arnold off and I could tell it made him angry inside, but at least he didn't take it out on me this time.

Pearl put the plates on the table, piled high with roast turkey and ham. The smell was wonderful, I wished it could last all day! Then she passed round the vegetable dishes and gave me a helping of each. I know most children don't like sprouts, but I loved them as I helped the gardener to pick them at Field House. The carrots and crispy roast potatoes were delicious, too.

'What's orange and sounds like a parrot?' Uncle John asked me.

'I don't know,' I replied. 'What is it?'

Uncle John stuck his fork into something on his plate and lifted it up.

'A carrot!'

After that, Pearl, Uncle John and Grandma talked about various things together, while I concentrated on eating as much as I could. Arnold still looked a bit cross and I noticed he was mostly fiddling with his food, rather than eating much of it.

'What do you think, Arnold?' his mother asked him at one point in their conversation.

'I think it's all idle chit-chat,' he replied, pushing the rest of his food to one side and crashing his knife and fork down so hard that I was worried they might have broken the plate. He stood up and strode out of the lounge.

'I expect he's gone to have a cigarette,' said Pearl, trying to excuse him.

As soon as he was out of earshot, Uncle John turned to me and said, 'What did the big chimney say to the little chimney?'

'Tell me, tell me!' I pleaded, jumping around in my seat.

'You're too young to smoke!'

We all laughed at that, though Pearl looked nervously towards the door in case Arnold might have heard.

The rest of the day went well. We had a lot of fun and we even had a bit of a sing-song, with Uncle John playing the old piano in the corner where Joey's cage used to stand. Arnold didn't join us for that, but soon it was time for him to take Grandma and Uncle John back home again. I helped Pearl to take things out to the kitchen and went back to pick up all the bits of paper and rubbish from the crackers while she started to clear up.

'Did you enjoy your Christmas?'

'Yes, it was a lovely day. I liked Grandma and Uncle John – she was kind and he was very funny.'

Just then, we both heard a car in the drive and Pearl gave me a look. I knew what that meant and raced upstairs before he came in. After closing the bedroom door I sat down on my bed, looking at all the things Father Christmas had brought me. I wanted to put the record player on again, but couldn't remember how to do it, so I ate a toffee while I thought about everything that had happened that wonderful Christmas Day.

I heard them talking downstairs, then Pearl's light footsteps coming up the stairs.

'I think you'd better stay in your room now, but I'm glad you enjoyed your day and had plenty to eat. If you feel peckish, you can eat your apple, can't you?'

'Yes. Can you show me how to work this record player so I can do it myself?'

'Of course.' She showed me slowly what to do and set the record going, then listened through once with me, singing along, before going back to Arnold.

This time I put the record on myself and it worked. I listened to it again and again while I munched my way through another two toffees. I was so happy to have my music playing and things to eat and what a lovely day it had been that I didn't hear his heavy footsteps up the stairs.

The door burst open and he barged in, full of pent-up rage. 'I told you not to make any noise!' he shouted. 'I'm trying to rest downstairs but all I can hear is that terrible noise.' He pointed to my record player: 'Turn it off!'

I could feel my bottom lip trembling and my heart beat faster. All the happiness drained out of me as I realised I only knew how to turn it on.

'I don't know how to do it,' I said in a quavering voice.

'Just do it!' he shrieked, towering over me.

So I went over to the record player and tried to put it off, but the more he shouted, the worse I fumbled and panicked.

'I *can't*,' I said, shaking now.

He took two strides over to the record player, still playing, tore it from its socket, picked it up high and threw it against the wall with all his might. It fell into pieces to the floor, the arm coming off and scratching the record as it went, but at least it was now silent.

I was desperately upset, but just hoped this would be enough and he would go and leave me alone with my tears. But no, he grabbed me by the arm and dragged me downstairs, across the hall and into the sitting room, throwing me on the floor in front of the Christmas tree, where he started in earnest. He punched and kicked me, with his shoes still on, so it hurt worse than ever before. Like a madman, he was beating and beating me relentlessly, then he picked me up off the floor and threw me into the Christmas tree, the tree that Pearl and I had so lovingly decorated the day before. The whole thing tottered and fell, its branches crashing down and the baubles smashing into pieces and strewn all around.

'Now look what you've done!' he shouted. 'Look at the mess you've made.' His anger built up anew as he kept on punching me amid the ruins of our tree. 'You've spoilt Christmas for everybody!' he yelled. 'It was alright before you came.'

At this point, Pearl came running in, imploring him to stop. 'Please, Arnold,' she begged, 'you've done enough. Leave the poor little boy alone. You'll kill him if you don't stop now.'

As suddenly as he had started, he stopped and marched out, leaving me lying, bleeding, in the midst of the chaos of our Christmas.

Pearl extricated me from the remains of the tree and lifted me up in her arms.

'The tree,' I murmured, pointing forlornly at its sorry state.

'Don't worry, I'll clear all that up later – at least we had it to enjoy today. But I want to tend your wounds first, you're much more important than any decorations!'

As she carried me into the kitchen I gave her a weak smile through my tears. I was battered and sore and hurting all over. The kicks had made cuts and perhaps worse.

'We might have to take you to the doctor's this time,' she said, gently dabbing cream on almost all of my body. 'Do you hurt anywhere inside?'

'I don't know,' I sobbed. 'I just hurt everywhere.'

Pearl was crying too. 'Well, perhaps we can wait till tomorrow and see how you are then.' She picked me up from the kitchen chair and carried me carefully up the stairs to my bedroom. 'Now, you'll have to go to bed and you'll need to keep quiet,' she warned. 'Don't make him angry again.'

As we reached my room and she carried me through the door, she stopped, shocked by what she saw.

'What happened?'

'He didn't like the record playing and told me to turn it off, but I didn't know how to, so he picked up the whole record player and threw it at the wall to stop the noise,' I explained.

Now Pearl was in tears and so was I. Looking back, I expect she bought me that record player herself. It was such an exciting present, but it only lasted a few hours. She was certainly upset to see it smashed to bits on the floor.

'Oh dear!' She gave a deep sigh. 'What a terrible end to a lovely day. I'm so sorry, Richard.' She paused, then tucked me in bed, turned out the light and shut the door, leaving me sobbing for the present I would never enjoy again and the attack I had to endure because of it.

I couldn't find a comfortable position to lie in, with most of my body throbbing to remind me of my first Christmas with Arnold and Pearl.

CHAPTER 10

The Tricycle

E ver since I arrived in Greystoke Avenue, starting school was always going to be 'after Christmas'. Well, now it *was* after Christmas and Pearl helped me to prepare for this momentous new step in my life. Hodge Hill Primary School was just around the corner, behind our house, so it seemed familiar to me by now.

Pearl took me on the bus to a special shop that sold things for school. The first thing she bought me was a little brown leather bag with a flap and buckle.

'It's called a satchel,' she told me. 'This will be your school bag and you will take your things to school in it every day.'

Next, she picked out some pencils, crayons, a little note-book, a ruler and a rubber and put them all inside the satchel for me. I also needed some special black gym shoes and shorts, so they also went in the satchel.

I tried the satchel on for size and I felt very special with it on – I was a big boy now.

'Can I wear it home?' I asked.

'Yes, of course,' she said with a smile and went to the cash-ier's desk to pay.

THE TRICYCLE

I was very excited to be starting school, especially as my friends Johnny and Martin were going to start on the same day as me. The day before, Pearl walked me round so that I could see how close it was. Although I had heard the happy noises of children playing, I had never seen the school itself before because my bedroom was at the front of the house, so I was quite surprised to see such a long building, with its curly red roof, which I later realised was corrugated iron. There were windows all the way along it in both directions.

'They are the classrooms,' explained Pearl. 'I expect you will be in one of those.'

'Where do all the children play?' I asked her, anxious that I might have to stay inside all day.

'In the playground behind the building,' she said.

'Don't they have lawns to play on?'

'Not lawns, no. But they do have a field that they use in the summertime.'

'Oh good!' I said, relieved.

I always seemed to have so much energy and there wasn't much space in our garden. When I was running around, I felt almost as if I was running away, as if I could leave the bad things behind me. I couldn't wait to start.

Going to school on the first day seemed almost like a day out. Pearl packed my satchel for me in the morning and slipped in a little packet of cheese biscuits.

'These are a snack for you to eat at playtime,' she explained. 'I'll take you to school myself as it's your first day, but there are no roads to cross so after that you will be able to go and come back on your own, or with Johnny and Martin.'

The night before I could hardly get to sleep for excitement, so much so that for the first time ever I forgot to worry that Arnold might come in to attack me and spoil everything. Fortunately, he didn't.

'Time to go,' said Pearl with a warm smile. She helped me on with my coat and my satchel, then put on her own coat and scarf. 'Brrr!' she said as she pulled the front door to and off we went down the avenue. 'I'm sure you'll have a lovely time,' she told me. 'But, just in case anything happens to upset you, I'll be at home all morning. I'll come and fetch you at lunchtime and take you back afterwards.'

We arrived at the main entrance at the same time as all the other new children. I waved at Pearl and went inside. Some of the children were crying, but I felt quite confident – I suppose I was used to being with lots of other children and I knew I was good at making new friends. Straight away, I noticed the polished wooden parquet floor, which looked very similar to some of the floors we had at Field House. It was made from hundreds of small pieces of wood in diamond patterns, all the way across the entrance area and all the way down both the long corridors at each side. I seem to remember that one side was infants and the other side juniors. We had separate playgrounds too.

My name and Johnny's were read out together, so we were in the same class. He knew some of the other children too. Sadly, I don't remember my first teacher's name or much about her, but she led us down the long, long corridor that seemed to me as if went on for ever. All of the teachers were lovely.

Our first classroom had pictures round the wall with big letters on them. I recognised 'R' for Richard. Very soon I knew them all, singing the rhyme and the colourful numbers one to ten. At playtime we all had a little bottle of milk to drink. That was exciting! A helper came and took off all the tops and I licked the cold, thick cream at the top, before greedily drinking the rest.

Mmmm, delicious!

We had to put our coats on to go outside and run around. When we came back in, we learnt to sing 'Old MacDonald Had a Farm', which I already knew from our walks to the Clent Hills when we used to pass the monkey man. That all seemed so long ago now. Next, we played with plasticine and tried to make some of the farm animals, but they all looked very wonky, like Uncle John's joke about the donkey.

At lunch time, Pearl was there, waiting outside for me. She walked me home and made me special toasted sandwiches to warm me up. Then she took me back for afternoon school, before picking me up again at the end of the school day.

'Did you enjoy your first day at school?' she asked as we strolled back to our house.

'Yes, it was fun. Can I go again tomorrow?'

'Of course,' she laughed. 'You can go every day except Saturday and Sunday.'

'Goodie!' I did a little jig along the pavement.

After that, I walked round to school on my own or with Johnny, feeling very grown-up. As far as I can remember, every day at Hodge Hill Primary School was fun and it was an escape from all the bad things at home. I felt I couldn't get into trouble when I was at school, but I did feel sorry for Pearl as she didn't have me for company in the daytime. She must have felt sad on her own, sewing on Arnold's buttons or darning his socks.

We always started the day by going to the big hall with all the other classes, where we stood up, said the Lord's Prayer and sang a hymn (my favourite was 'All Creatures Great and Small'). Afterwards we all had to sit cross-legged in our short trousers on the beautiful floor to listen to the headteacher speaking to us.

I loved racing round the playground being aeroplanes with Johnny. Also, splashing about with paintbrushes because I had always liked painting at Field House. I was in heaven with all the lovely picture books to look at in the reading corner as I had hardly any books in my bedroom and I enjoyed learning new things. Most of all, I loved that little bottle of playtime milk and Pearl's cheesy snacks.

At weekends and after school, when the weather warmed up a bit, we carried on playing outside. Most of the children had tricycles, but I didn't – until one day. It was a weekend and Arnold had been out in his car. I saw him come back and stop in our drive, so I tried to hide behind some of the other children on a low trolley (I didn't want him to be angry with me in front of my friends).

'Richard, come here. I've got something for you,' he called out in an almost friendly voice. 'I bought you something today,' he continued, leaning into the back of his car and pulling something out. 'There!' He stood back. 'It's for you, so you can be like the other children and have your own tricycle.'

Amazed, shocked, I could hardly believe it. *Was this some kind of trick that he would pull away and take back to the shop?* But it wasn't, not this time.

'Go on,' he urged, 'give it a try. I want to see if it's the right size for you.'

THE TRICYCLE

It was a dark green tricycle with shiny silver handlebars. I could see that it wasn't brand new, but it looked wonderful. *Perhaps things were changing, maybe he did like me after all.*

'Thank you, Dad,' I said as I got on it and started to ride it around. Johnny and Martin ran up to look as well.

'That's a good trike,' said Johnny, which made me feel proud.

Every day I cleaned and polished my tricycle before riding it down the avenue. We played traffic games with one of the children as a policeman, directing us which way to go at the pretend roundabout, stopping and starting at the traffic lights one of the other dads had drawn on the road surface with chalk. It felt good to know that Arnold had been like a dad to me when he bought me that trike, though it still felt a bit strange that he let me play on it so much. When the weather was fine, I rode it outside with the others, but when it rained, Pearl would open the door that led from the kitchen to the garage and let me ride it in there.

'I can keep an eye on you from the kitchen,' she said. 'So you can ride your tricycle as much as you like in there.'

It was a very long garage, with hardly anything in it, so one day she helped me set up some sort of obstacle course in the garage for me to ride round. That made it more interesting and I had a lot of fun.

Every now and then, Pearl would put her head round the door and ask if I wanted a cup of tea or an orange squash and nine times out of ten I did!

One day, during my first half-term holiday, when I was riding my tricycle around the obstacle course in the garage and singing away merrily to myself, Arnold came home, stormed through the kitchen and burst through the door leading into the garage like an angry gorilla, shouting obscenities at me – all the usual nasty words.

I froze where I was, still sitting on my trike.

He strode straight across, his face bright red and his eyes bulging.

'I'm sorry, I'm sorry,' I mumbled in fear. I knew I had done nothing wrong, but I also knew that, as far as Arnold was concerned, just my being there was a torment to him. He picked up my beautiful tricycle with me still on it and threw us both as hard as he could at the brick wall.

I must have blacked out as soon as I hit that wall – I don't remember the impact or the pain. By the time I came to, in a daze and wondering what had happened, he was shouting and screaming at Pearl and at me, while she was on her knees beside me, on the hard concrete floor, gently cradling what she could reach of my little body.

'There, there,' she tried to soothe me, while also trying to keep him away.

He continued to rant and rage, though he sounded distant to my befuddled brain.

'Leave him alone,' she pleaded, protecting me with her body. 'You've gone too far this time.'

He stormed off and slammed the kitchen door behind him.

I couldn't comprehend what had happened or why. I don't know how long it was before the pain started to kick in and I realised my plight. I was lying in an awkward position, all tangled up with the parts of the tricycle, which had fallen to bits in a jagged mass of metal all round me and underneath me.

Pearl tried her best, as gently as she could, to extricate me from the wreck. But I was now regaining consciousness more fully and the slightest move made me cry out in pain. Eventually, she managed to free from the debris and carried me carefully back into the house.

'We'll have to take Richard to the hospital,' she announced as firmly as I'd ever heard her speak.

'He's not getting in my car in that mess,' growled the ogre. 'I don't want blood on my seats.' He paused. 'And I'm certainly not taking him to hospital – he's only got a few little scratches.'

'Well, I can't stop him bleeding,' she persisted, trying to bandage up and put pressure on the worst of my wounds. 'And he was unconscious for a few minutes, so he definitely needs checking.'

'I'm not taking him anywhere now. Let him sleep it off, he can go in the morning if he's not better.'

'Please take him now,' she begged, but he steadfastly refused.

By this time I was hurting all over – in so much pain that I didn't care where I went. I had a huge, throbbing, splitting headache and all my bones seemed to hurt too. My whole body felt as if it was pounding with pain and I still felt quite woozy. She carried me upstairs and into the bathroom to wash my wounds as tenderly as she could and I vaguely remember her applying cream, plasters and bandages. Then she got me into my pyjamas and into bed. It must have been about teatime, but she didn't offer me any food and for once, I don't think I could have eaten any.

'Be very quiet,' she told me before she left the room and I heard her go back down the stairs. As I lay there, battered and bruised, it was the shock that overwhelmed me. I thought we'd almost turned a corner when Arnold bought me that tricycle and he'd let me play on it, but he suddenly changed back into the monster again, hell-bent on destroying it. I couldn't understand it and I knew then that I would never again be able to see any good in him.

The following morning, Arnold went off to work and left Pearl to cope. Overnight, all my joints had stiffened and I could hardly move, let alone walk. She helped me to get up and dressed, then carried me down to the sitting room and laid me down on the settee.

'You stay there,' she said. 'I'll go and make you some breakfast and a nice cup of tea. Later, we can turn the television on, if you like and see if there are any children's programmes for you to watch.'

My eyes filled with tears. I suppose it was a mixture of how weak and shocked and in pain I still felt and her kindness to me in contrast to Arnold's violence.

After breakfast, Pearl checked my wounds and, one part of my body at a time, gently tested to see whether I might have broken anything.

'I think you've been lucky,' she said. 'I don't think you've broken any bones, as far as I can see, but I still want to take you to the doctor to make sure and to dress some of your wounds properly. I know you can't walk very well, so we'll have to wait till Arnold gets back.'

'Sorry,' I said.

Even at that young age I understood something of how difficult this was for Pearl and I felt it must be my fault for making Arnold so angry and being the cause of all this worry for her.

It was my fault for playing, for making a noise, for enjoying myself.

My fault for being there.

When Arnold came home from work that afternoon, Pearl pleaded anew with him to take me to see a doctor. He must have realised how badly he had hurt me and finally agreed to drive us there – 'But I'm not coming in.'

We travelled in silence and when we arrived outside the surgery he turned to look at me and wagged his finger. 'Don't tell him anything,' he ordered me. 'Not a word or you will be in trouble, more trouble than ever before. Do you understand?'

'Yes,' I agreed meekly – I didn't want to say anything anyway.

Then he turned to Pearl: 'You must tell the doctor he fell down the stairs and onto my metal toolkit.'

'Yes, Arnold,' she nodded as she lifted me out of the car and took me in.

The doctor was very kind and concerned about me as he removed all Pearl's First Aid plasters and bandages.

'I'm surprised to see Richard has so many wounds and bruises. Tell me what happened.'

'I didn't see it happen,' Pearl explained, 'but my husband says he fell down the stairs and landed on his metal toolkit in the hall.'

'No wonder he's in such a state,' replied the doctor. 'Did Richard lose consciousness, do you know?'

'Yes, I ran to him when I heard all the noise and I think he had blacked out.'

All the time they were talking, I didn't take much notice of what else they said – I just watched and winced as the doctor checked me over carefully.

'Do you think he's broken anything, doctor?'

'I'm not certain – there are so many bones in the human body. But I think he must have been very lucky not to have any breaks, having seen how deep some of these cuts and bruises are. I'll just call in my nurse to come and dress them properly for you.'

Both the doctor and the nurse were so kind and gentle that I soon began to feel better.

'There,' he said with a smile. 'I think you're all done now, almost as well wrapped up as an Egyptian mummy!' He laughed as if he had told a joke.

I must have looked puzzled.

'When you get home, you can ask your mother to tell you what an Egyptian mummy is!' Then he turned to Pearl as we were about to leave. 'That boy needs careful looking after for the next few days. I hope there will be no more falls down the stairs.'

At that moment I wondered whether he knew Pearl hadn't told the truth.

CHAPTER 11

Jekyll and Hyde

I must have been poorly for several days, the rest of the half-term at least. Some of my friends came to the door and asked for me to come out and play, but I heard Pearl telling them kindly that I wasn't well and wouldn't be able to come out for a while. It was a bad time for me, with my physical injuries gradually improving, but my mental health scarred. I had hardly any books to look at and nothing much to do as even drawing and painting was painful at first, so I used to watch the television sometimes when Arnold was out, but mostly I just lay in my bed or on the settee with my thoughts. Sometimes Pearl came and sat with me, when she didn't have too much housework to do, but of course, she had to keep everything spick and span for Arnold.

When it came to Sunday, some of my bruises were beginning to fade, but Pearl and Arnold must have decided that their Salvation Army friends might ask questions if they noticed anything.

'Arnold will go to the meeting on his own today,' Pearl told me. 'We don't think you're well enough to go, as you need to build up your strength to go back to school tomorrow, so you and I are going to stay home together today and maybe there will be something good to watch on television this afternoon, perhaps a cowboys and Indians film. Would you like that?'

'Ooh yes, please! I've never seen cowboys and Indians.'

We had our Sunday roast and, for the first day since going to the doctor's, I got dressed and came down to eat with them in the back room. As usual on Sundays, the food was delicious and Pearl had made extra gravy for me.

Throughout the meal, Arnold and Pearl talked to each other, excluding me from their conversation. This time it was about another Salvation Army family who were experiencing troubles. Looking back now, I can see the irony in Arnold's criticisms of others' faults and problems, seemingly without any awareness of his own. Pearl listened and seemed to stick up for the family in their plight, but Arnold showed his impatience with her defence of them by making exasperated snorts every now and then. I stayed silent, of course, and concentrated on enjoying my roast pork, gravy, roast potatoes and vegetables, followed by my all-time favourite, apple crumble. My appetite was definitely returning.

When she saw my clean plate, Pearl gave me a big smile.

'Well, I hardly need to wash that plate, you've all but licked it clean!'

Usually, after Sunday lunch, I would have to help her with the washing-up, then go upstairs and keep quiet while they had a rest, but today would be different.

'Back to school with you tomorrow,' barked Arnold, without even a look in my direction.

'Well, he's staying home and resting this afternoon, so that maybe he'll be well enough tomorrow,' agreed Pearl with a twinkle in her eyes. I could tell she was looking forward to a lazy afternoon with me in front of the television with Arnold out of the house for the duration.

Even at that age, I thought it was strange how Arnold could go to church and say he was a Christian when he never behaved like it at home. He would sometimes rant on about the Ten Commandments and all the 'Thou shalt not' commands and obviously saw me as a captive audience in the car. He used to say them all out loud, one at a time, with due emphasis, ending with a lecture on the devil and the need to guard against evil. I didn't understand a lot of the words, but I certainly got the message that there were a lot of things that I mustn't do, even though I didn't yet know what they were. I felt sure that he didn't keep to them all, though, and as for guarding against evil, *he* was the evil I had to try to guard against – if only I could.

If I wanted to be kind to him, as the adult I now am, I suppose I could say he had the right intentions, but there was obviously something different going on in his mind. Not just to provoke his raging violence against such a defenceless little boy, but also the vile language he used and all those terrible accusations against me that sapped my confidence and drove my self-esteem to the floor. As I grew older, I realised that religious people should not do those things, nor talk like that, but at the time I just thought there must be something about me that made him hate me so much: it must be my fault.

Every Sunday afternoon, Arnold would put on his navy blue Salvation Army uniform, buttoned right up to the top, with epaulettes and a peaked cap. Pearl always wore one of her floral dresses – not too colourful, with a dark coat and a neat little hat. Although she was the one who had been brought up in a Salvation Army family, she wasn't a 'soldier', so she didn't wear the uniform with the funny bonnets that some of the other women wore. But she did always wear gloves to the meeting – black gloves – they were a must, and on her arm she carried a small handbag.

I used to have to dress up, too. Pearl had bought me a little jacket, a jumper and a tie, which I had to learn to do up. Until I was about 10, I always had to wear short trousers to the meetings, no matter what the weather was like.

All the adults took their Bibles with them into the meeting and they picked up their songbooks as they went in. I don't know why, but they didn't call them hymns, though that's what they were. They were usually rousing songs, accompanied by the brass band. My favourite was 'Onward Christian Soldiers', because the band played that in such a jolly way and everybody sang it loudly, accelerating the noise level with each verse, the sound rising right up to the roof and beyond. That was the song that seemed to fill everyone with joy.

In between the songs there was always a sermon, delivered in a deliberately rousing way, working up to a crescendo, like American Gospel preachers do. It seemed to go on and on, the visiting preacher accelerating the pace by raising his voice up and up, more and more insistently stirring the emotions and raising people's fears, until visitors in the meeting felt the urge to come forward themselves to be saved.

Pearl once told me that Arnold had been a visitor to the meeting, when they were courting, and he had gone forward to be saved. I'm not so sure that it worked in his case as he clearly didn't take any notice of his promises to God when he attacked me. He can't have felt any guilt, as far as I could see, as he really seemed to get enjoyment out of hurting me. It took away his tension and anger with everything. The more he hit me and called me names, the better he felt himself, or so it seemed. If only his fellow 'soldiers' had known, but I'm sure he hid his true self well and I don't suppose anyone suspected a thing. To everyone in the congregation, he was an upstanding member of society. He was the treasurer, strutting about the hall, collecting the money and doing the accounts. He had a Salvation Army wife, he had a good job in insurance, a house and a car. He had taken in a motherless child and he was respected by everyone in the meeting.

What a contrast to the person he was at home, the monster inside him coming out and terrorising our lives. I don't know whether he ever physically attacked Pearl, but I could see she was frightened of him. He was the king of his castle and Pearl had to pander to his every need. She worked so hard every day, trying to please him, but I never heard him thank her. He carried on beating me whenever he felt like it, often with great ferocity, but he never expressed any remorse or sorrow. Afterwards he never even mentioned it, as if it never happened. I think he must have needed the feeling of power, so he had to control us both in different ways, yet when he attacked me, he lost control of himself.

It was Pearl I felt bad about. Right from the start, while I first felt sorry for myself, I hated seeing her so upset every time she was left to sort me out and pick up the pieces, sometimes literally. As her tears flowed, she became more and more affected by it all and increasingly anxious and nervous – and it was all my fault. It had only happened since I arrived, so I thought it must be my fault. Pearl was the one who was kind to me and she was always in trouble because of me. When she was upset, I feared she wouldn't like me any more, but the amazing thing was that she did. I don't know why, but she carried on being kind and motherly to me.

Every Sunday, after the meeting, we used to go to Auntie Ethel's. Her husband, Uncle Jim, was Pearl's brother. He was a lovely man, very quiet. I loved Auntie Ethel too – she was the lively one. He was small and she was tall, and both of them were very welcoming. They lived in a tiny back-to-back house in Aston, with two bedrooms upstairs and one room downstairs, so they cooked over the open fire. It was near our Salvation Army citadel, so it was very convenient.

Throughout the last song at the meeting, I couldn't wait to go there because Auntie Ethel always put on such a lovely big tea for us. In those days I rarely had enough to eat at home, so I couldn't wait to tuck into her generous feast every Sunday teatime.

Auntie Ethel and Uncle Jim scraped by on very little money, unlike Pearl and Arnold, with his high salary from working as a branch manager in insurance, so there were a lot of contrasts. And theirs was a happy, loving family home; that was the biggest contrast of all.

They had two children. A teenager called John, who already played in the Salvation Army band, and a younger lad named Michael. He was the same age as me so we had a lot in common and we got on very well indeed. The difference was that Michael was very well looked after and very much loved.

There were no mod-cons at their house. Their tin bath-tub hung on the wall in their downstairs room and was taken down once a week, put in the middle of the floor and filled with pans of hot water, so that they could each take turns to take baths. They had a toilet at the bottom of the backyard, which they had to use in all weathers. For me, this was part of the excitement of going there every Sunday. In winter they would put a little paraffin heater there to try and stop the water turning to ice, but oof, the smell! They even used to hang orange crepe paper wrappers on a string to use as toilet paper when we came instead of their usual newspaper squares.

When we arrived for tea, we would crowd into the downstairs room, sitting on stools and chairs round the table, which was covered with a plastic tablecloth. The table itself was always covered with piled-high plates of cheese or ham sandwiches on brown bread, together with freshly baked cakes. They were all delicious and I could eat as much as I wanted. There were cups of tea and jugs of lemonade to help the food go down and I used to play with Michael while the grown-ups talked. This was a house full of laughter. I never looked forward to the Salvation Army meetings, apart from the brass band, but I greatly looked forward to tea at Auntie Ethel's.

Michael was a bit taller than me and quite sporty, which I wasn't really. He liked kicking a ball around in the yard with the lads who lived in the other back-to-backs, so that's what we did sometimes on Sundays, if it was fine. We used to talk a lot too.

'What are your parents like?' I asked Michael one time, when we'd got to know each other quite well.

'They're so lovely,' he said with a grin. 'They couldn't be better.' He paused. 'What are Pearl and Arnold like?'

'Not so great. I'm in such trouble sometimes.'

'What do you mean?' he asked. 'What kind of trouble?' He looked concerned for me, as if he might have guessed something wasn't quite right.

'It's probably all my fault – he hits me a lot.'

'Oh, that's not good.'

'No, it's hard and it upsets Pearl as well.'

'You should say something,' he suggested.

I thought about it for a moment. 'No, I don't think I can,' I explained. 'It would only make more trouble for Pearl and more danger for me.'

'Hmm, it's tricky, isn't it? But it's not right. Somebody needs to know so that they can do something about it.'

'Please don't say anything to your mum and dad,' I asked him, 'because they might tell Arnold and then I'll be in even worse trouble.'

I don't think Michael said anything straight away, but he might have done at some stage, because I got an inkling that Uncle Jim suspected something. After all, he was Pearl's brother, so he would want to protect her too. There were just little clues.

'You don't seem very bright today,' he said to me one Sunday evening.

Unbeknown to him, this followed a bad attack from Arnold on me the night before. I hadn't even wet the bed, so I felt particularly indignant as well as bruised and traumatised.

'Are you not very well, or …?'

'Oh, I'm OK,' I replied.

He nodded and sat with me as we ate, trying to cheer me up. Michael saw us and came and sat the other side of me. I was grateful for their concern, but uncomfortable and fearful in case Arnold suspected anything.

* * *

I'd been with Arnold and Pearl for a year or so by now and some of my friends' parents down the Avenue started showing their concern, too.

'You don't look very happy,' said Johnny's mum. 'Are you all right?'

'Yes, I'm fine, thanks,' I said.

This was my stock answer and it seemed to work most of the time.

'You know, you can come round here any time, Richard, and have a cup of tea and a piece of cake,' Johnny's mum continued, so perhaps she had picked up on the fact that something wasn't quite right.

It was around now that social services got in touch for the first time. One day, Pearl and I were having our tea and biscuits at the kitchen table after school.

'Mr Watts is coming to see you after school tomorrow,' she began. 'He is your welfare officer and he wants to come and meet you. He will have a chat with you, your dad and me, so Dad will come home early. Mr Watts will make visits every few months to see how you are doing.'

'Oh?' I was curious. 'What will he ask me about?'

'Just easy questions, like whether you enjoy school and whether you are happy at home,' she replied.

This last one was not an easy question to answer. I began to think about it that evening. Would I have the chance to tell him the truth? For a moment I had a spark of hope. I had wanted to tell someone for a long time, to be rescued – but what would I say? Would he believe me? What if he told them what I'd told him? I feared the terrible punishment that would follow – I had a headache with the worry of it – but at least I could be reasonably confident that Arnold would not come and trouble me that night, in case of any bruises showing, so I slept well.

The next afternoon I walked home from school, wondering whether I would like Mr Watts, but as soon as I came in sight of my house, I thought I probably would. There on the drive, next to Arnold's car, stood a bright, shiny red Mini. This was a brand-new car and the first one I had seen in our street: anyone who had a Mini, especially a red one, must like cars, and so did I.

The front door had been left ajar so that I could get in and I could hear muffled voices in the front room, so I put my satchel down and went into the kitchen to reach a glass and pour myself a drink of water. I could just about reach the taps now, on tiptoes. They were still talking, so I went out to the garden to water my vegetable patch with my little watering can, then I sat on the concrete steps and watched a butterfly flitting from flower to flower.

'Hello, Richard,' said Pearl in her sing-song voice, coming out to find me. 'Mr Watts is here and he would like to meet you.'

I stood up, still unsure what I would say, yet half-hoping this was my chance. But I needn't have worried, or hoped. Arnold was still in the front room with him when Pearl led me in and introduced me.

'This is Richard, he's just come home from school.'

I gave the bald man a smile and he grinned back at me. Pearl sat down again on the settee and Mr Watts looked at the papers in his lap.

'Did you have a good day at school?' he asked.

'Yes, thank you.'

He ticked something on the top sheet of paper, which I suppose was some kind of welfare form.

'Do you like school?'

'Yes, I love school – it's just around the corner.'

Tick.

'Have you made some good friends?'

The ticks continued and so did the simple questions, until we got to the crunch: 'How do you like being a part of this family?'

I shot a glance at Arnold, who gave me a piercing look – I knew what it meant. Then I looked at Pearl and she was smiling at me.

'It's fine,' I said. 'Mum looks after me well.'

'And Dad too, I'm sure.'

I took in a breath, then nodded, as they all expected me to do.

'Yes.'

Any minute now, I thought, Mr Watts would ask them to leave the room and talk to me on my own – but it didn't happen.

'Well, you're obviously growing well,' he said. 'And I'm glad to know you are happy.' Then he turned to Pearl and Arnold. 'So, I'll take the paperwork back to the office and see you again in six months.'

And that was it – any hope of finally having the chance to tell someone what was really happening disappeared just as quickly as he did.

CHAPTER 12

Another Nail in the Coffin

Although I was always a loner to some extent, often forced on me when Arnold was at home, I think I was a naturally gregarious child with a thirst for learning, so I always loved school and I was lucky to have some very good teachers. School was my escape, my one refuge from Arnold and all that, so I made the most of it. I don't recall ever missing a day of infant school, though sometimes suffering after the night before – I don't think any of my teachers noticed, or if they did, they said nothing. School became my normality, compared with my general state of confusion at home, not understanding what was happening to me or why. School allowed me to laugh freely and feel safe. For me, that was a godsend.

We did a lot of painting, I remember, and the teachers read us stories. This made me very keen to learn to read so that I could take home books to devour in my lonely evening hours between Arnold coming home and my bedtime. I soon discovered I could get lost in another world in a book.

One of our infant teachers used to have a 'show and tell' time at the beginning of the day, when we were all encouraged to tell our news. The other children often used to talk about their mums and dads, their day at the zoo or the lovely holiday they'd had. I listened with a touch of envy, I suppose, but when the teacher asked what had happened to me at the weekend, I couldn't say anything – I think I did feel a bit depressed about that.

I'm not sure whether any of my infant teachers guessed that something wasn't right. Sometimes one of them would try to get me talking.

'How are you getting on?' or 'Are you feeling all right? You seem a bit sad today,' they would say. So, perhaps they did notice, especially if something had happened to me the night before.

I can't remember what I said, but it was probably something along the lines of 'I didn't sleep very well' – which was true.

My last Christmas at the infant school we did a nativity scene for the parents. We had to learn what to do and some of us had lines to learn too. I loved all that, acting and performing. I was glad to see Pearl in the audience, smiling proudly at me, but no sign of Arnold, which was a great relief. We sang 'Away in a Manger' so I didn't even have to learn the words to that, having sung it at Field House.

The best thing of all was the special tea we had afterwards in our classroom – orange squash and cakes from the local bakery. I had two cream cakes and three doughnuts! This was the only party I was ever allowed to attend. I had lots of invitations from my friends to parties where they played games, ate cake and all the rest. One of them even had a magician. But my instructions were always to go straight home from school, so that's what I had to do. I didn't dare go, even to Johnny's party for a short while – I was too afraid of what would happen if I did.

I was not allowed to have birthday parties either. Pearl always gave me one birthday present, while Arnold was still at work. She would bake me a birthday cake and light a candle to stick in it.

'Blow it out and make a wish,' she would say.

My wish was always the same – but it never came true.

I know my friends must have thought it strange that I couldn't go to their parties, but I suppose they just assumed my parents were strict or overprotective. Even at this young age, I quickly realised other children had a lot more joy in their lives than I did. Most of them weren't religious and didn't go to church, but they still seemed to have happy and fulfilling lives. They would go off for days out with their dads or for family holidays by the sea and tell me afterwards about all the fun they had – I never had any such stories to tell.

Despite my home problems, I did very well in my last year at the infant school. We were allowed to sit with whoever we liked, so Johnny and I always sat together. He was a good boy and always focused on doing his work. This had a good effect on me and I always tried to do my best, too. I suppose I craved praise and encouragement. It didn't matter what I did at home or how good I had been, I never received any praise from Arnold, and only from Pearl when he wasn't around, but I soon learnt I could earn praise at school and be proud of my achievements. Consequently, I was never really naughty – I had more than enough trouble at home to deal with, so I knew how to stay out of it at school. I was never bullied either, I think I just got on with everybody. Perhaps

I'd learnt to do that at Field House and it stayed with me at school.

In the summer holidays we moved house, to Windleaves Road in Castle Bromwich. This was a better house, in a quieter, more affluent area on the edge of the countryside, and I was thrilled that I could see some woods and hills from my bedroom window. I wondered whether maybe these were my beloved Clent Hills, so I asked Pearl, but she told me that Clent was far away on the other side of Birmingham. Whatever hills they were, I treasured the view. The residential area we lived in had wide, tree-lined roads and long drives, so it felt much more spacious. I later found out that Arnold had invented a new way of doing things in the insurance business, so his salary had increased and he'd gone up in the world. But, for me, he would always be low in the things that really mattered.

This house move was good timing for me because I started junior school in September that year, 1961. Of course I missed my old friends, especially Johnny, but I soon made new friends, both in my road and at school. I remember one of them was a big blond-haired lad called Robert. We got on very well, right from the start.

I felt slightly anxious about starting at a new school where I knew nobody except Robert, but I was getting used to change by now, so I knew I'd fit in somehow. The headmaster looked rather stern, I thought, in his tweed jacket and thick glasses, but I liked my new teacher.

Arnold had a workshop in the back garden at this new house and he prided himself on being able to make or mend things, although he'd never had any training in woodwork.

He was always making new furniture out of old bits of wood. One weekend, Pearl and I were sitting in the kitchen having a mid-morning cup of tea when the hammering stopped and he brought in a stool he had made. As usual, he ignored me and put it down to show Pearl. The seat part of the stool was made out of a polished piece of what I think must have been mahogany and he had cut out a shape on either side. He had nailed in four short legs, so it was more like a footstool than one for an adult to sit on. Because the legs were all a bit different and only nailed on, he had added a wooden strut, which he nailed in underneath, perhaps to give it strength or stability.

'What do you think?' he asked Pearl.

She inspected it, then turned to face him and gave him a smile.

'Very nice,' she said. 'I'm sure it will be very useful.'

Happy enough with that, off he went, back to his workshop.

I didn't know anything at all about woodwork yet, but I do remember these awfully big nails, hammered in, which seemed to be holding everything together.

'Is that how it should look?' I asked Pearl.

'Well, Arnold doesn't know how to make proper joints,' she replied, 'so this is the way he always does it.' She reached down and moved the stool to test its strength. 'It's a bit wobbly,' she added, 'but I think it will be fine.'

A few days later, I was sitting on the stool, playing with my cars on the kitchen floor, while Pearl sang the hymn 'Jesus loves me, this I know' as she cooked a pie for Arnold's tea. It felt warm and cosy. I loved the aroma of the pie, even though I knew I would not be allowed to eat any of it.

Suddenly, Arnold stormed into the kitchen, sending the contentment temperature plummeting. Home early, he tore off his raincoat and threw it across the table, dropped his briefcase on the floor and his hat on the back of a chair, then sat down. He didn't seem to have noticed me, so I kept completely silent and still.

'That bloody accountant!' he began telling Pearl and he ranted on about invoices and extra expenditure.

All this went over my head. I wished I'd known to get out of the way before he came home, but I couldn't escape now.

'Make me a cup of tea,' he ordered Pearl. 'Thank God it's Friday and I don't have to see that fool tomorrow! He'd better watch out, I'll give him a piece of my mind first thing on Monday.' He turned and took a rolled-up newspaper out of his raincoat pocket and flattened it out on the table. While he had a look at the headlines, Pearl turned to me with her finger to her mouth. I understood what she meant, but it was too late.

'Look at all this bloody nonsense!' he shouted, scraping back his chair and standing up in a rage, presumably at the state of the world. That's when he spotted me, sitting still on the little stool he had made.

'What's that brat doing here?' he shouted at Pearl, not waiting for an answer. 'He should be up in his bedroom. You know I don't want to see that shitbag when I get home from work – I'll show him!'

With that, he strode over to me, picked the stool up, with me on it, and hurled it across the kitchen.

I remember my horror when I was still in the air, as if it was happening in slow motion. I could see the wall coming towards me.

Crash!

Then the searing pain. The stool had partly disintegrated, leaving me to fall on a long nail that was now sticking out from the debris. I was in agony, but even worse was the fear. There was so much blood spurting out of my foot, I was frightened I might lose all my blood, pouring out like that. It shot out in every direction – on the floor, up the wall and streaks of it were on the table, the chairs and the cupboard nearby.

Pearl rushed to get out a clean tea towel and wound it tightly round my foot, applying pressure on my wound, which made the pain even worse. By now I was feeling faint and my head was spinning. I turned cold with shock.

Pearl kept the pressure on as much as she could, but it didn't staunch the blood.

'He's still bleeding!' she shrieked at Arnold. 'I can't stop it! We'll have to go straight to the doctor's this time, it's going to have to be stitched.'

He hesitated, perhaps realising that this situation, which he had created himself, had now gone beyond his control.

'Quick, start the car!' she told him. 'I'll carry Richard out.'

Soon we were on our way, the tears falling down my face in pain and fear of what would happen to me.

'What are we going to say?' Pearl asked Arnold, hugging me to try and warm me up, while still exerting pressure on my foot as we drew up outside the surgery.

Arnold turned to face me: 'You tell them you fell on a stool.'

Knowing I had no choice, I nodded.

* * *

'Now, what have you been up to?' asked this new doctor, directing Pearl to put me down on the high bed in his surgery, where he immediately undid the bandages. 'How did you do this?' he asked, using swabs to apply pressure to my wound and stem the bleeding.

I looked at Pearl and she looked at me.

'I fell onto a stool,' I said, obeying orders.

'What kind of a stool did this to you?' he asked in surprise.

'A homemade stool,' I replied, still feeling faint.

'My husband made it,' added Pearl. 'He thinks he's good at making things, but he doesn't know how to make joints so he just nailed the pieces of wood together and when Richard tripped, he fell on the stool, which came apart and a large nail pierced his foot.'

'Well, what an unfortunate accident,' commented the doctor, turning back to me. 'But you were lucky it was only your foot.' He gently lifted the swab. 'I think that's done it,' he added. 'It seems to have stopped bleeding so much now, but I'm a bit worried your wound may become infected, so I'm afraid I'll have to give you a tetanus injection.'

That was another shock for me. Nobody likes having injections and I burst into tears again.

'Do I have to?' I sobbed.

The doctor nodded and Pearl put her arms around me while he administered the injection, which didn't hurt half as much as I expected. Then he carefully stitched up my wound. When it was time to go, he turned to me: 'You've been a brave soldier today,' he said, and reaching into his desk drawer, he got out a mint humbug and gave it to me.

'Thank you,' I said, beginning to feel better at last.

'Now, you take care and try not to have any more falls,' he advised me with a smile as we left.

Outside, Arnold was drumming his fingers impatiently on the steering wheel. It was an ice-cold journey home, or that's what it felt like to me, and another night of throbbing pain, but at least he didn't trouble me that night.

Perhaps even he realised he'd done enough damage for one day.

Any injuries I sustained as a result of Arnold's attacks were usually not very noticeable, but this time the wound on my foot made me limp, so I couldn't hide that.

'Why are you limping?' Robert asked, with a mixture of curiosity and concern. 'Have you hurt yourself?'

'I fell on a stool at home,' I replied. 'It was a homemade one and there was a nail sticking out of it and …'

'You fell on a stool?' he asked in disbelief. 'How? Surely you knew it was there?'

I fended off his questions and he didn't mention it again that day. However, I do wonder whether he told his parents because the next day at break he started to ask me more: 'Are you sure it really happened like that?'

'Yes,' I replied, slightly embarrassed to have to talk about it again. 'I actually fell on the nail sticking out of the stool – it went into my foot.'

'Did it bleed a lot?'

'Yes, I had to go to the doctor's and have stitches.'

'Well, you'll have to be careful, won't you?'

'Yes, I know.'

He paused, then said: 'Well, if anybody hurts you, you can tell me. I'll come and sort them out!'

I'll never forget his response. I was so touched that he would defend me like that, but of course, he didn't know what it was really like.

'Don't worry, I'll be fine,' I insisted.

If only I could have told him. For a moment, I nearly did. I'm sure that would have been a great help to me, to have somebody I could trust to talk things through with – but it was too dangerous. Whenever I woke after one of Arnold's attacks, the impact was still there with me – in my mind and my body. I carried it with me into school. It definitely affected my concentration in lessons so I didn't listen to the teacher as well as I should and sometimes had to ask Robert what we were supposed to do. He never complained and the teacher rarely seemed to notice. On the way home part of me was desperate to keep talking and tell Robert everything, but I didn't dare.

There were a lot of good things about junior school and many new experiences. For one thing, we had bigger wooden desks with inkwells and brass sliding lids. Each of us had a sheet of white blotting paper to dry up any blots we made as we learnt how to use our dip pens. From now on, pencils were only for drawing and all our writing had to be in pen and ink. I really enjoyed this, despite making quite a mess sometimes while I was learning, but I soon got the hang of it.

We had new subjects to learn too and I especially liked geography and history. People didn't travel to other countries as much in those days, so it was exciting one day when the teacher showed us a huge map of the world, which she pinned up on the wall. As she pointed out the continents and the oceans, I was amazed.

'This is Africa,' she said. 'Here is the Atlantic Ocean and that's America.'

It reminded me of the lovely time at Field House when my housemother brought me a globe to look at – I'm sure that's where my love of learning began.

'But isn't the world round?' I asked the teacher.

'That's right, Richard. Well done! We can have a look at a globe tomorrow.'

In history, my favourite topic was transport. I loved looking at the pictures of old cars and lorries. Another topic I enjoyed was Earth and other planets. That was amazing. Sometimes at night I would look out at the moon and the stars and wonder: would anyone ever be able to go there?

Although I had loved running around and climbing trees at Field House, I now had a complicated relationship with PE at school, because I was always afraid that if I changed into the school PE kit, other children and the teachers might notice my bruises and I didn't want any awkward questions or strange looks. I didn't know how to deal with them, so as art was my favourite subject, I went to ask my teacher if I could do extra art instead. I can't remember what excuse I gave for wanting to do this, but she was a lovely lady – very understanding of children's problems, even when she didn't know what they were, though I'm sure she might have guessed (in those days, nobody intervened in what went on 'behind closed doors').

'You can just sit out and watch this time,' she suggested. 'Would that be all right?'

'Yes, thank you,' I said gratefully.

'Then I'll look into it and see whether that's allowed.'

I suppose it would not have been possible in most primary schools, but we had the luxury of having a special Art room, where there was always a teacher in the room, which was very spacious and relaxing. I don't know who my class teacher spoke to – probably the headteacher, I suppose – but she kept me back one break time for a few minutes to tell me what had been agreed.

'I know you're a talented artist,' she began, 'so I've arranged it for you. Every PE lesson, you can just go straight to the art room and the art teacher knows about it, so she will make a little space for you and give you a drawer with paper, pencils and anything else you need.'

This was wonderful news for me and it worked out very well. I liked both drawing and painting, but most of all, I loved to do drawings of cars or buildings. I think the beauty and elegance of Field House had inspired me in that direction, so the art teacher let me look through *Country Life* magazines and draw some of those houses, or sometimes cars from *Motor Sport* magazine. For me, these were joyful interludes when I could forget all my troubles and develop my creativity.

It was strange, thinking back, that none of the other children ever questioned me about this arrangement. I suppose they all loved PE, so perhaps they felt sorry for me that I wasn't doing it. I would probably have enjoyed it myself under different circumstances.

One of the many things I had missed about my time at Field House was having bedtime stories. Pearl rarely read anything to me and the only books on their bookshelf seemed to be an old dictionary and their Salvation Army Bibles. The only books I had were my picture Bible (Pearl had read out stories from this when I first had it) and the little car book that Father Christmas had brought me when I was first with Arnold and Pearl. I wasn't even allowed any comics to look at.

At my infants' school, I had loved reading all the funny or interesting picture books, with just a few words, then progressing to those with more text. Now that I could read well at the junior school, I asked if I could borrow books from the school library to take home.

'Yes, of course,' agreed my teacher with a smile.

This was a wonderful opportunity for me. I went straight to the library and for my very first book, I chose *Our Friend Jim*, a hardback with a picture of two young boys on the front. I took it home, up to my bedroom and started to read it that evening. It was a simple story of children on their summer holidays, finding some pirates on an island, but to me it was an exciting adventure and I imagined I was there with them. I enjoyed it so much that I read it from cover to cover before I put the light out.

That book was the beginning of my passion for reading.

Two or three times a week I took out another book from the school library. Pearl used to clean my bedroom and she must have noticed one of the books there because she offered to take me to our local public library.

'Ooh, yes, please!'

The local library was like a sweet shop to me – full of colourful goodies for me to choose from. Every Saturday morning, Pearl and I went to renew my book or borrow a new one. Every evening after school, I read those books, alone in my room, keeping quiet and well away from Arnold. As well as being the best thing to occupy the hungry and previously empty hour or two before going to bed, reading became an escape away from my difficult life into other worlds, where everyone always had a lot of love and enough food to eat.

CHAPTER 13

Adoption – Hope
or Despair?

While I was playing outside in the road with one of my friends, Mr Watts, my welfare officer, made one of his regular visits to check up on my progress. He got out of his Mini and gave me a cheery wave before he went into the house. As usual, he didn't stay very long, mainly talking with Pearl, who then called me in to join them. He asked me a couple of questions and wrote something down before getting up and leaving.

'I'll be back again a bit sooner than usual,' he said as he left. 'That will probably be my last visit.'

I didn't take much notice. He was in and out of my life in a flash each time, but he was quite a kind and jolly man and I liked him.

2nd April 1963
Richard was his usual happy self and after staying indoors for a while to talk, he went off to play with his friend. He is always full of life and has plenty of scope for activity in his foster home. Mr and Mrs Gallear were pleased that at long

last their intention to adopt had been registered and they are eagerly looking forward to completion of the adoption proceedings.

Welfare officer's notes

Apparently, Arnold and Pearl had started the process to adopt me from when they first took me home with them, when I was almost five, but something made it impossible until I was nearly nine. I'm sure it was Pearl who really wanted to adopt me and maybe Arnold wanted to look good and claim status among the Salvation Army folk, especially since one of the other members had recently adopted a boy and everyone praised him for giving a good home to an orphan.

To the outside world, Arnold was a good Christian man, married and with a respectable job. This front must have fooled the Child Care Department and the adoption agency. He and Pearl seemed like the perfect couple to foster and adopt a young, defenceless child. Now at last they were able to go ahead with the adoption and later that day, after I'd eaten my chips and sausage tea (a rare treat), Pearl began to explain.

'You know, don't you, that Arnold and I are your foster mum and dad?'

'Yes.' I wondered what this conversation was going to be about.

'Well, we wanted to adopt you when you were younger, but we had to wait till now.' She paused. 'Do you know what adoption is?'

'No, not really.'

'Well, you are our foster son, which means we are allowed to have you to live with us and look after you, but Mr Watts has to come every six months or so and make sure you are healthy and happy with us.'

I nodded, wondering, with a flutter of hope, whether perhaps he had at last found out about Arnold and I would be taken away to a safer place. But then I realised that I didn't want to leave Pearl, who had truly been like a mother to me and had done her best to protect and look after me, though rarely allowed to fulfil that role until too late. *If I wasn't there, would she be unhappy? Even worse, would the monster beat her instead?* All these thoughts were battling with each other in my head.

'Now,' she continued, 'we have been told that at last we can adopt you, if everything turns out all right and you tell the judge you are happy for us to adopt you. That would mean that you could properly become our son. Then we would be your real mum and dad. Wouldn't that be wonderful?' Her whole face lit up as she waited for my response.

As young as I was, at just under nine years old, I had become very good at interpreting what other people's intentions were and what they wanted of me. I'd had to develop that skill to help me cope with my scary, unpredictable life. I instinctively knew how much Pearl wanted us to be a happy family and I wanted to make her happy.

'What do you think?'

'Do I have to be adopted by you and Arnold separately?' I asked.

'Oh,' she looked surprised. 'Well, adoption is for both parents together.'

'The thing is, I would like you to adopt me, if it was just you, but ...' I tried to work out my next few words the best way I could. 'I don't think Arnold wants to adopt me. He keeps telling me he doesn't want me here and wants to get rid of me.'

Her smile faded. 'But Arnold always says things he doesn't mean when he's angry. He doesn't know what he's saying.'

I took a deep breath. 'Why does he hit me?'

She groaned and put her head in her hands, then looked up at me. 'I'm so sorry, Richard.' She gave a deep sigh and her eyes welled up. 'I wish I knew.' She paused. 'I just can't stop him.' She tried to smile and put her hand on mine. 'But I'm sure that adopting you will change all that.'

Luckily, we heard his car pull into the drive just then, so we had no time to discuss it any more as I had to dash up to my bedroom as usual to be out of his sight.

That evening, I felt too confused to read my book. I just mulled it all over, upset that Pearl had defended Arnold, but realising she was obviously trying to persuade me that it would be all right. If I refused, her wish would not come true, I suspected. Worse still, she might lose me altogether. I couldn't do that to her – she was the one who cared most for me. If I was taken away from Pearl, what would happen to me? There was no going back to Field House and I was afraid of the unknown alternative. But this might be my one chance to stop Arnold abusing me. Oh, what an awful situation! My head was whirling. What should I do?

The next stage was Mr Watts's final visit. I always used to look forward to him coming in the hope that he might talk to me alone this time and I could tell him – I desperately needed to tell someone. I'd be at the window, waiting for him to appear up our road in his car. Maybe this time … I could start by telling him how well Pearl was looking after me, but Arnold was cruel and often hurt me. Would he believe it? He had to believe me, surely? But the other side of my brain was telling me probably not. And if he thought I was telling the truth, would he be able to do something about it? I always kept that tiny spark of hope, but every time it turned into despair. Yet ... maybe this time?

I remember the night, after one particularly violent beating, when I shouted out, 'I'll tell Mr Watts what you're doing to me!'

Arnold carried on punching me, even harder and shouted back at me: 'No, you won't, because you know I'd do something worse! Anyway, nobody will believe a little bastard like you. Your mother didn't want you, your father is in prison ...' I tried not listen to the rest, but I can see now that it was a kind of brainwashing and sometimes I did start to believe it and it made me feel worthless and depressed. Yet I supposed he was right: who would believe me?

I realise now that child abuse was an unmentionable phrase in those days.

Pearl had told me that Mr Watts would come that afternoon and eventually I saw his little red Mini whizzing down the road. He rang the bell and she let him in. I thought they would call me down, but first, they went into the front room and talked. Pearl wanted the adoption very much, I knew, but it wasn't her that I was worried about.

After a while, Pearl called me down and she stayed while Mr Watts looked me over and smiled.

'I can see you're growing up nice and tall,' he said, jotting something down on his form. 'How are you getting on at school?'

'Fine, thanks.'

'Now, come and sit next to me,' he said in a serious voice. 'I want to talk to you about something important.'

'Is it adoption?' I asked.

'Yes, do you know what adoption means?'

'Mum told me a bit about it,' I nodded.

'So, you probably know that your foster mum and dad would become your real mum and dad?'

'Yes.'

'It wouldn't change anything else. This is where you would live and you'd carry on going to the same school with all your friends.'

'How does it happen?' I asked.

'Well, you talk to a lady, who will come and visit you. She will be your Guardian ad Litem and her job is to make sure that adoption is the best thing for you.' He stopped to blow his nose rather noisily. 'She will check that you have toys to play with, good food and nice clothes to wear, as well as making sure your foster father is in a job and your foster mother keeps the house clean and tidy. And she will talk with you all and make a report to say what she thinks should happen. Then your foster parents and you will go to court and the judge will ask you if you are happy for them to adopt you, so you will have the chance to say yes or no. And when you've said yes, he will sign the document for you to be adopted.'

I didn't like the sound of that, especially as he assumed I would say yes. I was so confused by it all, I needed some advice to help me cope – but who from? I was desperately hoping this lady guardian person would let me talk to her alone so that I could explain everything and see what she said.

'Will she come soon?' I asked.

'The Guardian ad Litem? Yes, quite soon, I should think.'

And that was all he said about it. Pearl stayed in the room the whole time, so I was never alone with him.

'Good, that's all done,' he said, putting his papers in a battered leather briefcase. 'I'll be off now.' He gave me a final grin and Pearl showed him out.

I was left sitting there, deeply disappointed to have missed another chance. I liked Mr Watts – he was a friendly man and he seemed to like me. I think I could have talked to him, but he missed all the signs. I don't think he ever suspected anything. It was his job to safeguard my welfare, but he just filled in the forms and that was that. However, I refused to give up hope. I had to make my voice heard – preferably without destroying Pearl. If I didn't, my silence would destroy me.

22nd July 1963
Richard is growing quite tall now and is clearly keeping very
well. He is a very active and happy boy and fits in extremely
well in his foster home.

Welfare officer's notes

It was a few weeks later when the Guardian ad Litem came to our house. I was so excited that here was a woman, someone more like my housemother at Field House, someone I could more easily talk to. This was my big chance: surely she would want to see me on my own?

Like Mr Watts, she talked to Pearl and Arnold together first and I could understand that, but I couldn't wait for my turn. I was thinking out what I would say. This Guardian woman was a lot longer with them than Mr Watts had ever been – I suppose it was because she had to write everything down for her report and she was probably more thorough than he had been. When I was called in to join her, my heart sank: Arnold and Pearl stayed in the room with us, listening to every answer I gave.

To start with, she mainly asked me questions that just needed yes or no answers, like my having been at Field House and coming to live with them when I was nearly five and checking she had written my name and birth date right.

Again, she explained the whole court process to me.

'All this would have happened sooner,' she said, 'but a lawyer had to find your birth mother to give her consent and now they have it.' She carefully avoided mentioning this woman's name, however the information embedded itself in my memory. It was the first time anyone other than Arnold had ever mentioned her to me and he had told me she didn't want me, so I was glad she had agreed to my adoption. Of course, I didn't know then whether the awful things he said were true, but I was young enough not to worry about that for now – it was the adoption itself that I was anxious about.

'When you go to court with your mum and dad, the judge will want to ask you all for your consent to this adoption going through. So, Richard, that means that first he will ask you if you understand what adoption means, and then he will ask you that important question about whether you agree to be adopted. All you have to do is to answer each question with either yes or no in a loud, clear voice. Do you think you could do that?'

'Yes.'

'And I'm assuming you will agree to your mum and dad adopting you?'

I glanced at Arnold's fixed expression and then at Pearl's hopeful smile. I knew I had no choice but to go along with it for now – I couldn't let Pearl down and I feared a beating like no other from Arnold, so I nodded.

'Yes.'

Would it have been different if I'd had the opportunity to speak to this lady on her own? Yes, I really believe it might have been, but in those days nobody seemed to think it important to find out what the child really wanted.

I felt shocked and empty when she left, robbed of my right to make a free choice and change my life. *How could everyone ignore me like that?* Back in my room again later, knowing how much Pearl wanted to adopt me, I was torn in two: I did not want to let her down. After all, she had always shown me kindness and had done nothing wrong – other than marrying Arnold in the first place, of course – and I'm sure she must have regretted that. And so I resigned myself to waiting till we went to court. I would have to be brave and speak out there – I had no other option.

Leaving things unsaid pulled me down and I felt lonelier than ever before and depressed too, I suppose. But I did find the courage to talk to Pearl one day about what Arnold always used to say regarding my birth mother – that she didn't want me.

'Oh, you don't want to worry about that,' she said with a sympathetic smile. 'You're with us now because your birth mother had her problems when you were born and she couldn't keep you, so now, with the adoption, I'll become your mother instead.'

This answer might well have been true, I realised, but it

didn't make it any easier when Arnold kept accusing me of whatever my birth mother or father had done wrong.

If they were so evil, does that make me evil, too? I wondered.

Preparing for the adoption seemed to bring out the worst thoughts and feelings in me. It was all very confusing and upsetting for a boy of nearly nine, who was desperate to be happy and carefree, like his friends.

Our imminent appearance at court seemed to lessen the amount of physical and mental abuse Arnold heaped on me, but I feared it was probably only temporary, although I did harbour a small seed of hope that perhaps, as Pearl had said, he wouldn't feel the need to inflict such cruelty on me once I legally became his son.

The day came and as Pearl helped me get dressed and do up my tie, a huge smile lit up her face.

'Isn't it lovely?' she said in her musical voice. 'By the end of this day, you'll be mine and I'll be yours.'

I was too overwrought to reply, so I just smiled and nodded.

Arnold drove us to the court at Corporation Street in Birmingham. I had a nagging stomach ache when we arrived and my head was whirling. As we walked into this huge, imposing building, I remember thinking, *This is my last chance. Will I be able to say something? Should I?* I wanted to. But then Pearl, who held my hand, gently squeezed it. I looked up at her and she gave me a nervous smile.

'Isn't it exciting?' she whispered, smoothing down a wayward strand of my hair. 'After the adoption, everything is going to change. Arnold will be happy and stop hurting you. Won't that be wonderful?'

She seemed so certain that I think I almost believed her – I wanted to believe her. I looked up at her radiant smile and in that moment I felt like a traitor. She was so innocent in all this – I knew she genuinely loved me, and I loved her.

I can't … If I say something, I'll be in trouble and she'll be in trouble, I thought.

It seemed everything was against me. How could I betray her?

The courtroom was cold and dark, very intimidating. We took our seats and I listened to the voices of all those who spoke, as if in a fog, without really hearing their words. It all seemed quite distant. But then I heard my name; I tried to focus as the voice called my name again. I stood up and one of the lawyers took me to the centre of the courtroom.

Here was my chance …

'Hello, Richard,' said the judge in a kind voice. 'I will ask you three questions and I want you to think before you answer them. When you are ready, you may say either "Yes, I do" or "No, I don't". Please nod your head if you understand.'

I nodded my head.

'Here is my first question: do you understand what adoption means?'

'Yes, I do.'

'Do you agree to have Pearl Gallear as your mother?'

'Yes.' I looked across at her and she beamed back at me. 'I do agree to have Pearl Gallear as my mother.'

'Do you agree to have Arnold Gallear as your father?'

I hesitated, looking at Arnold's previously expressionless face, which seemed to grow more threatening with every second, staring at me, boring through me. The whole court seemed to hold its breath.

It was now or never …

Finally, I caved in.

'Yes, I do agree to have Arnold Gallear as my father,' I gasped.

Now it was done, all hope gone.

As we drove back home again, I was miserable: I had let myself down, but what else could I have done? It was a balancing act between what was best for Pearl and what was best for me – I couldn't spoil her special day. My stomach ache worsened and I was almost doubled up with pain by the time we arrived back home again.

'My tummy hurts,' I told Pearl.

'Just sit down and I'll find you something that will make it better.'

Arnold had gone off to his garden workshop as if it had been an ordinary morning. I sat on a kitchen chair and waited as the tears streamed down my face.

'Here you are,' said Pearl as she came back with a small brown bottle of liquid. 'Oh, you poor thing!' she added when she saw I was silently crying. I think she assumed it was my tummy that was making me cry and I didn't say anything different.

She took a glass from the cupboard and poured a little of the brown liquid in the bottom, then took it to the tap and filled the rest of it with warm water before handing it to me.

'Sip slowly,' she said. 'It will calm your tummy.'

So I took a sip. 'It's horrible!' I complained. 'What is it?'

'It's called brandy. But try not to worry about the taste, just drink it slowly and it will make you feel much better.'

I wasn't so sure, but I did as she said and she was right: it worked. My tummy had stopped whirling and my whole body relaxed. I had no idea what brandy was, but I was relieved it had sorted out my physical discomfort. Now I had to come to terms mentally with the fact that I was trapped with this evil man and his cruelty for the rest of my childhood.

That night he gave me one of the worst beatings ever, just because I had hesitated when asked to accept him as my father.

CHAPTER 14

Finny

Now I was officially Pearl and Arnold's son, but nothing changed. This was clearly a huge disappointment to Pearl, who I truly believe had high hopes, even certainty, that Arnold would treat me better and we would all be happier.

The terrible abuse continued as before, but now I sometimes heard him shouting and swearing at Pearl too. I felt trapped and the light went out in Pearl's eyes. This was the first time I became fully aware of her nervous condition. She no longer sang or hummed as she did her housework, which made me very sad. I took the blame because I thought it was my fault that she was so upset: it wouldn't have happened if I wasn't there.

Looking back, I can see that it was something about Arnold's personality. Resentments built up inside his head and he just had to find a release. Everything annoyed or frustrated him – often nothing to do with me, but I was his scapegoat, his whipping boy. He could regain his power and control by hurting me.

I'm sure Arnold thought he did his best to provide for Pearl and me. He worked hard and bought us a lovely house and gave us all that we needed – except love. It was as if there was something not quite right in his brain. I could see it in his eyes, the pleasure it gave him to take out all his pent-up aggression on me. I think he even found pleasure in seeing Pearl so distressed – God knows why. She was frightened of him and that fear, together with her inability to change things, turned her into a nervous wreck. I could see her agitation rising as the clock turned towards the time he was due home. I felt so sad to see her increasing unhappiness on my behalf, and somehow responsible for it.

Gradually, I found a way to cope with the beatings. I steeled myself to endure what was happening and somehow managed to distance myself from it. I couldn't stop him, but I could will myself to block the pain from every blow and, in a way, rise above it. This became my secret weapon. But it was too much for anyone to take and it did wear me down over all those years, until eventually I learned to block it out of my mind as well.

In the final year at my junior school, we all sat the 11+ exam and had to wait for the results to learn which school we would go to next. Once the exam was over, we could enjoy our last term in various ways. One of my favourites was when our teacher brought a cine-camera to school and showed us how it worked.

'Who would like to act in a film about World War II?' he asked, and everyone's hand shot up. There was great excitement across the class as he explained all the things we would have to do.

I was one of the actors who had to dress up as a wounded soldier, with bandages wrapped round various parts of our bodies and blood painted on. We were the walking wounded and we had to practise, some of us dragging our legs and others helping each other along. Some of my friends had their whole heads bandaged and had to be led with their hands on the shoulders of those in front. Once we had rehearsed enough, the filming began.

Finally, we were able to watch it on a screen in our classroom. It was so exciting to see ourselves on film and we laughed a lot at our escapades, especially wherever things had gone a bit wrong! Then it was time to show the rest of the school, so a big screen was put up in the hall and all the classes filed in and sat cross-legged, ready to see our very own film. We felt so proud as everyone watched, then clapped at the end.

In the last week of that summer term, we were intrigued as we walked to school and saw a lot of huge, colourful lorries, which had arrived overnight and parked higgledy-piggledy in a nearby field. What could this be?

By the time we walked home, the mystery was revealed. An enormous sign proclaimed this was a fairground and invited people to come and have fun on the rides and the stalls. This was a great excitement. We all agreed to go home and ask our parents if we could go to the fair when it opened the following evening. While I did agree and desperately wanted to go, I knew Pearl would say yes and Arnold would overrule her with an irrevocable refusal. Of course, that is exactly what happened; I also got a beating that night for daring to ask.

'Bastards don't deserve to go to fairs!' he yelled as he lashed me with his belt. 'You're a worthless bag of shit and that's all you'll ever be!'

On the last day of term, I walked to school with Robert, who was full of excitement as he recounted his experiences at the fair.

'Mum and Dad took me,' he said. 'And we had a wonderful time. Oh, you should have been there, it was fantastic! I won a goldfish.'

'How super to have your own fish,' I said, with a tinge of envy.

'The only trouble is that we're going on holiday tomorrow to Cornwall for a week and Dad said we can't take him with us.'

'Oh, what are you going to do with him?' I asked.

He paused. 'Would you like to look after him for me, just while I'm away?'

'Ooh, yes!' I agreed, without even a thought as to what Pearl and more importantly, Arnold, would say. 'I'd love to look after him for you.'

I felt nine feet high to be asked and entrusted with this wonderful responsibility.

'His name is Finny, I'll bring him round before we leave tomorrow. Will that be all right?'

'Yes, of course.'

I skipped the last few yards down the road to my house, light as air, with something to look forward to – some company for the holidays and something I could talk to and tell my worries to.

This was going to be perfect.

The next morning I was up early, looking out of my window, waiting for this special delivery. I saw Arnold putting something in his car, then going round the back to his workshop. A few minutes later, Pearl called me down to breakfast.

'You seem excited today,' she said. 'I expect you're excited about the holidays. We could go the library later today if you like and you can choose some books to read. Then we could go to Smith's and buy you some paper and a proper box of paints for you to do a painting that I can put on the wall.'

We chatted on, but for some reason, I completely forgot to tell her about the goldfish. Just as I was helping her to clear away the breakfast things, there was a ring on our doorbell.

'I expect that's one of your friends,' said Pearl. 'You might as well answer it.'

Sure enough, there was Robert with a big grin on his face, a plastic bag over his arm and proudly holding the new bowl of water with a bright orange fish swimming round inside it.

'Here's Finny,' he said, holding out the bowl to me.

'Come in,' I told him as I very carefully took hold of it.

'And I've brought you some special goldfish food. It says on the container when to feed him and how much. I have fed him already this morning.'

'Mum!' I shouted through into the kitchen, unsure where to put the bowl.

'I've got to go,' said Robert, in a rush. 'Dad's waiting in the car outside to drive us down to Cornwall.' He went through the open front door and turned at the last minute. 'Thanks very much for looking after him for me. Bye!'

And he was gone. Just at that moment, Pearl emerged from the kitchen, wiping her hands on a tea towel.

'Ooh, what's that?' she asked.

'It's Finny, Robert's goldfish. He asked me to look after it for him while he is away on holiday with his parents.' I put the bowl down gently on the kitchen table. 'I'm sorry I forgot to ask you if that's all right, but he only told me yesterday afternoon and he needed to know straight away, so I just said yes.'

'That's fine,' she agreed with a smile. 'But we'll need some food for him.'

'Robert gave me food.'

'Oh, good.'

'Where shall we put the bowl? I'll keep it in my room, if you like.'

'Why don't we put him on the hall table?' Pearl suggested.

'Yes, he would look good there.'

Pearl put a lace doily in the middle of the table and I put the fish bowl down on it.

'He's a handsome fish,' said Pearl as we both watched him swimming around. 'Maybe we should get him some stones or a little arch to swim through.'

'Yes, that's a good idea,' I agreed.

At that moment, Arnold came in from the garden. 'Where are the secateurs?' he asked Pearl, then he saw the fish in his bowl and his expression changed immediately, as if he'd switched on the nasty button. 'What's this smelly, stinking fish doing here?'

I didn't know what to say, but Pearl jumped in. 'Oh, Richard's friend brought it round for us to look after while he's away.' She paused. 'His name is Finny and he's not smelly at all.'

'You can't keep him,' ordered Arnold. 'I'm not having that creature in my house!'

'Well, he's got it now,' explained Pearl, bravely. 'It's Richard's responsibility to look after it.'

'Well, tell him to take it away. Tell him to take this bloody fish upstairs and throw it down the toilet!'

My first response was indignation and my second was helplessness. *Would everything I ever tried to do to help a friend end up like this?*

'But ...' I began.

'Ssh!' Pearl whispered to warn me as Arnold stormed into the kitchen and threw his gardening cap on the floor. She went after him.

'I am the master of this house, I will not be disobeyed!' he shouted. 'Get rid of it!'

'I can't,' I replied timidly. 'It's Robert's fish.'

'Well, Robert shouldn't have trusted a scumbag like you to look after his precious fish! You can't keep it here, so take it upstairs and get rid of it.'

'I'll take it up to my room, you won't see it again.'

'Oh no, you don't, you little bastard! You take it straight to the toilet and flush it away.'

'I'm taking him to my room,' I repeated, carefully carrying the bowl up the first two steps of the staircase.

Suddenly he was behind me. He pushed me on, hitting me hard on my back. I stumbled and fell, somehow holding onto the bowl and only splashing out a little of the water.

Finny was swimming more quickly now, darting to and fro, as worried as me. I struggled to right myself and took one more step upwards on the carpet running down the middle, clipped to the wood at each side. He pushed me so hard this time that I fell and dropped the bowl to one side, which shattered on the wood into several shards of glass. The water gushed out and Finny fell onto the wet carpet, flapping furiously.

All I could think of was that this was Robert's fish and I had to rescue him, so I tried to catch him in my hand to save him. I did my best to capture his desperate little body, but now Arnold started raining punches, which sent me sprawling. I caught my hand on a long, curved shard of glass. Then, trying to steady myself, I accidentally leaned on another jagged shard. Immediately, the blood spurted out everywhere. I didn't feel much pain at first, with the coldness of the water. Then he punched me even harder.

'Look at the bloody mess you're making! I wish we'd never chosen you, I wish you'd never been born!'

I sprawled onto the glass with the palms of my hands.

Pearl had been doing something in the kitchen, trying to stay out of it, but now came to see what the commotion was about.

'He's cut his hands!' she shrieked.

Single-mindedly, Arnold took no notice: 'Get that fish upstairs and down the toilet!' he shouted. 'Right now, it has to go!'

Pearl ran back into the kitchen and brought back a pudding bowl, half full of water.

My hands were hurting so much now, but I refused to give in until I had caught Finny, so I scrabbled about among the smaller smithereens of glass and finally caught him and put him straight into Pearl's pudding bowl, along with some of my blood.

Arnold kicked me. 'Go on, up you go!' he ordered me. 'Throw that stinking fish in the toilet and pull the chain! I want to hear it flush.'

He followed me up, towering right behind me, so I had no choice: I turned the bowl right inside the toilet so that Finny didn't have too far to fall, then pulled the chain. I watched as the water whirled, red from my blood and didn't clear enough to see whether Finny was still there or not. All the time I was thinking and hoping, perhaps he'll survive and I can get him out later and hide him in my bedroom. But when I looked again, he had gone.

Now at last I looked at my hands and saw all the cuts bleeding profusely. I must have fainted, because the next thing I knew, I was sitting next to Pearl in Doctor Callas's surgery. The nurse came in and wiped my hands clean with antiseptic, which stung, and injected me with local anaesthetic. Then the doctor stitched up the two deepest cuts. Finally, the nurse came back and bandaged up both hands completely.

'You must keep your hands clean and dry,' said the doctor. 'Can you do that?'

'I'll try,' I replied in a little voice, still a bit woozy.

'I'll make sure, Doctor,' agreed Pearl, her eyes glazed.

He sat back and gave me a quizzical look: 'How did you do all this damage?'

I looked at Pearl.

'He dropped the goldfish bowl,' she explained. 'Then he fell on the glass.'

'You'd better learn not to be so clumsy in future,' warned Doctor Callas.

'I will,' I said with bleary eyes, trying my best not to cry for the injustice of this situation. 'Will there be scars?' I asked.

'Yes, sure to be, I'm afraid, but they'll fade with age.'

I felt so bad about what happened to Finny. My hands throbbed continuously with pain, but more than anything, I felt ashamed.

Ashamed for how badly I had let my friend down.

'I know what we should do to keep those bandages clean,' suggested Pearl, as brightly as she could. 'Let's watch some television together, there must be something on that you would like.'

That cheered me up. I think it was mainly old films that were on during the day – we enjoyed those. My favourites were *Lassie* and some of the Westerns, like *Bonanza*. Pearl liked the wartime films that made her cry, but I enjoyed them too if they had spitfires or jeeps in them.

When Robert returned from his holiday, he came round to collect Finny and I had to admit to him that Finny was no more. I couldn't tell him the truth, so I just said that the table had been knocked and the bowl fell off and shattered.

'I tried to catch Finny and save him,' I said, 'but I couldn't. I'm very, very sorry.'

Robert, bless him, wasn't angry with me at all.

'Oh, don't worry about it,' he said.

What a good friend he was.

'Is that why your hands are both bandaged up?' he asked, with genuine concern in his voice.

A week or so later, when my bandages had been removed, I went to call for Robert. His mother answered the door.

'Come in,' she said with a beaming smile. 'Oh dear, look at your poor, scarred hands! How did you hurt them so badly? Was that when you tried to save Finny?'

'Yes, I'm afraid so. They're getting better now, but I'm very sorry.'

'You don't have to apologise, Richard.'

'I didn't mean to drop him.'

'You *dropped* him?' she repeated.

'Yes, I dropped him and his bowl broke and I fell on the glass, trying to save him.'

She paused for a moment. 'I'm a bit worried about you,' she said with a kind voice. 'Perhaps I should have a word with your mother.'

'Oh no,' I said, rather too quickly. 'There's no need to do that, it's all right now.'

Just then Robert came down the stairs.

'Come on,' he said. 'Let's go out to play.'

I don't know if she ever did say anything to Pearl.

The doctor was right about my hands. Even now, decades later as I write, I can still see the scars to remind me of that terrible day – the day that began with such excitement and ended in pain and misery.

CHAPTER 15

Schooldays and Holidays

It was the beginning of September, 1965, and I was looking forward to starting at Park Hall High School. It seemed like such an adventure to be going there. It was slightly further from where we lived, but Robert was going to the same school, so I was able to call round to his house on the way so that we could walk together. As he and I went through the gates on the first day, I felt full of pride.

We were all directed into the assembly hall, with its highly polished floor and huge lights hanging from the ceiling. When everyone was sitting down, the headmaster strode onto the stage.

'Good morning to all our new students,' he said. 'I want to welcome you to Park Hall High School. I hope every one of you will be happy here and will work hard to achieve great things.'

Next, we were sent to our new classrooms, where Robert and I found we were to be together again, which was very good news.

Park Hall High School was in the countryside, with fields at the back, so I immediately felt quite at home. A modern building, it was very impressive and it seemed like a massive school to me. It had all sorts of extra rooms, like libraries and science laboratories, where the old Bunsen burners bubbled away and flames leapt up. We had to put white coats on to go into the science labs. I remember feeling like a proper scientist in my white coat, working out how to change colours in a test tube.

Other subjects with their own rooms included woodwork and metalwork. In both these rooms we made things, like toasting forks out of metal; I also made a stool out of wood. Mine had tongue and groove joints, so it was a lot better than the one Arnold had made. I loved the warmth and smells of both these craft rooms, especially the smell of wood shavings.

Everything was new and exciting. My favourite place of all was the canteen. By now, I usually got just a slice of bread and dripping for tea. Or occasionally bread and Marmite, or a foul-tasting ginger jam that Pearl made. But I didn't mind not having a proper tea now that I had all this wonderful school food to eat. The delicious smells that emanated from that kitchen were overwhelming. It was all healthy, home-cooked food, so I was back to having all my favourite meals and a delicious new dessert: chocolate pudding with pink custard. There were second helpings for those who wanted them. Well, of course, this was heaven for me – I was that boy who always used to say, 'More, please!' That lunch filled me up and kept me going for the rest of the day. I absolutely LOVED school dinners!

They had a big gym too, and a football pitch. But I didn't want to play football – I didn't like ball games and, as usual, I was worried that the adults or other children would ask awkward questions about my cuts and bruises. Luckily, my art teacher spotted my talent early on and was keen for me to do some extra art, so he suggested I come to his studio instead of doing PE. I can't remember his name, but he was my favourite teacher. He had ginger hair and a huge Vanden Plas car. With him, I did sketching and painting.

'You can come up here in break-times too, if you want,' he suggested.

So, I often did.

On alternate weeks, I attended a separate class for technical drawing. I excelled in this new subject and enjoyed it greatly. Each of the teachers used to praise my drawing skills and some of my work was displayed on the walls of the corridors around the school.

'You'll be a good architect if you carry on and study,' my technical drawing teacher told me.

I hadn't thought of that, but I loved the idea. Having been surrounded by the elegance of Field House when I was younger, this had given me a thirst for beautiful architecture. Now I had a potential career in view for when the time came. Whenever we talked about what we wanted to do when we left school, my friends had various ideas. One wanted to be a jockey, another hoped to work at British Leyland and a third aimed to be a doctor.

'I want to be an architect,' I said, proud that I had a goal to aim for.

The more I said it, the more I liked the idea, and my teachers continued to encourage me in that direction so I borrowed books from the library about buildings and other structures, such as bridges, and developed a fascination for design and lines. I was in raptures looking at pictures of the finer details of windows, staircases and ceiling decorations in grand old houses.

Meanwhile, Pearl had bought me some good watercolour paints and brushes, along with thicker paper, so I painted watercolours in my bedroom most evenings. I usually painted houses and the countryside views from my window and pinned them to the wall. One day, I painted a watercolour of our house and when Pearl saw it, she looked quite surprised.

'Ooh, that's good, that is! I like the way you've done it.'

Now that I was older, I was more able to join in activities outside school. Arnold was working longer hours and Pearl just wanted me to be happy. I joined the cinema club on Saturday mornings, Scouts on Thursday evenings and the choir on Fridays after school. Anything to get me out of the house. But I have to be completely honest and say that I was a choirboy for the wrong reason, because we used to be paid for doing weddings on Saturdays!

From the age of 13, I was given an annual escape from Arnold's cruelties. Pearl explained that I would be spending my entire summer holidays with Arnold's brother. Arnold had two brothers – Uncle John, who lived near us, and Uncle Geoff, who lived in the country. For most boys my age, I expect spending the whole summer away from home with complete strangers would be the last thing they would want – and, of course, I was wary, too.

'He's very nice,' Pearl told me. 'He was an RAF pilot during the war, so you can ask him to tell you all about that. He has a lovely wife and three children – a boy and two girls.'

'Where do they live?' I asked.

'A little place called Botley,' she replied. 'Uncle Geoff has a market-garden business there. Arnold has booked a day off just after you break up for the summer so that we can drive you there ourselves. I'm sure you will love being in the countryside again, won't you?'

'Yes, I'd love that,' I said, quite excited at the thought, though still very wary about Arnold's brother.

What if he was like Arnold?

The day before, Pearl packed my case with all the clothes and everything else she thought I would need. I added one or two books and my sketchbook in case there was anything to draw. At the last minute she opened the case again and added a little blue packet of cheese biscuits.

'You might need these when you get there,' she said with her gentle smile.

The last few days of term, Arnold steered clear of me, so my days and nights were the most peaceful I'd had since they chose to take me in. Perhaps he didn't want to mark me with bruises in case his brother and sister-in-law might suspect anything.

Early on the morning of our departure, as I got dressed, I began to worry about the journey. This car was much more comfortable than the old van, but it still made me travel-sick on the long journey down south. Arnold had to keep stopping and starting the car, annoyed with me for being sick each time. He would haul me out, stand back, then haul me back in again, all the while shouting the vilest abuse at me, but for once his anger was pent-up and he refrained from physically hurting me. He obviously wanted us to look like a happy family and even warned me not to say anything about his violence.

'Don't you even think of telling anyone,' he said with a hostile expression. 'Nobody will believe a bastard like you!'

I nodded, but said nothing. I didn't care. Soon we would be there and I would be free of him.

Finally, I saw the sign for Botley. Seconds later, we drove up outside their bungalow and they all came pouring out of the front door to greet us. Pearl had been right – I could see straight away how kind and friendly this lovely family was.

'Come in, all of you,' said Auntie Betty. 'Come and have some lunch.'

Pearl looked at Arnold, who slightly shook his head.

'We can't stop long,' he said. 'I have to go back to work tomorrow, so maybe just a coffee.'

'Yes,' agreed Pearl meekly. 'Thank you, a coffee would be nice.'

'You must have one of my fresh-baked biscuits too,' added Auntie Betty.

Arnold was on edge the whole time and didn't really communicate with anybody, even his own brother. As soon as Pearl had finished her coffee, he was raring to go. I felt sad she was leaving, because I knew she would miss me, but perhaps she would have a quieter and less stressful time without having to try to protect me from her beast of a husband.

'Bye, bye,' said Pearl. 'Have a lovely time.'

But Arnold didn't even look at me: he just got in his car, slammed the door and revved the engine until Pearl joined him.

Uncle Geoff, Auntie Betty and their three children lined up beside me to wave them off. Of course, I was only waving to Pearl, though nobody else knew that. Neither did they notice, as the Ford Anglia disappeared down the lane, that I gave a huge sigh of relief. But in the short time since we arrived, I could already tell this was going to be a wonderful break for me. In fact, this was the best thing that could have happened to me.

I immediately warmed to the whole family. There was Uncle Geoff, tall and slim – taller than Arnold – with a wonderful moustache that I later discovered was typical of RAF pilots. He was softly spoken and a gentle, friendly family man who loved plants and the natural world. Auntie Betty was a smallish woman with straight black hair and a rosy complexion. She was always jolly and full of fun. It was quite obvious that they both adored their three children.

Susan was the eldest, three years older than me. Richard was a year older and Elizabeth was two years younger. All three of them were welcoming and friendly, taking me into their family and sharing their toys and games with me.

Then there was Dandy the dog. He was the size of a small poodle – in fact, that's probably what he was, except that he wasn't groomed or anything. His curly black hair was left to do its own thing. He did the same, although when I was there, he always seemed to follow me about – I loved that!

They lived in a country lane, with a stream at the bottom and a dairy farm at the top. 'Would you like to go up to the farm and ask Farmer Daniels for some fresh milk in this jug?' asked Auntie Betty after I'd taken my case to my cosy little room. 'If he's not in the house, just look round the farm – you'll find him somewhere.'

Eager to please, and to see the countryside, I took the jug and turned up the hill towards the farm gate. Halfway up, I thought I heard a sound behind me and turned to see Dandy, my little black shadow, following. As it happened, when I reached the top of the lane, Farmer Daniels was walking across towards his house.

'Hello, laddie,' he said with a beaming smile. 'Are you the new boy at Geoff and Betty's?'

'Yes, I'm Richard,' I said. 'I'm Uncle Geoff's nephew.'

'Well, they've been look forward to having you and you are welcome to come up here any time to play with the hay bales in the barn,' he said pointing across the yard, 'or on the old tractors, if you like. They won't go without their keys, but you can sit on them and play as much as you like.'

'Wow, thanks!' I said, very eager to do just that. 'But first, I brought Auntie Betty's jug ...'

'Yes, I thought I recognised it,' he laughed. 'Let's go and fill it with milk.'

Auntie Betty was pleased to see me back with the milk. 'Just in time for lunch,' she said. 'I was just going to call everybody in.'

I soon settled into this wonderful life, in which Auntie Betty's kitchen was open house to everyone who worked or helped in the fields or the greenhouses, as well as the children, including me, and all their friends. It felt as if I'd walked into the best kind of picture book.

I whiled away my days doing all kinds of things: playing five-stones with their Richard or going for long walks across the fields or down by the stream. Everywhere I went, Dandy always followed. He had such a sweet temperament – he never needed to have a lead on as he always just followed and sat with me, looking up with his soulful eyes.

On days when he wasn't too busy, Uncle Geoff used to take me down to the village, where we made a beeline for the Jaguar garage. Oh, how I loved sitting in those leather seats, in front of the polished wooden dashboard, trimmed with chrome, turning the steering wheel and pretending to drive those sleek, luxurious cars!

On busier days, I often used to offer to help. Uncle Geoff was always pleased and gave me jobs to do.

'It's great to have some extra hands,' he would say with a wink. 'But don't work too hard or I'll have to pay you!'

We both grinned.

So I worked alongside his workers, who showed me what to do. I used to pick ripe tomatoes and lettuces, sometimes other vegetables too, and put them into boxes, ready for market, which I think was one day a week. The night before, everything had to be moved out of the greenhouse and into the shed, ready to load up Uncle Geoff's big Commer van.

Working together like that, with lots of chatter, joking and a bit of singing, was a heart-warming experience, like nothing I'd ever known before. And the smell of those tomatoes! I shall never forget their wonderful scent. Even now, years later, I crave that smell. I can only get it, and I do so every time, by opening one end of a sealed pack of vine tomatoes and sticking my nose right inside. It takes me back to being in Uncle Geoff's greenhouse, the wonderful experience and the happy times we had there.

Ten a.m. was always coffee break, when a beaming Auntie Betty called all the workers into her kitchen for homemade biscuits, cakes and her delicious milky coffee. The three children used to join us as well. It was always a jolly occasion.

Weekends were the best times of all. The treat was that we were all going on an outing together. Before we left, Auntie Betty used to send me off up the lane to bring back some eggs and milk, then off we'd go. Sometimes it was to the New Forest with Dandy the dog, taking ball games with us to play, or I liked to climb the trees. Other times we went to the beach in Bournemouth, with buckets and spades. Occasionally we drove down to Southampton Docks, without Dandy, and watched the big passenger liners coming in or leaving – *The Queen Mary* or *The Queen Elizabeth*. They were such an amazing sight, gliding quietly by. One weekend, I remember us all going on a ferry to the Isle of Wight.

Every weekend was a joy: they took us to so many places, all of which were new to me. Wherever we went, we stopped and had a wonderful picnic that Auntie Betty had prepared for us. Those were happy, idyllic days, full of fun and laughter – we always came home exhausted!

I loved my carefree summers at Auntie Betty and Uncle Geoff's house and I went for three summers in a row. But as the end of the summer approached every year, I would dread the day Arnold and Pearl returned to pick me up.

One summer, as their Ford Anglia pulled up in the drive, my heart sank. Parting was awful for me. Auntie Betty would give me a big hug, with tears rolling down her cheeks.

'Come back again next year, won't you?'

'Yes, please. I'd love to,' I'd say.

I waved until well after they disappeared. Obviously thrilled to have me back, Pearl couldn't stop smiling at me. However, I couldn't say the same for Arnold.

'Take your bloody hand out of the way of my rear-view mirror!' he snarled as we drove away from Botley. 'You wait till I get you home!'

CHAPTER 16

Leaving School

At the end of the fourth year, when I was 14, I must have been doing quite well as I won the Progress Prize, which was for the student in the whole year group who had made the most progress and excelled across all the main subjects. I don't know how I did that as maths was definitely not my best subject, but perhaps everything else made up for it. There were particular mentions for technical drawing, art, geography and history. I had to go up on stage, in front of the whole school and all the staff, and the Headmaster, wearing an academic gown, presented me with this award and a book.

When I took them home after school, Pearl was delighted.

'I'm very impressed,' she said, with pride in her voice and her eyes, which had a momentary hint of her old spark in them.

When Arnold came back from work, Pearl was still looking at them and immediately showed them to him.

'Look how clever our son is,' she said. 'He won this important award, the only one in his year group, and the Headmaster wore a gown to present him with it, and a book as well.' She paused. 'Isn't that brilliant?'

But Arnold just brushed past without even a glance.

'Why is he still down here? And where is my tea?'

He deliberately walked past me and pushed me as hard as he could against the wall, his fist raised to my face: 'Get out of my way, you jumped-up bag of shit!'

'*No*, stop!' shrieked Pearl as she came to my aid and tried to pull him back.

Arnold shoved her away, unsteady on her feet.

I was bigger now and stronger, so he could no longer pull me down to the floor or beat me in the way he used to. But he took every opportunity to show he was still the boss and I was nothing to him: it was more a mental battle these days. But Pearl seemed weaker than before, both physically and mentally. In seconds, she had gone from happiness to utter despair. Silent tears trickled down her cheeks. I felt so sorry for her – Arnold seemed to hurt her even more than he hurt me. Her nerves were bad enough without such cruel and deliberate rejections, and I knew it was because he needed to exert his control on her as he could no longer get away with physically abusing me as much as in the past, perhaps fearing I might turn on him. However, he escalated the verbal abuse with all kinds of nasty accusations and slurs. But Arnold didn't know me well enough. I never retaliated – I would never have put Pearl through that, or made her choose between us. In those days, a wife had to put her husband first, no matter what.

I worried about Pearl and wanted to protect her as much as I could. She was an old-fashioned, dutiful wife, for whom divorce could never have been an option, so she had become more vulnerable than ever.

Just as I was about to leave the room, Pearl handed me back my award scroll and book, speaking through her tears.

'You'd better keep those somewhere safe,' she said.

I knew exactly what she meant.

I knew I had to get away from Arnold somehow, not just for my sake, but also for Pearl's. The longer I was there, with him subjecting me to so much mental cruelty, pushing me around and repeatedly telling me to go away, to get out of his life, that he didn't want me, the more ill Pearl became. I couldn't bear to see that happen because of me. Already, she was slower and less engaged than in previous years. Seeing her eyes grow blanker and her trembling lip at stressful moments, together with her slower reactions, it was like watching a fire going out. I felt certain my presence was the unstabilising factor in this house. Before they took me in, I think they'd had a happy, carefree life. Pearl once told me how shocked she was that first time Arnold attacked me as he had never shown any signs of that side of his character before, so things might change for her as well as me, if I wasn't there.

I began to hatch a plan: the new school year started in September 1969 and I would turn 15 in November 1969. From the September I would be starting on studies towards end-of-year O levels or CSE exams, but I came to the conclusion that it was too long a time to wait. Yes, I would have loved to gain the qualifications and move forward towards my career, but I couldn't delay. In those days, 15 was the earliest age anyone could legally leave full-time education, so that was uppermost in my mind. I kept all this to myself of course and started the fifth year along with my classmates, as everyone expected.

Some of us knew what we wanted to do, but others didn't, so in the first week we all had to go and talk with our form teachers about what type of careers we might aim for and what subjects we should take the following year to help us towards our goals.

Naturally, this had all become a bit tricky for me as I firmed up my exit plan, but I couldn't tell anyone yet.

'If you really set your mind to working hard and doing your best in these exams, Richard,' my form teacher told me, 'you will set yourself up for life.'

'Yes, sir.'

'Do you have a career in mind yet?'

'Well, the technical drawing teacher and the art teacher both told me they think I should become an architect.'

'And would you like to do that?'

'Well, yes, I'd love to ...'

'An excellent career, I'm sure you'll do well.'

'Thank you, sir.'

So that was that, as far as the school was concerned. For now, I had to bide my time. If I told anyone at school what I was planning, even my friends, it might get back to Arnold and I couldn't take that risk. This was my decision to make and I was fairly set on it now, so it had to be my secret. At the first opportunity, the first possible moment, I would have to go.

Looking back, I don't know why I was quite so set on not completing that exam year – just a few months longer, to gain my basic qualifications. But it was perfectly legal. At that time any pupil could walk out of school for good on the day they turned 15, usually to take on a job or an apprenticeship, but most would stay at least to the end of term.

* * *

At home in those first few weeks of term, the times I had alone with Pearl were quiet and cosy – probably like a typical mother-and-son relationship. She was a lovely woman, a gentle soul and a caring parent, as far as she was allowed to be. We enjoyed each other's company, as long as it was just the two of us. Despite her increasingly nervous disposition, she always seemed calm and relaxed with me.

By contrast, Arnold still took every opportunity he could to make my life a misery.

'Get out of my way, you bastard son of a criminal!' he would hiss in my face, as he rammed me as hard as he could into the wall. 'You're no good to anybody, just a useless waste of space. Get out of my way – and get the hell out of my life! Everything was fine before you came, but you've ruined our lives. Now, go off and ruin your own!'

In the background I could see Pearl's tearful face as she sat there, nervously picking at her fingernails. I knew she wanted to stand up for me, as she had always done, but she didn't have any spunk left in her.

She did still try sometimes – 'Oh, Arnold, please don't speak to Richard like that!' But it made no difference.

'Useless bag of shit, do you hear me?' he would bellow right in my face and jab his finger in my chest, as if to upset her all the more.

From being a little boy at Field House, watching all the insects, my friend the toad and the early morning rabbits, I had never wanted to hurt any living creature. I loved them all, even the wasps, though I might have felt differently had they stung me. In my childhood years with Pearl and Arnold I had tried very hard to find some good in him, but I found precious little. Indeed, he damaged me mentally more than physically these days, but in some ways that seemed even worse. By now I hated this man, not only because of what he had done to me, but for what he was doing to Pearl.

I could see it would never change between us, so the way I saw it, the only way to help Pearl have a calmer, easier life was for me to go as soon as I could.

It was with a heavy heart that I knew what I must do.

Straight after half term, as my 15th birthday was approaching, I went to see the school careers officer and told him I would be leaving as soon as I was 15. He looked up my notes and seemed surprised.

'But I can see you are doing so well at school.' He read on a little. 'And I believe you want to be an architect. Your teachers clearly think you have the talent and perseverance to do that, so why this sudden change of heart?'

'I can't tell you the exact reasons, but it's family circumstances.'

'Hmm, I see …' He looked even more puzzled now. 'I know I can't make you tell me, but surely your parents would be happy for you to stay on to take your exams, with such a promising career in front of you?'

'I haven't told them yet,' I explained. 'I can't until I after I've left. And I haven't told anyone else either. You are the first …' I paused. 'It's not what I want to do, but I know I have to leave. Circumstances dictate that I have to go to work, that's all I can say.'

'Let me see …' he looked back at his notes. 'So, you will turn 15 at the end of next month, November? At least stay on until the end of the term, only three more weeks after your birthday. That will seem a neater leaving date and better for you to have longer to find your first job, if you must.' He seemed genuinely disappointed for me. 'Are you sure there is no way you could stay on and at least get your O levels?'

'No, I'm afraid things have come to a head and I need to leave. But yes, I suppose you are right about leaving at the end of term, so I will agree to do that. I hope that maybe I will be able to come back to studying later, then perhaps I could still be an architect one day.'

'Yes, it may be possible, though that would be so much more difficult. But if you're absolutely certain that you have to leave and it's what you want to do, then you must do it with our blessing and our help.'

'Thank you.' I was about to go when I realised what he had said. 'What do you mean about help?'

'We have contacts with a lot of local employers, so we could help you to gain employment. If you come back and see me after school tomorrow, I can help you look for suitable jobs and apply for them. The school will provide you with a very good reference, I'm sure, after winning the Progress Award last year.'

I was amazed – I hadn't realised the school would actually help me get a job.

'So, shall I see you at 4 p.m. tomorrow?'

'Yes, please.'

I left that room with more hope in my heart than I'd had for years.

Unexpectedly, while walking home from school that day with Robert, he told me he was going to leave school at Christmas.

'But you have such a wonderful, supportive family. Don't they want you to stay on and do your exams?'

'I don't think they mind – they know I'm not fond of studying, I just want to start earning my own money.'

Just then Max, another good friend, caught up with us.

'What are you two talking about?'

'I've just told Richard that I'm leaving school at Christmas,' explained Robert, 'so that I can get a job and earn some money.'

'I'm going to be leaving at Christmas too,' I said, as casually as I could. I hadn't intended to tell my friends yet, but it seemed the ideal opportunity to keep this announcement low-key.

'Why?' asked Robert. 'I thought you wanted to be an architect?'

'I do – I *did*. But I have to leave, so maybe I'll go back to studying later.'

'Well, I'm staying on,' said Max. 'I'm going to do my exams and then go on to college. My mum and dad are good sorts – they can keep me in the manner to which I'm accustomed!'

So now it was out, I was definitely leaving and it felt like a weight off my shoulders. But it would also have been quite scary, had it not been for the careers officer's promise of help in finding my first job.

Sitting down for a cup of tea and a biscuit with Pearl when I got home, it seemed the right time to tell her my decision too.

'I've decided to leave school at the end of this term,' I began. 'I'll be 15 next month, so I can legally leave. I want to get a job and start earning some money. Robert's leaving too, so it's not just me. I've told the careers officer, so he's going to help me find employment.'

Pearl looked surprised, but not perturbed – she rarely showed strong feelings these days. 'Well, if you're sure that's what you want to do? I just want you to be happy, so it's your choice.'

'What do you think Arnold will say?'

'He will probably agree.'

I told her about my appointment with the careers officer the next afternoon after school.

'Oh, that sounds very helpful,' she said with a smile. 'It's important to get the right job that you will be happy in. Whatever you want to do will be fine with me.'

For some reason, Arnold came home early that afternoon in a foul temper. He threw his briefcase across the kitchen floor and dropped his hat and coat by the door, no doubt expecting Pearl to pick them up for him.

'Get the hell out of my kitchen!' he shouted at me.

'Richard has just been telling me he's leaving school at Christmas,' said Pearl, probably hoping to lighten his mood.

'Hoo bloody ray!' he cheered. 'About time he was off our hands.'

'I will be soon,' I told him.

He took a step towards my chair and pushed it as hard as he could. Because he took me by surprise, just as I was about to stand up, he caught me a blow and sent me and the chair flying.

'There!' he exclaimed. 'You see, you're not so strong as you think you are.' He gave me a kick while I was still sprawled on the floor. 'The sooner you get a job and earn your own money, the better. Then you can get out of my house and out of my life. I never wanted you and I never will, so good bloody riddance!'

He turned and stormed off to change, then go out to his workshop.

'I'd better start making his tea,' said Pearl, with tears in her eyes. 'He doesn't mean it, Richard – he's just had a bad day at work.'

'It's OK,' I said, feeling stronger than ever. 'I'll be fine.'

The following afternoon, I went back to the careers officer.

'What kind of job do you think you'd like to do?' he asked.

'Well, I love anything to do with art or technical drawing,' I told him. 'But I like people, so I think I'd be happy in a shop, or as an office boy, or something like that.'

He ran his finger down a list and stopped. 'Here's one,' he said. 'I think, with your background, you could do well in a larger shop environment and this looks just the right sort of job for you. It's at the Co-operative Department Store in the city, in the centre of Birmingham. They need to recruit a reliable salesman for one of their departments. They're a good employer – they'll give you a fairly basic wage to start with, but if you do well, they will give you a rise. Do you think you would like to apply for that one?'

'Yes, please!'

The Co-op was huge in Birmingham and all across the Midlands, with funerals, milk rounds, bread deliveries and their big store. And so the careers officer helped me fill in my application form and write a covering letter – I wouldn't have known about all that if I hadn't had his help.

Just before my birthday, I was invited to go for an interview. I put on my school uniform to look smart and caught the bus for the long ride into the city. I stopped someone to ask the way to the Co-op and when I arrived, I had to go up to the offices at the top of the department store (locally, they called it the 'Big Top in Town'). I was shown into a room, hardly knowing what it would be like to be interviewed, so I was nervous. There were three people there and a chair for me to sit in. After introducing themselves, they started asking me questions, one after another:

'What did you like best at school?

'How well did you do?'

'What do you think you would be like with people?'

'Are you good at getting up in the morning?'

All those sorts of questions.

I answered them all as best I could.

The next day, after school, I went back to see our careers officer.

'Sit down,' he said with a smile. 'I've already heard from the personnel department at the Co-op and they like you, so well done!'

'Thank you. Does that mean I've got the job?'

'Not quite,' he said with a grin. 'It means they will put you on their file to offer you a second interview after you have left school, just in case you change your mind or have a different offer that you prefer.'

'Oh, I see. So, it's quite hopeful then?'

'Yes, it's very hopeful, but not absolutely certain. Only the second group of interviewers can decide.' He paused. 'So, when you've left, if you're still interested in this job after Christmas, here is the telephone number to ring and they will arrange it for you.' He passed the sheet of paper to me with the number on. 'Now, keep that safe. Don't lose it!'

'I won't,' I said.

* * *

My fifteenth birthday came and went, then the Christmas and end-of-term fun at school. Finally, the last day came. We finished at lunchtime and then, without any fanfare, Robert and I walked out of Park Hall High School for the very last time. It did feel strange, but not so bad because we were together and both had possible jobs lined up for us. Over the following days, I had time to get used to the fact that I would never go back to school again.

After the festive season, every now and then, alone in my room and perhaps drawing a bridge or designing a house, I regretted not being able to stay on and continue on the road towards architecture. But now all my schoolboy dreams were dashed and it was not to be. I had made my choice, not just for myself, but even more in favour of Pearl's mental health, and I would never regret that.

CHAPTER 17

The Next Step

The Christmas holiday was always subdued because of Arnold's hatred of noise, fun, fuss and festivities, apart from on Christmas Day when his mother and brother, Uncle John, came to lunch, as every year, and brightened up our lives.

Soon after Christmas I took out the phone number from my hiding place in a niche at the back of my wardrobe and went out to the phone box down the road to phone the Co-op store's number. The telephonist put me through to the personnel department and I gave them my name. They seemed to know immediately who I was, which was very heartening, and arranged a date the following week for my second interview.

Those days dragged by. Most of the other boys had gone back to school and Robert had already started his job, so I just sat around at home, thinking about everything, which wasn't a very healthy start to the New Year.

Finally, the date of the second interview came around and I made my way back to the city centre and the Co-op department store. This time there were three different people interviewing me because they wanted to ask me some more detailed questions to help them decide whether I still wanted to do this job and whether they still wanted me to do it, so it was more like a double-check really.

'You will have to wear a suit, collar and tie for this job,' the woman interviewer said. 'Do you have one that you could wear?'

'I don't at the moment, but I'll ask my parents to help me with that,' I said. I wasn't so sure they would, of course – I'd have to ask Pearl.

All three of them were smiling at me, so I realised they liked me and they were talking as if I'd got the job – but they hadn't exactly said so. They asked a few more questions to help them decide what department I might work best in.

Then, out of the blue: 'Would you be able to start next week?'

'Yes, I can,' I smiled.

'Good! Well, we'd like you to arrive at 8.30 on Monday morning and find your way to the hardware department, where you will meet your boss. He will show you round the different parts of the department and train you on what to do.'

So, it seemed as if the job was mine!

'Thank you,' I said. I'm sure I must have had a silly grin on my face, but that was because I was so pleased they wanted me.

'We hope you will enjoy working here. Do you have any questions?'

I hadn't expected this.

'Er, yes. Do you have a staff canteen?'

* * *

I was so delighted that I couldn't stop myself smiling all the way home: I had achieved the first step in my plan. But then, as I got off the bus and walked the last bit to our house, I began to worry about the suit. I knew I would have to speak to Pearl when Arnold was out, but I had no idea whether she had any money of her own. If not, I was worried about what I would do. Perhaps I could ask Uncle John? But I didn't want to have to do that because I knew it would probably get back to Arnold.

Luckily, when I walked into the house it was quite early in the afternoon. Pearl was in, but Arnold was out, so I went straight into the kitchen to have a chat with her and tell her how the interview went.

'Tell me about it all, from the start,' she said, putting the kettle on.

I described the scene and the people, then told her what questions they had asked me and what they said at the end.

'I'm going to start at half past eight on Monday morning,' I told her.

'Ooh, how exciting!' She seemed so thrilled for me – it was the first time I'd seen that spark in her eyes since I'd won the Progress Award.

'There's just one problem,' I added.

'What's that?' Her face fell.

'They told me I must wear a suit, a shirt and a tie.'

'Ah well, we can do something about that. How would you like me to come shopping with you? You can try things on and I'll pay for your first suit, a couple of shirts, so you can always wear a clean one, and a couple of ties as well.'

'Oh, thank you, that would be amazing!' I said, relieved at her generosity. 'Are you sure you can afford it?' I asked. 'Any suit would do.'

'Yes, I can. My uncle gave me a little bit of money and I can't think of anything better to spend it on. You will have the best suit I can afford and I shall so enjoy the day shopping with you – that will be worth every penny.'

So that's what we did. She insisted on buying me some smart, shiny new shoes as well, so I was all set up for the following Monday.

I don't think Pearl told Arnold until after she'd bought me the suit. The following day, Saturday, he came in from the workshop and found me in the kitchen, chatting with her about my new job – I think he must have known by then.

'How much are they paying you?' he asked in a churlish voice. For once he was looking straight at me.

'Four pounds and 10 shillings a week,' I replied. 'But out of that I'll have to pay my bus fares, my lunches and ...'

'Two pounds a week board and lodging,' he said. 'That's what you've got to pay us for living here, not a penny less.'

'All right,' I agreed. But I knew Pearl would have let me off, for some weeks at least. I'm sure, if it was just her, that she wouldn't have asked me to pay anything at all.

Now I would have a harder job saving some of my earnings, but maybe I still could. I remembered the careers officer had said they might give me a rise if I worked hard, so that was what I intended to do.

Bright and early on the Monday morning, I set off and took the number 55 bus into the smoke and grime of the city, excited yet apprehensive and nervous, to get started on my very first day at work. The hardware department downstairs in the basement of the city store sold everything from saucepans and kitchen furniture to tools and wallpaper. It was almost like going into a huge hardware superstore today, with everything laid out in sections and labels to help customers find what they needed. The only difference was that we served the customers and showed them what we had and then we took them back to our counter for them to pay for their items. There were no trolleys and checkouts in those days!

The department manager would be my boss. Mr Holman was dressed immaculately. Oh yes, he was a very fine gentleman! From the way the others spoke to him, I could tell he was well respected and he was certainly nice to me.

'I'll start you off with an overview of the department,' he told me. 'Then after that, I'm going to hand you over to Mrs Martin, who will train you. Come with me and I'll introduce you.'

He led the way to the tool counter.

'Ah, Mrs Martin. Here is Richard, the young man I told you about.'

'Hello, Mrs Martin,' I said with a nervous smile.

'Welcome to our department,' she replied. 'If there's anything you need to know, come to me.'

'Thank you. I'm very keen to learn, so I will.'

'That's the ticket!'

By the look of it, nobody retired in this store till they dropped! Mrs Martin was a case in point – she must have been in her eighties and was quite slow-moving, but there was nothing wrong with her brain, or her sense of humour, and I could tell she was going to be a mine of information to me. She was a dear lady and the wink she gave me immediately eased my nerves as I followed Mr Holman on our tour of the department, explaining things as he went. I could see I was going to like working here.

'You're a quick learner,' he said with a smile, 'I'll say that for you. I reckon you'll do very well. Now, off you go and have your coffee break. The café is over in the other building, Mrs Martin will take you.'

'Off we go then,' she said, taking me to the tunnel under the road. It was a massive store and I'm sure I would have got lost without help. 'It's just up here,' said Mrs Martin. 'They do a nice cup of tea in the staff café, or do you prefer coffee?'

'I like both,' I replied. 'Do they have biscuits as well?'

'Oh yes, they're free for staff.'

As soon as we sat down in the café, she got out a cigarette, lit it and breathed out clouds of smoke between sips of tea. In fact, when we got back to the department, she lit another cigarette and held it under the counter between puffs – she always seemed to have a ciggie on the go!

'Now,' she said. 'I'm going to show you the ledger and how to enter numbers into it. These are members' numbers, you see, for their dividends.'

'Right.'

I nodded agreement even though I didn't have a clue what dividends were.

Next, she showed me things around the tool counter, which was quite eye-opening.

'Anybody can come into this department with a rusty old screw and ask for a set of six matching screws.' She took out a large box from behind the counter and opened it up – it was packed full of assorted screws. 'Look at all these,' she said, proudly tipping a few out onto the counter to show me. 'I can almost guarantee they will find their matching screws in this box. Have you ever done any woodwork or metalwork?'

'Yes, I did both at school and loved them.'

'Well, you'll be very useful with the customers,' she said, rifling through the box and picking out a few different types of screws. 'You'll probably recognise some of these.'

Next, she showed me all the different kinds of hinges and catches and how they are used – I was learning a lot from this lovely woman.

The other colleague I got to know that first day was Mr Collinson, who was also going to train me in other areas of the department. Dear old Mr Collinson, he used to spend all his money on gambling – for him it was putting bets on horses.

'You should have a go,' he suggested. 'I could place your bets for you.'

'Thanks for the offer, but I'm afraid I have to pay nearly half my wage on accommodation so I can't get into anything like that,' I told him.

I had to stick to my plan, which meant saving as much as I could, so no unnecessary spending – I was very determined about that. I very much liked and respected these people and I enjoyed working with them, but I knew what I had to do. The only exception I made was to buy myself a cheap radio from my first pay packet at the end of the week to have something to listen to – very quietly, of course, so as not to annoy Arnold – during the lonely evenings in my bedroom.

For me, the worst part of going to work was the bus ride, morning and evening. I've never been one for too much cigarette smoke and because it was the rush hour, I always seemed to be unlucky, always having to sit on the top deck of the bus, which was filled with thick smoke. You couldn't see from one end to the other. I tried to open the windows, but other passengers complained – sometimes not too politely! It was about half an hour's ride each way and sometimes it used to make me feel sick.

For me, the best part of working at the big Co-op store was the upstairs canteen, which was lovely – a bit like my school's canteen. The cooks made wonderful home-cooked food, the same as the meals they sent down to the store's cafeteria for the customers to eat. We had a staff section, where we could buy the same dishes at a much-reduced price – pennies, really. It was very much the thing at the Co-op to look after their staff. This meant I could eat well at midday, every day, as long as I budgeted for it, which I managed to do and still save some of my wages every week.

In charge of the canteen was a very bubbly woman of about 50 called Hilda. She had a big, blonde beehive hairstyle, huge earrings and her face was heavily made up. The most lovely woman, just thinking of her now makes me smile!

'Do you want some more?' she always asked me. 'You look like you could do with a bit of feeding up.' And she knew just what I liked. 'Ah, Richard, just in time! It's steak pie and gravy today, but it's nearly all gone.'

'Oh!'

My face dropped.

'So, I dolloped out a lovely big portion on a plate for you.'

She reached into an oven and brought out a piled-high portion of my favourite lunch.

'Ooh, that does look good!' I beamed.

When we met sometimes in the café in our breaks, we talked about all sorts of things. I confided in her about my home life and some of the things Arnold had said sometimes too.

'Try not to believe it the way he tells you,' she would say. 'By the sound of it, he's probably exaggerating. Perhaps your birth mother did love you, but she had to battle with hard-ships, money problems or maybe family pressures. She proba-bly had no choice, so she had to give you up.'

'For years I didn't even know what that word "bastard" meant, until I looked it up in a big dictionary in my High School library.'

'So, you remember what it means now?'

'Yes, it said my parents weren't married. I realised that must mean my birth parents. I know people think that's bad, but is it so terrible? It's a cruel word, isn't it? Especially when he shouts it at me while attacking me.'

'Oh, you poor boy! You have had a lot to put up with, haven't you?'

She paused and almost certainly saw me wiping away a tear – I'd never received sympathy like this before, but then I'd never told anybody before.

'Is it still happening now?' she asked with a look of concern.

'No,' I lied. I didn't like lying, but I'd said too much already and I couldn't let her get the police onto him, or anything like that. 'It finished when I grew too big and strong for him to beat me.'

Hilda's kind words have stuck in my mind ever since. A true diamond, she was. But I never told anyone Arnold's accusation about my father being a criminal – I suppose I felt ashamed, I couldn't bring myself to believe it.

I will always remember opening my first wage packet, a little brown envelope with the cash inside. That was probably the most exciting moment of my life! Every week, I counted it to make sure it was right and I set aside whatever I could afford to add to my savings, which gradually grew. I was quite surprised and proud of myself. This money was mine, it was the key to my future. Every now and then I would get it all out from my hidey hole – the half crowns, the 10-bob notes and just a few green pound notes.

Gosh, I thought, *I'm getting really rich here!*

It never occurred to me to open a bank or building society account – I didn't know how to and I didn't want to ask Pearl in case she told Arnold and he would come looking for my cash. As far as they were concerned, I used it all up on bus fares and meals at work.

When my savings became too much to hide in the niche in the back of my wardrobe, I looked around for somewhere else to put them. My room in this house was bigger than in the first house and it had proper carpet, so I started hiding the notes under a corner of the carpet, where one of the floorboards had warped. This was the most wonderful thing that had happened to me and it was all by my own efforts.

When I got home in the evenings, if Arnold wasn't in the way I used to pop my head round the kitchen door and tell Pearl I was home.

'Did you have a good day?' she would ask.

'Yes, thanks. What's for tea?'

'It will have to be something quick – how about beans on toast?'

"That will be fine.'

'I'll bring it up to you with a cup of tea when the coast is clear.'

'Thanks.'

Other nights, I went without, but I didn't mind a bit of hunger, knowing my savings were the reward for it.

It was several weeks before I realised I had done hardly any drawing or painting since starting work. How strange! Then I realised that I had been out longer hours each day and had been putting all my energies into work. When I was home in the evenings, I was tired out and just relaxed, listening to my radio at its lowest volume. If I thought of anything, it was preparing for the next stage of my plan, working towards my escape.

CHAPTER 18

The Motorbike

It was 1970, I had been working at the Co-op for nearly a year and had just turned 16 when David, a friend at work, told me about his new toy.

'You know, it takes such a long time getting to work each day, standing in the bus queue and being held up in traffic jams,' I complained to him in a coffee break.

'Oh, I don't have to queue for a bus any more.' He looked quite pleased with himself. 'I've bought myself a little motorbike and it's not fast or anything, but it gets me to work on time.'

'That sounds like a good idea,' I said. 'How old do you have to be to ride a motorbike?'

'You can get a provisional licence at 16,' he replied, 'as long as it's no more powerful than 250cc.'

'Is that like a bike with a little engine?' I asked.

'No, that's a moped,' he smiled. 'Mine is 250cc and it's a proper motorbike.' He paused. 'In fact, why don't you come out and see it at lunchtime?'

Sure enough, at midday there he was, standing next to a shiny silver motorbike.

'Come and sit on it,' he said. 'I'll show you what everything does.'

The lunch break flew by as he demonstrated everything and even had me starting it up, so I could see what it felt like to ride, except we kept the brakes on.

'I hope you don't mind my asking, but how much did you have to pay for it?'

It was a lot of money, but I had saved for a full year by then.

He gave me a few hints as well: 'Always the simpler the better,' he advised. 'All you need is for it to go. Get something reliable, like a Honda or a Yamaha.'

On the way to the bus stop that evening, I popped into a newsagent and found a magazine about motorbikes, so I bought it out of my precious earnings and took it home with me to study and learn all I could about them. If I chose wisely, a good, reliable used machine would probably save me some money on bus fares. I made a mental note to ask David about the cost of fuel and worked out how much of my savings I might be able to spare. At the weekend, I walked down to a small motorbike dealership at the Fox and Goose shopping centre to have a look round.

The first thing I noticed was the distinctive smell of oil and petrol. It wasn't at all like the glamorous Jaguar garage I used to visit with Uncle Geoff during those carefree summers. No, for one thing, this showroom needed a good clean. Motorbikes of various sizes and styles were propped up randomly, quite close together, with others ranked round the edges. There was hardly room to walk between them, especially as I wasn't the only customer in the place that Saturday morning.

Still, at least that meant I could take my time looking around, without being accosted by any over-eager salesman.

Finally, when I saw the manager was free, I went over to talk to him.

'I think I might like to buy myself a small motorbike,' I explained. 'But I know I would need to apply for a licence first. Can you tell me how I could do that?'

'Yes, of course. In fact, we can make it really easy for you. We have the forms here. Would it be a provisional licence you want?' he asked, obviously noticing I was very young.

'Yes, I'm 16 and it's provisional.'

'You're lucky,' he said. 'You're just in time – they're going to raise the age to 17 for riding a motorbike next year.'

'Oh, good! I'm glad I'm lucky in something,' I smiled.

'Well, all you'd have to do is fill in the form and leave it with me – I'll do the rest. I'll post it off and you'll get your licence back in no time. As long as you've applied, you can ride.'

'Mmm, if I do that, would it be possible to have the licence delivered here instead of to my home address?'

I was crossing my fingers, hoping he wouldn't ask me why. I had a sneaking suspicion that, if it came to our house and Arnold happened to see the envelope first, he might take it and throw it away.

'Yes, that won't be a problem. You'll need some L-plates as well – they only cost a few pence and you can buy them from us too. Now, what about a motorbike? I noticed you were looking around earlier. Did you see any that you liked?'

'Yes. A friend of mine gave me some advice – he said to look out for a Honda or a Yamaha. Would you agree?'

'Yes, that is good advice. Do you want new or used?'

'I can't afford new, I'm afraid, but I'm hoping I might be able to buy a second-hand motorbike.' I paused. 'Can you show me what you have?'

He didn't have a used Honda, but he did have a very smart-looking shiny, dark green Yamaha. He took me over to see it and talked me through all its features – it looked nearly new.

'The seat lifts up, look, and you can store things in here, and that's where you put the petrol in.'

Quite a straightforward little motorbike, it had been well looked after by the previous owner. It had done very little mileage, so that was good.

'Try it out,' the manager suggested. 'Don't worry, the prop will hold it steady. Hop up onto the seat and see what it feels like.'

'Yes, it feels very good,' I said, unable to suppress a big grin.

Then he took it outside for me to try out in the backyard.

I didn't go fast – there wasn't room – so I just rode it gingerly to see what it felt like. To be honest, I was quite nervous and I wasn't very good at first, but it felt great.

I asked him a few more questions and then we came to the price.

'How much is it?'

'£30,' he said. 'And we'll give you a full fuel tank and the L-plates for free. How's that?'

I was quietly relieved – this was the top limit I had set myself.

'Yes, I'll take it,' I agreed. 'But I don't have the money on me. Can you reserve it for me and I'll come back to fetch it this afternoon?'

'Yes, no problem,' he said. 'Any time before five o'clock and we'll have it ready for you. Would you like us to arrange the insurance for you as well?'

'Oh, I hadn't even thought of that. Will it be expensive?'

'I'll check it out and let you know when you come back.'

I stayed on to fill in the licence application form and he posted it off straight away. It seems strange now to think anyone could ride a small motorbike without taking a test. I didn't even need to have a crash helmet.

After a meagre lunch in Pearl's kitchen I returned to pay the full £30.

'Here,' said the manager, picking up a plain crash helmet from his desk. 'You might as well have this.' He handed it to me. 'I found it in the backroom. It's second-hand, but it will give you some protection. I know most people don't wear them, but I don't like to see you youngsters racing around on your motorbikes without crash helmets on.'

'Thanks very much,' I said with a smile. 'I will wear that.' Then I rode the motorbike very inexpertly the short distance home. I wavered around through our quiet residential area on an invisible carpet of air, trying to get used to the steering, but so thrilled with myself: this felt like my passport to freedom, I could go as far as I liked. Then it occurred to me that I hadn't even considered what Pearl and Arnold would say.

I parked my lovely new machine on the side of the drive and in I went. Fortunately, Pearl was on her own in the kitchen.

'Hello,' she said with a smile. 'Just in time for a cup of tea!' She put the kettle on and we sat down at the table. 'Have you had a good day?' she asked.

'Yes, a very good day. I've bought myself a motorbike to ride to work.'

'Ah, that was the sound I heard – how exciting!'

'Yes, I've parked it on the side of the drive, out of the way. Come and see it.'

'Ooh, it's lovely!' she said with an admiring smile, followed by a slight look of anxiety. 'But you'll have to be very careful on the roads,' she pleaded.

'Yes, I'll be careful,' I reassured her. 'Where's Arnold?' I asked, worrying about his reaction.

'He went round to his mother's to help sort out her finances – he's much better at that sort of thing than Uncle John.'

I took one more lingering glance at my shiny new motorbike before going back inside to have that cup of tea with Pearl.

Half an hour later, I was just crossing the hall from the kitchen to the stairs when Arnold burst through the front door.

'What's that?' he shouted, pointing out towards the drive.

'It's my motorbike, I've just bought it,' I said, defensively. 'I bought it for going to work – I paid for it myself out of my wages.'

'I don't care who bloody paid for it, you're not leaving it on my drive!'

'But I tucked it into the side, out of the way.'

'Get it off my drive! Get it on the road! Get rid of it, for all I care! I'm not having that heap of rubbish on my property. I'll throw it out in the road myself, if you don't hurry up and do it!'

I could see his rage was building and his face turned red. I didn't want a stand-up fight in front of our neighbours, so I kept my voice as calm as I could.

'But I've only just bought it and I thought you'd like to see it.'

'Well, you thought wrong. I want rid of it!'

'But where can I keep it?'

'Are you bleedin' deaf?' His voice was rising, along with his blood pressure. 'I don't care where you keep it, as long as it's not on my property!'

I got the message loud and clear and so, as calmly as I could, I wheeled my new motorbike off the drive and down the road, parking it where it wouldn't be in anybody's way. Fortunately, I could lock it, so I had to leave it there and hope for the best.

A few days later, Arnold was in such a foul temper that he told me to take it off the road too.

'I don't want to see that ugly machine anywhere in my road when I'm coming home after a hard day's work – and especially not at weekends!' he ranted, jabbing his finger in my chest and trying to ram me into the kitchen wall. 'Clear it right away or I'll take it to the rubbish dump!'

'But he's bought that motorbike with his own money,' Pearl ventured bravely, with a trembling voice. 'He's being careful, he's done everything right. Just let him use it so that he can go to work and back on it.'

I was a bit worried that he'd attack me and even more concerned that he would make Pearl suffer for defending me. *Why couldn't he see what he was doing to her, bullying her and undermining her health? Or did he see and not care?*

He gave her an odd look, then stared coldly at me, as if blanking me out of his mind, his life. I could see the hate in his eyes. He pushed and jabbed me, shouting as loudly as he could, with all the usual accusations, expletives and worse.

'Get your bastard arse out of my life!' he roared at me. 'I wish you'd never bloody well come here in the first place, we'll both be better off without you. Go and rot in hell!'

I didn't rise to it, which angered him more, so he struck me hard across the face and stomped off out to his workshop. My cheek stung, but more painful was poor Pearl's shocked expression – I feared she was going to faint and helped her to a chair.

I don't think I saw him for days afterwards. When I knew he would be about I kept out of his way and maybe he also steered clear of me. In my plan, it wouldn't be long before I would get out of his life anyway, so this was only a short-term situation now.

I started counting down the days.

1971–85:
THE ESCAPE

Chateau Impney © Malcolm Bagley

CHAPTER 19

A Room with a View

The next day I took my first real step to freedom. I went to a newsagent on the way to work and bought a local paper to scour for rental bedsits within reach of central Birmingham. With a red pen, I drew stars by a few possibilities but then one of the ads further down the page stood out. It was in Acocks Green, an area five miles south of Birmingham city centre and the Co-op Store – about the same distance as I was travelling now. It was one large room at the top of a house with parking for a bike or motorbike and the rent seemed reasonable. There was also a bus stop right outside, on the number 11 bus route, just in case I couldn't use my motorbike. It sounded perfect, so I phoned the number and made an appointment to go and see it after work the next evening.

I drew up outside a lovely old Victorian house in what was once an elegant terrace of individual residences, now mostly turned into genteel flats. It was a good first impression. After parking my motorbike, I looked at my watch: I was on the dot. I took off my helmet, stroked my hand through my hair to make it look tidier and walked up to the front door. The owner had told me to press the bell for flat number 1, so that's what I did, noticing while I waited that there was also a basement flat and four more above. The man who came to answer the door was quite small, around fiftyish, with mousey brown hair, and casually dressed, but clean and tidy.

'Hello,' he said, holding out his hand to shake mine. 'I'm the landlord.' He seemed calm and friendly, so that was a very good start. 'You found it all right then?' he smiled.

'Yes, your directions were spot on,' I replied, returning his smile.

As he took me up the stairs he told me the room to rent was on the top floor and everyone in the house was quiet and friendly.

'I live here myself, with my wife, so I like to keep the house nice and tidy and respectable,' he said.

'That sounds good to me,' I agreed.

When we reached the top, he unlocked the door and ushered me in. The first thing I noticed was how light and airy it was, with a high apex ceiling, a beautiful big sash window with a view across the tree-lined street, and a bed against one wall, so I could use it like a sofa. There was also a kitchen area on the other side of the room, with a modern, stainless-steel sink and a grey Baby Belling.

'This is what you cook on,' he explained. 'Have you ever used one of these before?'

'Oh yes,' I replied, breezily. I hadn't, but I didn't want to appear naive. Oh dear, I must have given the impression that I knew everything about cooking when the opposite was true!

'Here's the meter,' he said, opening a cupboard which also contained a broom and some cleaning things. Luckily, he didn't ask me if I knew how to use the meter or I would have been sunk. He assumed I hadn't and explained what to do. 'There's only the electricity here,' he said, 'and you put a shilling in this slot to pay for it. You can keep it topped up, if you like, or just add coins when you need to, when the electricity runs out.'

'Is there a toilet and bathroom?' I asked.

'Yes, the toilet is in the bathroom on this floor and you would share it with the tenant in the room like yours at the back,' he said. 'And the bathroom light is not metered because I pay for that.' He paused. 'We expect everyone to be in by midnight at the latest.'

'Oh, that would be fine with me – I don't suppose I will be able to afford to go out much.'

'How old are you?' he asked.

'Seventeen,' I replied, almost too quickly. I don't know why I said that, because I was only sixteen – I suppose I just wanted to appear a little older, in case it would help. As it happens, I think it did.

'The deposit is one week's rent,' said the landlord. 'So that is £2 in advance, and then £2 per week rent. Will that be all right for you?'

I noticed that when I first arrived we were talking in 'would' sentences and now it was 'will'. *Oh good, he must like me*, I thought.

'Yes, that will be fine. I'd like to take the room, if that's all right with you.'

'Yes, it's fine with me, as long as you keep it clean and tidy,' he said with a smile, shaking my hand to seal the deal.

'Oh yes,' I replied. 'I like to keep things tidy.'

We went back down the wide staircase to the bottom.

'Did you say you had a motorbike?' he asked.

'Yes, it's only a little one, right outside.'

'Well, you can park it in the space down the side if you like – it will be safer there.'

'Thank you.'

As I rode my motorbike back home, to the cold, austere atmosphere of Arnold's house, I was full of optimism for my move: I felt sure I had made the right decision.

I started to go through all my stuff, deciding what to take – it reminded me of packing my little case to leave Field House all those years ago. It was mostly just clothes and my radio. I made sure I included the long grey jumper and the woolly hat and scarf Pearl had knitted for me. I had very little space left, so chose just one thing to take for comfort – my old friend Jeffrey the bear, from my earliest days at Field House. I squeezed him in, but had to leave Billy, my cars and all the rest behind.

I had a lot to think about now and my head seemed to be full of it all.

I arranged to move in on the following Sunday afternoon, while I knew that Arnold and Pearl would be out at their Salvation Army meeting, so they wouldn't spot me stealing out of their house with a holdall stuffed with clothes. I'd borrowed the holdall from David at work. It wasn't very big, but it was just the right size to strap onto my motorbike.

On that Saturday morning, however, Arnold had a huge meltdown, ranting and raving and lashing out at me. Now that I knew I was leaving, I couldn't bear to stay a moment longer, so I prepared to leave after lunch that day, when they usually sat in the back room together, looking at the newspapers before falling asleep for an hour or two's nap.

I had thought of leaving a note, for Pearl's sake, as I didn't want her to worry, but decided against it as it would only anger Arnold and I didn't want to upset her any more than necessary, so I just crept down the stairs, across the hall and left, closing the front door as quietly as I could behind me. I felt bad leaving without saying goodbye to Pearl, but he was there, so I had no choice. In my hurry, I hadn't even managed to take all the things I needed, but I could go back and pick those up on the Sunday afternoon, so I kept my front door key for now.

I strapped the bag to my bike and got on, but then it hit me: where could I go? My room in Acocks Green wouldn't be ready until the next day, so I needed a place to spend the time until then. I thought of going and asking a friend if I could sleep on their sofa, but who? Because I could never have anyone back to my house, I had very few friends. Robert was too close to home and Grandma and Uncle John would certainly tell Arnold, so I couldn't go there.

I started up my motorbike and rode off down the road. Eventually, I turned towards the old Birmingham Elmdon Airport, where I knew there was plenty of space to get lost. I thought it probably stayed open all night, so I could buy something to eat and doss down somewhere to sleep. As I later found out, the airport building did close overnight. However, there was a groovy all-night café close by, so I went in there, which was considerably warmer than being out in the open on a winter's night. I knew I had to pay for something to stay there, so I had a cheap snack, then kept awake most of the night, drinking cups of tea. As I sat there, I imagined the scene of Pearl and Arnold waking to find I had gone. I felt very guilty to think of how distraught she would have been – if only I could have told her.

Finally, I slept very fitfully, for an hour or two, with my head on the table. Early the next morning, I had a quick wash in the gents' and then the airport opened up again. A few more hours of moving around, carrying my bag so that I merged with the crowd of travellers, and at last it was the afternoon and I could go and drop off my bag at the house in Acocks Green.

'I have a few more things to collect,' I told the landlord, 'so I'll be back with them in an hour or so.'

When I returned to Windleaves Road, the Ford Anglia was missing, so I assumed Arnold and Pearl were out at the Salvation Army meeting. I left my motorbike down the road and walked to the house, put my key in the lock and slowly turned it: there was a beautiful silence. I crept upstairs, collected my last few things and came back down again. This time, I hesitated for just a few seconds. I hated leaving for good without saying goodbye to Pearl. She wasn't there now, so I couldn't, but I knew this was the wrong thing to do. I felt very sad about leaving her without even saying goodbye. As I pulled the door shut and slipped my key through the letter-box, to drop softly on the mat, I realised it was final: I would never come back to this house, I would never see or speak to Pearl again. That haunted me for a long time.

When I got back to Acocks Green, I rang the bell for the landlord and he let me in again. 'Have you got everything this time?' he asked. 'You won't have to ring the bell again. Here is the key to your room and the other one is for the front door. Let me help you upstairs with your things.'

Taking hold of those two keys felt great. I'd made it at last – my own room. For the first time, I felt grown-up and ready to go! Of course, it wasn't quite like that, but in the euphoria of that moment of opening the door to the room for the first time as *my* room, I felt like I'd opened the door to my future.

That first night, I put a shilling in the meter, turned on my radio – the prized possession I had bought out of my first pay packet – and put all my clothes tidily away. There were sheets, blankets and a towel on the bed to start me off, so I made the bed and lay down on it to try it out. I'd never made a bed before and it probably wasn't the most comfortable bed ever, but it was good enough.

Due to the lack of sleep and food during that day, I was both ravenous and exhausted. *Food first*, I thought, going over to tackle how to work the Baby Belling. I had bought myself a loaf of bread, a packet of tea and some milk and put those in the cupboard. I kept out the tin of steak I had bought for my tea, but, ridiculous as it may seem, I thought all I had to do was put the tin in the oven and it would cook itself.

First of all, I wrestled with the Baby Belling and eventually got the oven going, so I put the tin inside and waited and waited. Finally, when I thought it might be cooked, I opened the little oven door to find that the tin was completely distorted. *How had that happened?* I went to reach in and take it out, but I'd forgotten how hot the oven would be, not to mention the tin. It was quite frightening to see the tin so misshapen, so I quickly closed the oven door again, in case it should blow up! *Oh no, it's all going wrong*, I thought. After a few minutes, when nothing happened, I turned the oven off and opened the door to cool it down. Meanwhile, I hunted for a tin opener and couldn't find one anywhere, so that meant I wouldn't be able to open it anyway.

When I was looking for the tin opener, I found a kettle with a whistle on the top, so I filled that with water and put it on the Baby Belling to boil, while I opened my packet of tea and looked for a cup and a spoon. It didn't take long to find those in the top cupboard and the drawer, so at least I could now sit down and have a nice cup of milky tea.

By now, my stomach was rumbling and I remembered the loaf of sliced bread, but I had nothing to put on it. This wasn't good, I thought. But I suddenly thought back to my favourite pastime at Field House, all those years ago, when I would often take a packet of bread from the kitchen and eat the burnt crusts. I opened the loaf I had bought that afternoon and was thrilled to find that there were some slices with burnt crusts, so I didn't mind at all eating them without any spread. That cheered me up and staved off the hunger that evening. As it was growing late and I knew I had to get up for work in the morning, I got ready for bed.

It did seem strange, being completely alone, despite the fact that I'd spent 10 years on my own for hours on end in my bedroom at Pearl and Arnold's: this was different. I was so tired, but I couldn't sleep. It was entirely dark and I could hear muffled sounds below in the house, as well as traffic outside. As I lay there, I wondered, had I done the right thing?

Instead of lying sleepless in the dark, I got up and switched the light and radio back on, which helped me feel less alone. So that was my first night of being independent and I did eventually fall asleep.

Going off to work the next day, then back again to my own place, I had mixed feelings. It was a relief, going 'home', where Arnold could not get at me any more, to hurt me and drag me down, yet I was alone at the top of a house where I had not even met my neighbours yet, where I had a lot to learn about cooking and shopping and looking after myself. When I made a cup of tea for my breakfast, I had found I did have a tin opener after all, at the back of the drawer, so for my second evening, I bought myself something to cook in a pan, which was a great improvement.

One step at a time, I thought.

Those first few nights I kept the light on for company as I went to bed, but of course I soon realised that this was burning up the electricity, which I couldn't afford. It took me two or three weeks to feel I was settling in. I gradually met the other residents in the house, who were all people working in the city. One man was a little bit awkward and used to blank me, but I soon realised he did that to everybody. The others were all busy with their own lives and didn't speak much, other than 'Hello' or 'Are you using the bathroom?' But nobody was noisy or difficult, so that suited me fine.

Years of having to stay in my bedroom had made me into a bit of a loner, but now I couldn't afford to go out and socialise, and all that time alone in my room sank me into depression. I'd done this very grown-up thing and moved away from home, but in doing so, I seemed to have overstretched my funds. I had to find the money to buy petrol for my motorbike to keep that going, I had the rent to pay and the electricity to top up. Then I still needed to buy food to eat, not to mention toothpaste and shoe polish and all that kind of thing, so there was no money for entertainment or going out and meeting people. Everything, even food, cost too much, so I had to economise and I found it all quite a struggle.

Why hadn't I thought all this through beforehand? Well, I knew the answer to that: it was getting away from Arnold that drove me into living independently before I was really ready, but I didn't regret that. At least now I was safe. And I liked to think that Pearl's life must have been more peaceful without me there to make Arnold angry.

Every day was a struggle, financially. I made sure I paid the £2 rent each week and I had to set aside three shillings and seven pence for petrol. I could budget for those, but to start with, I could not predict how much money I would need to feed the electric meter each week, or how much my shopping would cost me, so sometimes I just had to do without.

I had taken on too much, too soon and in my lonely room at night, I missed Pearl. I missed her cups of tea and biscuits – I couldn't afford biscuits. I missed Sunday lunch – I couldn't afford a roast. I missed our cosy chats in the kitchen – I only had the radio for company, and that took up electricity too. I wasn't going to be able to afford this lifestyle – in fact, it wasn't really a lifestyle!

Missing Pearl made me think of what else I had been missing all my life. I had never known my real parents, never had the benefit of a true mother's love and protection. All I knew of them was their absence – the hole they had left in my life – and the accusations Arnold had always poured out on me because of them; words I didn't even understand.

So often through my 10 years with Pearl and Arnold I had felt alone, empty inside. Looking back, I felt as if I was grieving, but I never knew what for. This feeling had never left me. I felt guilty and yet I didn't know why; loneliness became my punishment.

It wasn't doing me any good having to do without food

some days, especially at weekends. And when I had food, it wasn't always the right kind of food. Back then I didn't know about needing a balanced diet.

I was often hungry, which sometimes made me feel weak, so the hunger, the weakness, the loneliness – it was all a big dent in my self-esteem. I had been so confident I could manage, so finding out I was wrong was making me more and more depressed. Everything seemed to get harder, week by week. I knew I was going downhill and everything was getting out of control, but I didn't know what I could do about it, until …

One day, as I was about to leave for work, I picked up a discarded newspaper, left on the wall near where I parked my motorbike. For some reason, I tucked it into the box under my seat and set off as usual. I remembered to take it in with me and when it was time for my coffee break, I took the paper out to look at it.

There was nothing wrong with my job – I liked the people, I enjoyed talking with the customers, and the Co-op were good employers. I earned a fair wage too, even though I found it so hard to make it last all week. Despite all this, something made me turn to the jobs page. I suppose I was looking for some kind of inspiration, a way of getting out of my difficulties – an answer to my prayer?

The very first job advert I saw was for a residential job, working in a hotel, where everything was paid for and there was a wage on top as well. It was like a light going on for me. *Wouldn't this be the answer to my predicament?* So now I had a new goal to aim for.

It wouldn't solve my immediate problems, but it was a ray of hope for the future.

CHAPTER 20

Crash!

One cold evening after work in October 1971, when I was nearly 17, I was riding my motorbike back home to my bedsit. I was going through the Swan underpass in Yardley when I felt very tired – and that's the last thing I remember. I must have blacked out, because I have no recollection of what happened next.

I came to with a blinding headache, propped up in a hospital bed. I was in a daze, disoriented. *What was I doing here?* I tried to look around, but my head wouldn't move. When I lifted my hand to my head, I found a strange, cage thing around it. From what I could tell, it seemed to be fixed to my head, keeping it rigidly in one position. It was free of my face, but all round the rest of my head and right down to my shoulders. Then I realised I had some kind of ear muffs on as well – no wonder I could only hear muffled sounds.

In fear and confusion, I sat there, calling out.

'Help! Can somebody please help me?'

My voice sounded distorted, but it was enough to bring a nurse over to my bed.

'What's happened to me?' I asked. 'Why am I here? What's this cage thing?'

'You've been in a road accident,' she explained in a kindly

voice. 'You've got a head injury and we're checking you out – that's why we've had to put this cage on your head; it's to keep your head still. The fact that you're talking is a good sign that the injury isn't as severe as we feared.'

'What happened?' I panicked. 'Where's my motorbike? What day is it?'

'It's all right,' she said, trying to calm me down. 'The accident happened yesterday evening and you're now in Dudley Road Hospital. You're in the right place. We will help you to get better, but it will take time.'

'Why can't I lie down? Is that because of the cage?'

'Yes, and you will have to keep that on until we can be sure it's safe to take it off.'

'Do you know what happened in the accident?'

'Only that you crashed with a minibus. Some of the witnesses told the police that they saw you meandering about on the road. Do you remember that?'

'No.'

'I'm afraid I don't know any more. When you're feeling well enough, the police will probably want to come and talk to you, so they should be able to explain a bit more about what happened.'

'Was anybody hurt?' I asked.

'Only you,' she replied. 'I think the passengers in the minibus were jolted, but nobody was injured as far as we know. It could have been a lot worse.' She poured some water into a plastic cup and held it up for me to sip.

I tried to move up the bed a bit, to be more comfortable, but I couldn't budge.

'I can't feel my legs!' I wailed, trying my best to make them move, to no effect.

'That's not unusual with a head injury,' she said. 'But the feeling is likely to return within a few days.'

I was really frightened now. My head was banging and pounding, my heart seemed to be beating far too fast and I felt very confused. I think I must have fallen into a shallow sleep again, which was probably just as well.

Perhaps a few hours later, I was woken by the scraping of a chair near my bed. There was an unknown woman sitting herself down with a notepad and pen.

'Ah, Richard,' she greeted me with a warm smile. Her calm voice soothed me. 'My name is Anne Kenwood and I'm a social worker, based in this hospital. I'm what you call an almoner.' She paused. 'How are you feeling?'

'Very confused! And my head hurts.'

'I'm not surprised – it was quite a crash. The police think you may have fallen asleep.'

'I'm not sure,' I explained. It was beginning to come back to me now, talking about it. 'I can remember a red minibus coming the other way in the underpass, and then I think I must have sort of blanked out.'

'Were you tired?'

'Yes, I was coming back from work, but I'd been feeling tired for a while. Things have been getting a bit on top of me, I think, and I probably wasn't eating the right things.' I didn't want to admit to this social worker that I didn't know how to cook and I couldn't afford to look after myself properly.

'Well, I think your head brace is on as a precautionary measure, so hopefully, you have come away from the accident without any serious injuries. But I'll leave that side of things to the doctors!' she said with a smile. 'What I really came to see you about is what will need to happen when you are well enough to leave the hospital.'

'Oh.' I groaned inwardly. I hadn't thought that far ahead yet, but I dreaded what she might say. I tried to sort things out a bit in my brain, but it wouldn't co-operate properly.

'When you are ready to go home, do you know where you want to go?'

'I live in a bedsit in a lovely house in Acocks Green,' I said, and gave her the address.

'Hmm,' she continued. 'I think you'll find you won't be able to go back there, because you won't be able to work for quite a while.'

'How long?' I asked, alarmed to hear what I dreaded.

'Oh, at least a few weeks, I should think. Maybe longer.' She paused. 'I'm sorry, I know that's not what you wanted to hear.' She had a very sympathetic manner and I appreciated that, so I couldn't blame her that this was happening to me – if it was anyone's fault, it was mine.

'How would you pay your rent?' she asked.

I tried to shrug, which was awkward with the cage resting on my shoulders. I couldn't answer that. I was already depressed, but now reality set in. *What had I done?* I knew the answer: I'd taken a big step backwards.

'Well, I see on your notes that you have parents who live in Castle Bromwich and they're coming to see you tonight. You'll have to …'

'No, I can't go back there! I've left.'

'Well, you're under 18, so I'm afraid you have no choice. You'll have to go back there.' She tried to break it gently, but there's no gentle way to break news as bad as that. 'You will need looking after while you recuperate and regain your strength. You'll have to go back to live there until you are well enough to manage on your own again.'

I gave her a forlorn smile.

I must have slept again through the afternoon as a nurse woke me to eat some nourishing food for my tea.

'That will help you on the road to recovery,' she said, trying to cheer me up.

It was a lovely plate of shepherd's pie. It looked delicious so I tucked in with relish but was hugely disappointed, then shocked to find that I couldn't taste anything. It was like eating cardboard. *What had happened to me?*

After tea, a doctor came on his rounds and stopped at my bed.

'How are you feeling today, Richard?'

'Battered and bruised, I suppose.' I tried to smile. 'I have a terrible headache and I still feel a bit woozy. But I'm very worried about my legs – I can't move them at all.'

'There's no need to worry too much,' he reassured me. 'The cage round your head is a brace to stop you moving it until we are absolutely certain that there is no other, hidden injury. However, you had such a big bang on your head that it certainly would have been much worse if you hadn't been wearing a helmet so well done for that!'

'Thank you.'

'You will probably find that your head injury will cause you some slight hearing loss and possibly affect your eyesight too.'

'What about my taste buds?' I asked anxiously.

'Yes, your taste can also be affected but it should only be temporary.'

Phew, that's a relief, I thought.

'You will have some balance problems for at least a week or two and your legs may seem to be paralysed now, but we have done tests and there's no permanent damage to your spinal cord, so it's mainly the shock of the impact. I'm sure you will find that the feeling gradually returns in both your legs, though it may take two or three months before you can really walk normally again, especially with your balance problem.' He paused and smiled. 'Don't worry, we'll get you up on your feet before you leave the hospital, just to make sure.'

About half an hour later, at visiting time, the ward doors were opened and in flocked visitors to most of the patients along the two rows of beds. I hadn't spoken to any of the other patients yet – I couldn't even move my head to see the people on either side of me. I wondered whether Arnold and Pearl would come, since he wouldn't let her learn to drive. I hoped he wouldn't, but I suppose he had to bring Pearl.

Finally, at the back of the line, I saw them walk into the ward. Pearl took a quick look round, saw me and made a beeline for one of the chairs placed beside my bed. Arnold trailed behind. I was surprised to notice the shock on their faces as they saw me, immobilised and trapped in a head cage.

I could see that Pearl wanted to embrace me, which I wouldn't have minded – it would at least have made me feel less panicky.

'You poor boy! I'd like to give you a hug,' she said as she sat down, 'but I'm rather afraid that I might break or move your head cage, or hurt you somewhere else. They told us they didn't yet know the extent of your injuries so I'll just hold your hand instead,' she explained.

Arnold said nothing, but at least he didn't look through me, as usual. If I hadn't known him better, I would almost have thought he had some sympathy for my plight. But I knew not to trust in that for long.

'You should have told us you were leaving,' he said in a gruff voice. 'You made Pearl very upset.'

'Yes, I worried about you every day,' she agreed. 'You should have told me what you were planning and why you wanted to go.'

'I'm sorry, Mum. I didn't mean to worry you, I just had to go. I couldn't say anything or you would have tried to stop me.' I chose my words carefully. 'I couldn't tolerate the situation any longer, especially as the longer I stayed, the more upset you were when things were difficult. I didn't want you to be upset any more.'

'Well, she was, and it was all your fault.'

Arnold's expression became more severe for a few seconds, then he seemed to think better of it and sat down next to Pearl.

'Never mind,' she said. 'You're here now, so we know where you are and can come and visit you each evening.' She gave me a lovely smile but then I noticed the anxious look had come back in her eyes.

'How did you know I was here?' I asked.

'A lady from the police station came round first thing this morning, just before Arnold left for work.'

'She made me late,' he complained.

'Ssh, Arnold! She came in and asked if we knew you and we said yes. Then she wanted me to tell them your date of birth and all that, just to make sure. She came into the front room and explained about your accident – she said you'd had a bad case of shock and a head injury, but hopefully not too bad—' She broke off. 'Is that why you're wearing a cage round your head?'

'Yes, that's what the doctor told me – he said he doesn't want me to move my head until they have checked to make sure it's safe.'

'The hospital almoner visited me this afternoon,' said Pearl. 'She explained that you would be in hospital for a few days before they would let you come home.'

'But I have a home,' I said, indignantly. 'I rent a lovely bedsitter at the top of a Victorian house.' I wanted them to see my pride in being self-sufficient and looking after myself, but I think they knew.

'The almoner told me you would need a lot of care and support,' added Pearl. 'So I will look after you every day and feed you up so that you can start to get better. I've got to help you get your balance back and walking again, a little further every day.'

That sounded good to me and I knew Pearl was totally genuine in her aim to help me recover, but I wasn't so sure about Arnold.

'We'll be a proper family again, the three of us,' she said. 'Won't we, Arnold?'

He grunted a reluctant 'Yes', looking away from me.

I was confused: *surely this leopard wasn't about to change his spots?*

'What happened to my motorbike?' I asked Pearl.

'Apparently it was a write-off. But don't worry, we have your kit back and I expect you'll get a bit of insurance money, so you can always save up to buy yourself another one.'

'But how can I do that,' I asked, 'if I'm not able to work?'

'Yes,' said Arnold, with heavy emphasis, 'the sooner you get yourself back to work and off our hands again, the better – we'll all rejoice!'

Whatever he said, he couldn't get out of the fact that they had chosen to adopt me. So now they had to have me back, like an injured fledgling, until I could fly again. Of course, that was the last thing Arnold wanted, but it was Pearl who would do the nursing and caring. My one hope was that he would stay well away from me for as long as it took.

Over the next few days, I worked hard on trying to remember the accident. I could remember everything before it, but not the actual impact or the next 24 hours, but I supposed I was unconscious or sedated for most of that time. It was infuriating, and it meant that I wasn't at all helpful when the policeman came to see me in hospital.

'I'm sorry, officer, all I can remember is feeling tired on the way home from work and then this red minibus coming towards me in the underpass. Everything else is a blank.'

'So, do you think the minibus drove into you, or did you ride in front of the minibus?'

'I just don't know. Did anyone else see?'

'Yes, some witnesses in the minibus and other vehicles said you were meandering along the road, encroaching on the other side of the white line. Some said that you had ridden into the front of the minibus. A couple of others thought you were meandering because you were trying to avoid the minibus. According to one man, the minibus was going too fast. However, we have no concrete evidence at the moment,' he explained. 'Both vehicles are being inspected to see if they can shed any light on the cause.'

'Thank you,' I said. 'I only wish I could remember.'

'Never mind, sir. If it should come back to you in a few days' time, will you please give us a bell and I'll be round to take your statement.'

'Yes, sure,' I agreed. 'Will it go to court?'

'Too early to tell, but we'll let you know about that as well.'

Time dragged slowly in the hospital. After about eight days, they removed the head cage, which meant I could at last lie down to sleep. That was bliss! The nurses got me out of bed every day to try and get me walking again, but I made very slow progress. I couldn't keep my balance at all, even with two sticks, so they had to take me to the physiotherapy department in a wheelchair so that I could hold onto the bars at both sides while I tried to lift my legs and plant my feet, and all that. Any improvement seemed painstaking and my slowness was depressing, but gradually my legs began to get the hang of what to do; if only they could reliably do it. Eventually, the nurses weaned me off the bars and encouraged me to use sticks instead, which meant that I could now go 'home'.

Most patients would have been thrilled to be discharged so that they could go back to their normal lives, but in my case, I was downhearted.

Where I was being discharged to was the last place I wanted to be.

An ambulance came to take me back to Windleaves Road, to the house I thought I would never enter again. I walked in with my sticks, through the doorway and into the hall. Pearl was there, guiding me in with her warmest, welcoming smile, while Arnold stood in the shadows behind her, his face expressionless at first, until Pearl turned to speak to him, right there, in front of me.

'You must leave Richard alone this time, Arnold. Leave him alone. He's got to get over his head injury and learn to walk properly again, so he needs rest, relaxation and care.' She paused to turn and look at me. My face must have looked a picture, my mouth almost certainly hanging open with astonishment. I had never heard Pearl talk to Arnold like this – whoever invented the expression 'Wouldn't say boo to a goose' must have modelled it on her.

Strangely, he said nothing. He didn't even show any anger in his eyes. It was as if he was trying his hardest to rein it all in. But I knew him of old. It wouldn't take long before some petty thing angered him and he'd be off again, with me in the firing line.

Pearl helped me up to my bedroom. Opening the door was a shock. There was nothing left of mine. Arnold had obviously stripped it of everything I'd had. My cars were gone, all the pictures I'd painted and pinned on the wall were gone too.

'He threw everything away before I could stop him,' she explained. 'The only thing I managed to rescue was Billy the dog and I brought back Jeffrey the bear with the things from your bedsit and hid him.'

'Thanks, Mum,' I said. If I hadn't felt so wobbly, I'd have turned and given her a hug.

Arnold kept to his truce for three or four days, then suddenly it all started again.

It was a weekday morning and I was in the kitchen with Pearl, washing up the breakfast things, when Arnold came back to collect a document he needed. He stormed into the kitchen, straight towards me.

'Get your bastard body out of my sight!' he yelled, spitting in my face.

As I tried to move round him, still unsteady on my feet, he pushed me and I lost my balance, sprawling on the floor. He kicked me hard, two or three times.

'Why don't you go and rot in hell?'

He stormed out and slammed the door.

Pearl wept with disappointment and frustration.

If ever I had doubted Pearl's feelings, now I knew with certainty that she loved me. The fact that she hadn't always been able to show it was down to Arnold's rigid control. If nothing else, this enforced stay in their house truly opened my eyes to how she felt. She had dared to stand up for me in front of Arnold and she was even more upset for me than she was for herself. All the little things now came together to show me that she *had* been a mother to me in her own way, as far as she had been permitted. I feared for her, both mentally and physically, when I was ready to leave again, which I certainly would. Already I was planning my second escape. And this time, it was to be my final escape, my final break with the monster.

For the remainder of my recuperation, Arnold forbade me from watching the television or coming downstairs, other than for drinks and meals. He probably saw this as a punishment, but to me it was a good thing as it meant I was much less likely to be in the same room as him. I had my radio, brought back from my bedsit, which I played on low volume; also, a few books and some paper to draw on, so I tried to keep myself busy.

When Arnold was at work, I would walk up and down the hall and when I'd regained more strength, down the road and back. At first, I used both sticks, then just one – that was a happy day. I still didn't have much stamina and my balance wasn't yet totally reliable, so the second stick was still essential, but I felt every day was a day less that I would have to stay in the same house as Arnold.

Somebody must have told them at the Co-op about my accident. One of the bosses wrote to me and told me not to worry as they would hold my job open for me, when I was ready to return.

You are an invaluable member of our sales team and your colleagues in the hardware department miss you. Everyone sends their best wishes for your speedy recovery and hope to have you back with us soon.

I was touched by this letter and truly appreciated their support, but my new plan didn't include the Co-op. No, I had a better idea in mind.

CHAPTER 21

A Second Escape

My first escape from Arnold's clutches was a disaster because I'd done it all wrong. This was the conclusion I had come to during those weeks recuperating. I'd tried to be grown-up before my time and made some simple but harmful mistakes. I didn't want to do that again, but I'd learnt a lot from it, so this plan was very different.

What I needed to do was to find a job that would feed me and give me accommodation, so that the money I earned would be spare money. During my convalescence I'd given this a lot of thought and had come to the conclusion that the best jobs where that might be possible were in the hotel trade. My first goal was to walk every afternoon as far as I could in the direction of the post office, which also sold newspapers.

The first day I didn't get far at all – barely halfway, before, almost exhausted, I had to turn around and try to make it back to the house again. That was a struggle in itself. My legs were gaining strength, but I had little stamina as yet. Worse still, I wasn't very stable as I still suffered from lapses of balance. But one thing I wasn't short of was determination. I knew I had to do this. It might take a long time, which was a depressing thought, but it was a challenge I had to achieve.

'Would you like me to come with you?' asked Pearl as I set out on one of my first forays.

'No, thanks,' I said with a smile.

I didn't want to offend her, but I had to do this on my own. I think she just assumed that I was being a typical awkward teenager.

Gradually, each afternoon, I walked a little better and a little further. I couldn't push it as much as I would have liked, because I was always fearful that if I ventured too far before I was ready, I might fall on the way home and knock my head again, or I might not make it back at all. But I kept going, day by day, until one day I almost made it. The next day would be the one, I hoped. When I made it at last, I was so proud of myself. I went straight over to the shelves where the newspapers were displayed and picked up the local paper, the *Birmingham Mail*. I didn't buy it, which was a bit naughty, I know, but I had so little change left and I knew I would need to keep that for bus fares to interviews – if I had any. I opened the paper and pretended to be browsing, but I had turned to the jobs page and studied all the ads, one by one, until I saw it – quite a prominent ad so it stood out:

Major new hotel opening soon. We are looking for live-in staff to work in the restaurant, kitchen, bars, accommodation and reception.

All food and accommodation provided. Brand-new staff block under construction. Wages commensurate with the role.

Contact the hotel manager at Chateau Impney, Droitwich Spa.

At the base of the advert was a telephone number. I had taken with me a stub of pencil and a scrap of paper, just in case, so I took them out of my pocket and quickly noted down the number to call. Then I put the newspaper back and left the shop, walking to the phone box on the corner.

With a mixture of excitement and trepidation, I dialled the number and asked for the hotel manager. I had to have some extra coins ready in case there was a delay in finding him, but I needn't have worried.

'Hello, I'm the general manager. Can I help you?'

I suddenly had cold feet, but only for a moment.

'Hello?'

'Yes, hello, my name is Richard Gallear. I've just seen your advert for jobs at Chateau Impney. I would like to apply for one of them, if I may.'

'What sort of job would you be interested in?'

'Well, almost anything,' I said, not knowing what might still be available. 'Perhaps a waiter or barman, or I could work on reception. I'd be happy to discuss that with you.'

'All right,' he replied. 'Why don't you come along for an interview?'

'Yes, please!'

'How about next Monday at 10 o'clock?'

'Yes, thank you. That will be perfect.'

'Good! I'll show you round and we can talk about it all then.'

'I'll look forward to it,' I said, which was something of an understatement – I couldn't wait!

* * *

Over the five weeks since I'd been discharged from the hospital, Pearl fed me every day, but it was never much – one large roast and trimmings on Sundays, but only light meals during the week. And when Arnold was out, we'd have our cups of tea and biscuits. Luckily, Monday followed my best-fed day, so I had some energy and was ready for the fray.

I took an early bus, then had to change buses in Birmingham to get to Droitwich. It was a very long journey, so on the way I thought through my home situation. It seemed to me like a bad marriage: both partners think, oh, we'll try again, but it's not working, so it would be best to end it and move on. That was me – I'd chosen the time to leave all that behind and start afresh, but first I had to get the job.

I thought through all the questions the manager might ask me and decided not to tell him about my accident – about my poor balance, my weakness and headaches. I didn't want anything to spoil my chances, I just had to hope he didn't notice.

I was relieved to arrive at Droitwich on time. I didn't know this area, so I was about to ask somebody the way when I saw it. I couldn't have missed it, really: the Chateau Impney Hotel was a very imposing building, standing on a rise in the ground, its turrets rising majestically up to the sky. This hotel was huge!

I arrived and gave my name.

'I have an interview with the general manager of the hotel.'

'Yes, Mr Garrett is expecting you. I'll show you the way.'

'Thank you.' I followed the receptionist along the wide, plush carpeted corridor. I'd never been anywhere like this. Even Field House, wonderfully elegant as it was, didn't have such opulence in its decor as this hotel.

The manager got up as I went in, and stepped forward to shake my hand.

'Welcome to Chateau Impney,' he said with a friendly smile, putting me sufficiently at ease from the start. 'What do you think of the hotel so far?'

'Amazing!' I replied with genuine enthusiasm.

'Now, I'll just ask you a few questions and maybe you might want to ask me some too. So, let's get started, if you're ready?'

'Yes, that's fine.'

'How old are you?'

'Seventeen,' I said, this time truthfully. 'I'll be eighteen in November.'

'Good! Now why would you like a job at this hotel?'

'Because I want a change, and maybe a challenge.'

'Would you say you are good with people?'

'Yes, I always enjoy talking to new people.'

'Which of the advertised jobs do you think you would be most interested in?'

'Well, perhaps a waiter, but I really wouldn't mind any of them.'

'Would you be prepared to work in the kitchens, if we needed?'

'Yes, I would.'

'Would you be prepared to go front of house, if needed?'

'Yes, I would.'

'Would you be prepared to work in the banqueting suite and serve at tables?'

'Yes, I would be happy to do that too.'

'Well, there might be a bit of heavy lifting sometimes, if we do a banquet and the carpets have to be rolled up and all the tables moved around and laid.'

'That will suit me fine – I like variety and I'm sure I could do that.'

Of course, I knew that I might find the heavy lifting or carrying difficult at first, but I'd just have to make sure I carried on regaining my strength and then I'd be able to manage.

He paused and gave me a long look. That was a bit uncomfortable, but I sat it out.

'Well, Richard, you seem like the sort of person we are looking for, so you've got the job. Congratulations!'

He put his hand out and I shook it. I can remember the great excitement I felt when he said that – I could hardly believe it.

'Can you let me have references?' he asked. 'I know I should have asked that before, but better late than never!'

I gave him the Co-op as my referee. Fortunately, they had already offered, so I knew that would be all right and I thought they would give me a good reference.

'All your accommodation and food will be free,' he confirmed. 'And we'll pay you a wage of £3 on top of that.'

I was amazed! This seemed to me to be the dream job. I really liked Mr Garrett and felt I would enjoy working for him. I couldn't believe how well it was all working out.

'As you know, the hotel is still under complete refurbishment and the new staff accommodation will not be ready for a few weeks, I'm afraid, though they will be the height of luxury when they're finished,' he explained. 'Meanwhile, we have a small fleet of brand-new caravans standing on the car park for you and your colleagues to sleep in. You will each have your own, so you should have plenty of space and privacy when you want it.'

'That sounds great,' I said.

'Oh, I forgot,' he paused. 'I should have asked you, will you take the job?'

'Yes, please! I'd be delighted to take it the job,' I agreed, with my widest grin.

'Time for the boring bit,' he said. 'Filling in forms!'

'Oh, that's all right,' I laughed. 'I'd like a pound for every form I've filled in.'

'Me too!' he agreed. 'When can you start?'

'Whenever you like,' I said.

'How about a week today, next Monday at 2 p.m.? Could you manage that?'

'Yes, I'm sure that will be fine.'

'Now, Richard, let me take you on a guided tour of the hotel. There are some areas that are not finished yet, but they soon will be. We have a gang of talented tradesmen working on it every day.'

'That sounds good.'

'Meanwhile, we have put together our core team of staff, including you, to help us get everything in order and all the finishing touches done, ready for our grand opening in a month's time.'

'Oh, good!' I said. 'I'll enjoy doing that. I did art and design subjects at school and wanted to be an architect.'

'That's excellent news – you might be able to give us some ideas of your own.'

'I'd love to.'

Finally, it was time for me to make my long, weary but highly excited way on the Midland Red bus, back to Castle Bromwich, to Pearl and Arnold's house for just one more week. I knew it was going to seem a very long week, but it would be worth the wait to work in such a great job.

As I was walking down the hotel drive, towards the bus stop, a white Daimler Jag stopped beside me and the window came down. A man leant across and spoke to me.

'I saw you in my hotel just now,' he said. 'I know you were being interviewed. Did you get the job?'

'Yes,' I said, a little bewildered. Then I realised who this was. I'd seen his photo on the wall in Reception, labelled 'Mr Jackson, Co-owner of Chateau Impney'.

'Where are you going now?' he asked.

'Back to Birmingham,' I replied.

'I can drop you. I'm going that way, so hop in!'

Well, I was in my element in this glamorous car with the co-owner of the hotel, chatting away as if we were old friends. Astonishing, really – I felt I ought to be pinching myself, but it was all real.

Mr Jackson told me how he'd found this hotel and seen the potential in it when everyone else seemed to want to pull it down. He bought it as a wreck and immediately set about designing all the luxury interiors to turn it into a palace, while overseeing his builders and tradesmen in rescuing this imposing building and restoring its exterior shell.

'It's looking wonderful already,' I said.

'Well, we're aiming to finish all the main rooms and public areas within the month. That's when we're going to have the official opening.'

'Ah yes, that's what Mr Garrett told me.'

'In the meantime, we have key members of new staff starting with us next Monday, including yourself, I believe?'

'Yes, that's right.'

My self-esteem shot up to hear that he already considered me to be a key member of staff. I was determined to do my best in every way to reward his trust in me.

'We want to do our staff training programme first, then you will all be part of our team to prepare for the opening, ready to welcome and serve our first guests.'

'I'm really excited to be working at your hotel.'

'That's great. I hope we can all stay excited and make it the best hotel in the region!'

He dropped me off in the city centre, which was a great help as I only needed one bus ride from there to Castle Bromwich.

As that bus trundled me back to Windleaves Road, I thought through everything that had happened that morning. I felt jubilant that my plan seemed to have succeeded so quickly and that this was not any old job, but an exciting opportunity for me to shine. However, I had to appear calm and 'normal' when I got back. Arnold would be out, but Pearl would no doubt ask where I'd been and I decided not to tell her that I had a job, the best job I could imagine. If I was to make this second escape work, I had to cover my tracks.

Sure enough, when I got in, it was mid-afternoon and Pearl welcomed me with a smile.

'I'll put the kettle on,' she said. 'Let's have a nice cup of tea.'

At that moment, whatever happened to me in the future, I would always remember with fondness Pearl's cups of tea and cosy chats.

'Did you have a good day?' she asked, opening a new packet of biscuits.

'Yes, thanks.'

'Where did you go?'

'Oh, I just got a bus into the city to meet up with a couple of work colleagues,' I said.

I didn't want to lie if I could help it and indeed now that I'd been given the job, Mr Jackson and Mr Garrett *were* my work colleagues.

'Oh, that's good! I'm glad you are able to get out and about so much better now.'

'Yes, I think I'm almost back to full health now,' I agreed, 'so it's time for me to think about my future again.' I wanted just to sow a seed, without giving anything away, to see what she thought – I always valued her opinion.

'Will you go back to the Co-op?'

'No, they did offer to take me back, but I think I should look for a different sort of job this time.'

'Oh yes?'

'Ideally, a job where I would have accommodation and food provided and a wage as well. What do you think?'

'What kind of job would that be?'

'Well, maybe a care home, or a hotel.'

'Oh yes, that does sound like a good idea.' She paused for a sip of tea. 'If you're bent on leaving home, then that would probably be the best way to do it this time – as long as you're safe.'

'I've given it a lot of thought,' I told her. 'If I had that kind of job, I wouldn't need to buy another motorbike, because I would be living on the premises, so yes, it would be much safer.'

'If it's what you want, it's fine with me – I just want you to be safe, healthy and happy. I'd miss you, of course, but you could always come home on your days off.'

I felt mean not to tell her I already had the job, but it was the only way. Tired but exhilarated, I went up to my room. This was the day that started my new life.

The week went slowly. I couldn't wait to get started, but I was feeling very positive – happier than I'd been since my early childhood, so I sat in my room with a permanent grin, drawing while listening to the radio and picturing myself in my new uniform, waiting at tables.

On the Sunday night, I packed all my stuff again. I was so excited that I couldn't sleep much, so I was up very early, adding last-minute things to my bag, including my beloved radio – the first thing I had ever bought with my own money. Because I didn't have enough space for everything, I didn't take any of my childhood mementoes this time and I regret that now. There wasn't room for Jeffrey, my battered old bear which Pearl had rescued for me. I have nothing from Field House, except for my treasured memories, but they are all I really need.

When I heard Arnold leave for work as usual, I went down for some breakfast with Pearl and a last cup of tea. I felt very guilty that I had to pretend that nothing was happening, but it had to be. I waited until she took the washing out to hang on the line and seized the moment. As I pulled the front door to, as quietly as I could, once again I slipped the keys through the letterbox and walked away. This time it was my final escape – the very last time I would leave this house, the last time I would ever see Arnold. I felt like skipping down the road, though the neighbours might wonder why, but I knew neither my legs nor my balance were yet strong enough for that!

On the bus I reflected on how the past year had failed me. I had got it all wrong before, getting a job that paid barely enough for me to live independently. I couldn't cook. I couldn't budget. I knew I was unprepared. I'd made some bad decisions and nearly paid for them with my life, but I had learnt a lot from all that. Now at last I felt confident that I had made a more sensible plan. This time I was much better prepared and I knew it was right.

CHAPTER 22

Crossroads ... and
a New Life

I was pretty exhausted by the time I arrived at Chateau Impney, but my excitement overrode my fatigue and kept me going. Mr Garrett and his wife were in the hotel foyer, ready to greet me.

'Ooh, that's good timing, Richard,' said the hotel manager with a firm handshake and a welcoming smile. 'The head chef has just arrived, so I'll take the two of you over to find the accommodation we've earmarked for you, then you can unpack your things and get settled in before coming over for your evening meal.'

Mrs Garrett said little, but seemed charming. I immediately warmed to them both.

They took us over to the car park, where there were several small caravans. Mr Garrett took Gaston the head chef across to his and Mrs Garrett led me to mine.

'Here we are,' she said, handing me the keys. 'This will be your home for the first few weeks until the staff residence block is completed – that will be deluxe accommodation. I'm afraid a caravan doesn't rate so highly, but it is clean and tidy, with more space than you would think. Now, let's look inside.'

I mounted the step and turned the key in the lock. Mrs Garrett followed me inside.

'As you can see, this is the little kitchenette, with a kettle for hot drinks and everything you might need in the drawer and cupboard to make yourself a snack, though I don't suppose you'll want to cook very often, when you have all your meals provided.'

I smiled at the thought. 'That will be a great boon,' I said.

'The settee converts into a double bed for you at night. There are lockers and drawers for your things and here's the shower,' she said, opening what looked like a cupboard. 'But I'm afraid you'll have to go into the main building for the toilets. We've given you a heater for when it's cold.' She paused. 'I hope you will be comfortable here.'

'I'm sure I will,' I replied.

'And if you're ever feeling a bit down or needing a chat, come and knock on our door. We're very good listeners and we both want you to be happy here.'

'Thank you, that's very kind.'

I spent the next hour unpacking and trying things out. The settee folded down and the seat cushions, which doubled as a mattress by night, were surprisingly comfortable. I put the settee back up again and sat looking out of the window to see the view beyond the car park, of mature trees and countryside views. This place was like a dream for me. I sat back with a huge smile on my face, which extended even further when I spotted the little television screen on a bracket that jutted out from the wall: I could sit there and watch it whenever I liked.

What a bonus! My only concern was, being in a caravan on my own; would I feel lonely, like I had in my bedsit? But that thought soon vanished when the friendly head chef came over and knocked on my door.

It was still light, so the two of us went on a little tour round the outside of the hotel. We saw the half-built staff-residence block and various other features, but then he had to dash off after half an hour to cook our evening meal – I was getting quite excited about that.

Back in my caravan, I turned on the television and watched a teatime children's show on BBC. It wouldn't have mattered what it was, it was a real luxury to have it.

I thought I'd better change and then, at seven o'clock sharp, I proudly locked up my caravan and went over to the hotel dining room for dinner.

'We won't normally eat in such splendour,' explained Mr Garrett, 'but we can this week, before our first guests arrive. We're trying it out on their behalf,' he grinned.

The swing doors to the kitchen opened and out wafted the most delicious smells. I was in heaven! On our first night we had two courses, all sitting round a large table together – I suppose that was what we'd call a team-bonding exercise nowadays. The main course was meatballs in a herby gravy with creamy mashed potatoes and lovely fresh buttered vege-tables – delicious! Dessert was superb too: a chocolate pudding with blackcurrants and Chantilly cream. I savoured every lovely mouthful!

If I'd had any doubts about taking this job, they were dispelled by that first meal. They'd won me already! What-ever else happened, I knew I would always be fed well. That night, I went to bed full and happy and even though I wasn't

on a proper mattress, it was the best night's sleep I'd had since
Field House.

The training went well and the hotel opened on time, with a
lot of guests and a smattering of dignitaries, one of whom cut
the ribbon.

Everyone had a guided tour around the plush, opulent
interiors. The whole place was a triumph of design: it was all
done in a classical French style, apparently similar to the
Château de Versailles. There were marble pillars, mirrors and
gilding everywhere and chandeliers all the way up the grand
sweeping staircase. Everything was stunning.

By the time the hotel opened, all the rest of the staff had
moved in to the caravans and it was a bubbling place to work
or stay in, like nothing I'd ever experienced before. We all
worked well together as a team and soon got to know each
other, forging friendships. In our times off-duty, a group of us
would stroll down to the village and have cups of tea or coffee
and delicious cakes in the tea shop. Of course, we could have
had all that in the hotel, but it was good to get away sometimes and chat among ourselves.

Not long after the hotel opened, the new staff quarters
were completed. It looked good from the outside – a bit like a
mini-university campus. We each had our own room,
centrally heated and beautifully equipped with built-in furniture, and a common room to relax in with each other – we all
loved it. Soon we all got to know each other very well and I
made a lot of good friends.

I loved everything about my job. I loved the guests and I
loved their generous tips – we all did. We used to put them
in a pool and share them out. What with the tips and my

pay, I was able to save quite easily and still go out whenever I wanted to. In fact, the word was 'flush'! For the first time in my life I was well off, so much so that I didn't have anything to spend all the money on, so it kept on accumulating. Meanwhile, I felt safe and happy and fulfilled. I was optimistic and trusting, with so many good friends, and my confidence bloomed as I was promoted up the scale and into management, despite being still very young – not yet 19. It was at the Chateau that I learnt to live again – it changed my life.

One day in 1975, out of the blue, the hotel manager asked me to come and see him to discuss an approach he had received from a TV company. I went to his office and Mr Joynes, one of the co-owners, joined us, too.

'I had a phone call this morning from ITV – it was the director of a popular programme called *Crossroads*. Do either of you know it?'

I shook my head. 'I haven't even heard of it, I'm afraid.'

'My wife watches it,' said Mr Joynes. 'I think she's quite hooked on it. Apparently, some of the characters are very good.'

'Well, I'm like you Richard – I know nothing about it,' said Mr Garrett. 'But I shall try to watch it as soon as I can.' He paused. 'The storyline is coming up to a big wedding and they want to stage it in an actual hotel. The director said it would take up the whole of one episode and their first choice of location is here, at Chateau Impney. What do you think?' He looked at Mr Joynes first.

'Why not?' he answered with a broad smile. 'It would mean a lot of work for us, but it would be a great advert for the hotel. Apparently, so my wife tells me, millions of people watch it and are glued to every episode. So, as long as they agree to a prominent credit for the hotel, I'm all for it.'

'Yes, I agree,' I said. 'It could boost our bookings no end, especially as a wedding venue.'

'That's true,' agreed Mr Garrett. 'But I would like to watch it first, just to make sure, and provided I'm happy with the tone of the programme, shall I give them the go-ahead and tell them it's a yes?'

We all agreed.

'But not a word to anybody until we have it in writing.'

How exciting, I thought to myself as I walked down the corridor and back to my duties. I didn't breathe a word, but I did watch a couple of episodes of *Crossroads* and couldn't wait for it all to happen.

The filming was scheduled to go ahead, so it was all systems go. When everything was arranged, we had a meeting of the staff to tell them the news. The whole place was buzzing with excitement – *Crossroads* was such a big thing in the Midlands in those days.

'Who's supposed to be getting married?' one of the reception team asked me.

'Apparently, it's the fictional wedding of the main character, Meg Richardson, and Hugh Mortimer.' (I'd read the director's memo to us by then!)

The day dawned and we all got up early to be ready for the arrival of the cast and crew. We couldn't wait! The camera crew were the first to arrive and their vans with all their equipment. Next came the directors and producers, the make-up team, the technicians and the caterers, all with their huge vans to be parked where they would be needed, but out of shot for the filming.

All the production teams milled about in their casual clothes. While all of this was interesting to watch, what most of us really wanted to see were the stars – and Noele Gordon (who played Meg Richardson) in particular. We didn't have long to wait. First came the supporting actors and bit-part players in a luxury coach from Birmingham. We craned our necks as they came down the steps, out of the coach, and we recognised some of them, usually by their cast names.

'Look, there's Amy Turtle.'

'Isn't he the policeman?'

'Where's Noele Gordon?'

'Oh, she won't be on the coach!'

We could hardly believe all this was really happening in our own hotel car park.

There was a short lull and then a white Rolls-Royce was driven in by a uniformed chauffeur. It pulled to a halt at the front and out stepped Noele Gordon herself, waving at us all.

Only moments later, another white Rolls swept in and out of the back stepped Larry Grayson, who most of us knew as a comedian at that point, although of course he would later become more famous for presenting *The Generation Game* on the BBC. He came as Noele's close friend. She had apparently arranged for him to have a small part in this episode so that he could come and keep her company on location.

My role that day was to look after all the needs of the leading actors, so I welcomed them into the hotel and led them through into the lounge bar and brought them tea, coffee or other drinks, plus nibbles, snacks and anything else they wanted. I had other staff to fetch and carry for them, so I stayed with them and looked after them all day and I spoke to them all.

I suppose they didn't usually do much filming on location, so they all seemed quite excited to be here, on a big budget for a change. Larry Grayson was a lovely, warm character – not at all like he was on television. He was especially interested in the history of the hotel and its renovation, so he was asking me all sorts of questions about it and had a friend in the village, so we had lots to talk about. Friendly and pleasant, he was very easy to talk to and always said please and thank you. He was not at all big-headed either, but I suppose he wasn't all that famous then.

'I'm really excited about being in this hotel,' he said. 'I had to persuade Noele to get me a part as an extra at the wedding,' he explained, 'so that I could come and see the interior. All this marble and glass – it's so beautiful, isn't it?'

Noele Gordon herself was a gem. For some reason, she seemed to take to me. She had brought her mother with her and introduced her to me. 'This is my mother, Jockey. I usually take her with me whenever I can – she likes a good outing!' Jockey was very nice and just stayed in the background, watching and occasionally chatting to someone.

Noele of course was very glamorous and theatrical – lots of make-up, some amazing jewellery and a mink pelt slung, or perhaps carefully positioned, over her shoulder. She had a natural smile all the time, which was very engaging. Throughout the day she spoke to all the cast and crew, as well as the hotel staff, calling everyone 'Darling'. She was very friendly, with a warm personality and extremely professional – not a single re-take all day.

The director and crew were all focused on their jobs, so I didn't talk as much with them, but they were easy to talk to in their breaks. They worked very hard and sometimes needed things moving, so they told me and I made sure it was done. But everyone was also accommodating to the fact that this was a real, working hotel, with guests staying and mingling with them in the bars.

At one point in the day, when I was serving drinks to Noele and her screen son Sandy Richardson (played by Roger Tonge), they had obviously come up with an idea.

'Why don't you serve some drinks to us at the wedding reception?' asked Roger.

'Yes, darling, we'd love you to be part of this episode,' added Noele.

'Oh, I can't do that.'

'Yes, you can, darling,' she said, trying to persuade me. 'Just come on with a tray of drinks, like you usually do. You'd be perfect for the part.'

'Well, all right then, but only if the director is happy about it.'

Noele Gordon had only to click her fingers on that set and it was done.

So, the scene was set at the wedding reception for me to come to their table with my tray. The director gave me instructions, I brought the tray of drinks to their table and served them and then walked out of shot again. It was just a walk-on part and I didn't have to say anything; it felt just normal to me and I didn't even have to do a re-take, which surprised me more than anyone. I did enjoy it, but they didn't pay me for it! Just as well that I was happy to do it for nothing and it was really good fun. Afterwards they asked me to join them for coffee, which I did for a short while, with Mr Garrett's permission, but I felt awkward about it as I was meant to be working and I was supposed to be setting a good example!

It was truly a day to remember.

A week or two later, we heard our episode was to be aired and we got as many of the staff together as we could to watch it. I cringed when I saw myself – 'I look terrible.'

'No, you don't. You look just the ticket, as you always do!' said one of my friends.

'Yes,' agreed Mr Garrett. 'You're a good advert for the hotel.'

Of course, my name wasn't in the credits, but the hotel was and we got a lot of publicity after that as it was the most popular episode, watched by many millions! It resulted in a lot of additional guests, who had seen the hotel on *Crossroads*, thought it looked fabulous and wanted to come and experience it for themselves. What these guests loved best of all was getting us to regale them with stories of the day *Crossroads* came to the Chateau!

I'd been working at Chateau Impney for about three years and life was great for me now. I had a circle of good friends and I was going along quite happily when one day I was headhunted.

What happened was that Stephen Joynes, co-owner with Mr Jackson of this hotel, was going to sell it. 'But don't worry,' he told Mr Garrett and me, 'because I've bought somewhere else. It's an absolute wreck of a place, but I've got big ideas for it – I'm turning it into a luxury hotel.'

I had absolutely no doubt that he would do as he said and create another triumph of a hotel, but I had an inkling of what he was about to propose and this new place was in Walsall, a place I'd never been to. Before I could think any more, he looked straight at me and came out with it: 'Mr Garratt has already agreed to come and take on the role of general manager and I would very much like you, Richard, to come with him. I know that is what he wants, too, if you're willing?'

I turned to look at my boss, who nodded and smiled.

'We make a good team, Richard. You have become my right-hand man here and I'd really love you to come on board with us at the new place. I know you have many good friends here, but I would hope you can still keep in touch with them and make new friends too. What do you think?' he asked.

'It will be a good challenge for you, and a promotion,' added Stephen Joynes. 'We'll keep paying you in the interim, if there's a break between the two jobs.'

They both looked at me.

'Can I have some time to think about it?' I asked. 'It's a big decision, so I want to be sure – either way.'

They both agreed and said they didn't want to rush me, so they'd give me a few days to decide and let them know.

The rest of that day, I kept turning it over in my mind. I asked a couple of my friends what they thought.

'It sounds like an interesting opportunity,' said one.

'It's another step up for you,' added another.

'You're both right,' I said. 'But do I need a change right now? I'm happier here than I've ever been, so why would I want to move on?'

'That's true, but if the Chateau Impney is sold, it's quite likely to change a lot and the new owners might want to get rid of us and put their own staff in.'

'Oh! I hadn't thought of that,' I said, suddenly realising I should take that into account. 'But what about all of you, if you lose your jobs?'

'We'll find other jobs, and we can all stay friends, wherever we have to go. Hopefully, it won't be too far for us to get together every now and then.'

That conversation made my mind up for me and so I told Mr Garrett in the morning that I had decided to come with him – 'And please could you pass that on to Mr Joynes?'

'Yes, of course. I'm so glad, Richard. You're a good man and a hard worker – I don't think you realise just how far you've come since that day when I interviewed you. I value your support and I'm glad we will continue to work together as a team on this new project.'

He shook my hand and I left his office on a high.

If only I could tell Pearl without Arnold knowing. I hadn't been in touch with them or anyone they knew since the day I left. Reluctantly, I realised it would have to stay that way, or I'd have Arnold coming after me and ruining everything. But I knew she would have been thrilled for me and that helped a lot.

True to his word, Stephen Joynes, the owner of the wreck in Walsall, renovated, converted and extended it all, and transformed it into a beautiful, luxurious hotel. The time came to leave Chateau Impney and it was a sad goodbye to all my friends and colleagues but I was also excited to be working on building up this new venture, the Baron's Court Hotel. I remembered Stephen Joynes telling me his own rags-to-riches story: he had started off as a drapery salesman in Walsall and now owned an exclusive hotel worth a fortune! I respected him greatly for making so much of his life.

When Mr Garratt and I arrived to take over, it was indeed beautiful – a very glam place. We both enjoyed appointing staff and melding them into a team, just as we'd done at the Chateau. For a while I kept up with my old friends and met up with them a couple of times, but we all worked long hours. That and the distance between us made it difficult and a lot of them moved on and lost touch. However, I made a lot of new friends and soon had another close group around me. As before, I stayed in this job for about three years. It was more than a job really. I loved building the new business up and bringing in a new clientele, so the time went quickly and we continued to be a successful team.

I was in my early twenties now and the clue was in 'more than a job'. Hotel work is long hours and utter commitment. Yes, I socialised within the hotel, but I could rarely get out and meet new people, go out for dinner or a party, or as I would have liked, so I made another decision.

I secured a new job and gave in my notice at the Baron's Court. I explained to Mr Garratt and I think he understood. He certainly gave me a wonderful reference and a good send-off.

I used a small part of my savings to find a lovely flat for myself and I started my new job in a Birmingham plant rental company, supplying flowers and plants to retail outlets all over the country. They trained me and just as I was starting, the American company McDonald's was expanding in Britain and they gave us a huge order to supply all their restaurants with plants. A huge coup for me, it gave me some valuable experience too.

After that I started my own businesses and built them up. One was buying and selling houses, linked to a building company, which gave me the much-longed-for opportunity to draw house plans and design new extensions, which I loved. So, in a way, I had come full circle.

If only I could have told Pearl, perhaps over tea and biscuits in her kitchen, but not if Arnold was there. I'd grown up and moved on since those lonely, fearful years; I'd changed from the enforced loner I was to the outgoing, confident man I had become. My only regret was leaving Pearl behind, but I sincerely hoped and believed that she would be having an easier life without my presence to cause a rift between them.

I enjoyed a good social life and built up another group of close friends, who have now become a family to me. This was a happy, carefree period of my life and so it continued. However, things don't always turn out as expected, do they? There was always a nagging question at the back of my mind, but it would take me another 20 years before I began to unravel the answer.

1986–2019:
THE TRUTH

Child Found Under Bridge

Birmingham Police Seek Information

A newly-born male child wrapped in newspaper was found under the bridge on the canal side in Gas Street, off Broad Street, Birmingham, at 9.15 last night.

The child was taken to the Accident Hospital, where medical opinion was given that it had been born about two hours previously. Shortly afterwards the baby was transferred to Dudley Road Hospital and is expected to live.

Birmingham police appealed early to-day for information to be given to the superintendent at Thornhill Road Police Station or any other police station.

n of atomic have now rance from o far as the ivilian pur-

or the next luction and re 9]

ick to 75

n Old h'

on his old-Mr. William enue. Alvas-resign the ton branch Association ent, he has or a pension has had to ort himself

as awarded World War.

axle-box from the smashed guard's van was hurled into a field nearly 100 yards away.

Anou

Socialis A

By Our

The Opp its second c directed t Governmen television. in the Hou day and t issued.

The Scu alarm at tl Television requests th forward le repeal the A be subject t ment.

The ba complaint Independen its choice o had appoin which are Party as ha

CHAPTER 23

Opening Pandora's Box

In 1986, 32 years after I was born, I wanted to apply for a passport, but needed a birth certificate. I mentioned this when I was talking with Malcolm. He had worked for me in my business and gradually become such a great friend that we had decided to share a house.

'I don't even know who my birth parents were, or anything about their lives,' I told him.

'Well, maybe it's time to find out the answers,' he said. 'Your birth certificate will tell you their names and a bit about them. It should be easy to find out – you just have to go to the register office for the area where you were born to get your birth certificate.'

'But I don't know where I was born.'

'Well, you could start with Birmingham Register Office – I'll come with you, if you like. Then we'll have something to begin your family tree with.'

So that's how my quest began.

We arrived at the Register Office the next morning and a woman explained about the births, marriages and deaths records – 'It's all been put on microfiche now, at the library.'

So, off we went to the library and a very helpful librarian found us the correct reel and showed us how to use it, so we searched 17 November 1954 – my date of birth – but immediately came across a hitch: the entry had been removed and only the word 'adopted' remained. Well, I knew I'd been adopted, but I needed my original birth certificate as well.

'I'm afraid we will have to do manual searches and send your original certificate by post,' said the librarian. 'You should receive it within eight days.'

By the seventh day, I was on tenterhooks. The eighth day came and went. It was three weeks before the envelope finally dropped through our letterbox.

'Here you are,' said Malcolm. 'It's for you, from the Register Office.'

He sat down with me while I opened the envelope and slipped out the crisp sheet of folded paper. I opened it out and read it quickly.

'So, at last I know my mother's name,' I said. 'Lucy Cunningham.'

I repeated it twice, trying to imagine what she might look like. It seemed surreal, after all these years of not knowing, to see it there in plain black and white: Lucy Cunningham.

Then I looked across at the next column: 'Why is the father column blank?'

'It's not quite blank,' Malcolm pointed out. 'It's got a line through it, so that's deliberate. I think it means that the father was not known, or they weren't married.'

'Oh,' I said, letting out a long breath. I felt like I'd just had a punch in my chest. 'So, Arnold *was* right,' I muttered, 'I am a bastard.' It felt like an awful thing to say. It was a big shock. 'He must have known.'

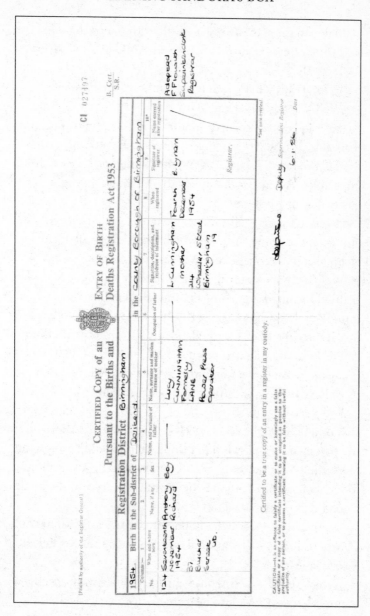

Malcolm came to my rescue by diverting my attention.

'I didn't know your first name was Anthony!'

'It isn't!'

'Look, that's what it says here: Anthony Richard.'

'Well, nobody's ever called me that!'

'And look at your birth mother's address,' said Malcolm. 'Isn't that near where you used to live when you were a child?'

'That's crazy!' I said. 'That's only a mile or so away from Greystoke Avenue, where I started school. I might have passed her in the street!'

I couldn't take it all in: I was fixated on that one column and I kept running those words through my head again and again, like a microfiche reel: *Not married. Bastard.*

We hardly spoke for the rest of the day – I think Malcolm realised I wanted some time to think and take in what we had found out. It wasn't much, really, but it came as a bad blow to me: Arnold had been right about my birth mother, but how could he have known anything about my birth father, when his name wasn't given on either of the records, so surely he must have been wrong about him being a criminal?

It was another eight years (1994) before I felt up to revisiting my past again. In fact, I didn't think there would be anything else to find, but Malcolm had been talking to his sister-in-law, Toni, about it. She had done her family history and she made a good suggestion, so he ran it by me.

'Toni said they have the phone directories at Birmingham Central Library, so if you want, we could look up Arnold and Pearl Gallear.'

'What for?' I asked with a shrug. 'I don't want to phone them, I don't ever want to hear that sadist's voice again!'

'No, I know. But it's not for their phone number, it would give us their current address, so maybe we could write to them and ask them to send us your adoption papers.'

'I couldn't write to them,' I said abruptly.

'No, I know. But maybe I could write and pretend I'm acting officially on your behalf and ask them if they have any of your documents. What do you think?'

'Well, you can go and look if you like,' I agreed, reluctantly. 'I don't suppose you'll find them.'

Part of me was hoping he wouldn't. However, after checking out local phone books without any luck, he was advised by one of the librarians that he might have more luck checking the electoral registers, so he started on that task. It took him several visits to the library, but his dogged determination on my behalf eventually came up with their details.

He came home triumphantly. 'I've found them!' he shouted down the hall. 'They moved to a little village about 50 miles away, that's why it took so long. It looks like they're both in some kind of retirement or care home.'

'Well, that's a surprise!' I said. 'Well done for finding them, now you can write that letter.'

So that's what Malcolm did. We composed the letter together and he went straight out to post it before I could change my mind. I didn't suppose anything would come of it – I really thought that as soon as he saw my name, Arnold would have screwed the letter up and thrown it into the fire or the dustbin. However, several days later, the postman knocked on our door with a big brown envelope. I took the package into the lounge and turned it over so that I didn't have to keep seeing Arnold's handwriting. It was addressed to Malcolm anyway, so he could open it later. I was in two minds as to whether I wanted to see its contents.

Finally, Malcolm came home and opened it to find a brief covering letter, asking that Arnold and Pearl's address must be kept confidential and not divulged to me – referring to me only as 'the above named'.

Once I'd got over that shock and learning that he and Pearl had found it 'very upsetting' to receive Malcolm's letter, we began to delve into the handful of documents Arnold had sent. There was a summary of my inoculations and illnesses from Field House, together with some brief notes made by the welfare officer Mr Watts, following his visits, all saying how happy I was in my foster home! If only he'd actually asked me …

The next document was a photocopy from the Birmingham Children's Department – a request addressed to the Matron of Field House Nursery, asking for assistance in tracing my birth mother, giving her last known address in South Yardley, where she no longer lived. Judging by the date of the letter, I was still at Field House then – not yet three years old. I do know I never had any visits while I was there, so the Matron probably didn't have that information.

The following piece of paper I picked up showed my birth mother's signed permission for the adoption, five years later, so the authorities must have found her eventually.

There were a handful of other documents relating to my adoption in 1963. Also included among the papers was a letter from a doctor at Dudley Road Hospital, signing me off as healthy, just 12 days after my birth (see page 8)! It was only as I set it aside that I wondered why on earth I was still in a hospital 12 days after my birth. Maybe I would find out one day.

'Well, that didn't tell you much!' said Malcolm.

'Not much at all,' I agreed, putting all the paperwork aside while he made me a much-needed cup of tea.

'I should think you'll be glad of a biscuit too!' He smiled as he handed me the packet.

'Yes, please!'

Malcolm knew me well.

Another 15 years went by. Then, in 2009, aged 55, I finally felt ready to try and find out more about my origins – but where to start?

I was sitting with Malcolm, his sister-in-law Toni and Craig, a journalist friend, listening to Toni telling us the latest snippets of interesting information she had found on the *Ancestry* website to add to her family tree. Then she turned to me.

'What about you, Richard? Have you done any more research into your family?'

'No, I haven't – I wouldn't know where to start,' I said.

'Well, there is so much online now. *Ancestry* is a brilliant website to begin with.'

'But I don't even know what I'd be looking for!'

'I've got an idea,' interrupted Malcolm. 'Do you remember we were going to find out whether Birmingham Children's Services might have all your early records from Field House? Why don't we start with them?'

'Yes, good idea,' said Craig. 'That could be just a phone call.'

Far from being that simple, so began a long to-ing and fro-ing of phone calls and getting nowhere – all very trying. As one of the Children's Services staff put it: 'We don't deal with that sort of query any more, I'm afraid we can't help

you.' I was just about to put the phone down in disappointment when she added: 'But you could try the After Adoption
charity, here's their number.'

'Oh, thank you very much, I'll give them a ring,' I said, my
faith in human nature restored.

By this time, it was a little late in the day, so Malcolm
helped me find the charity's website and I read through what
they did – I was quite excited! The following morning, first
thing, I called them and a lovely lady answered the phone. I
explained the main points that I knew of my childhood and
told her that the Children's Department couldn't help me, but
possibly their charity could.

'Yes,' she agreed. 'I think you've come to the right place.'

'Oh, good! Can I arrange to come and see you about how
to access my records?'

'Yes, we should be able to gather some documents for you,
but before we can show them to you, we always arrange a
counselling appointment first.'

'Why?' I was quite surprised. 'I would definitely have
benefited from counselling or therapy earlier in my life, but
not now.'

'Yes, I understand your reaction, because that's what most
people feel. But some of the information we hold on adopted
individuals can be distressing to them. Such information can
seem very stark on a document, in black and white. I'm not
saying there will be anything bad in your records, but it's just
possible there might be something you didn't know, that
might upset you, so it's always best to be prepared. We cannot
take the risk of sharing your records with you until we make
sure you are ready to go ahead.'

'I see.'

I hadn't thought of this, but I was willing to have the coun-selling as I was sure there couldn't be anything else to upset me. After all, I already knew that Arnold was right when he used to call me a bastard – what could be worse than that?

'When can you fit me in for an appointment?'

She gave me a date and time.

The counsellor introduced himself and explained the purpose of our meeting. He seemed very calm and had a soothing voice. It sounded quite sensible, though I still didn't think I really needed counselling. He started by asking me some questions.

'How would you describe your attitude towards finding out whatever facts we have?'

'Well, I've been thinking about it for a long time and didn't do anything because I was unsure. But now that I'm older and had the chance to digest one shock already, I feel more positive now about seeing my own paperwork. For most of my life, I've felt the lack of identity that happens when you don't know anything about your origins. I wasn't happy in my adoptive home and escaped as soon as I could. I had a terrible start at being independent, but soon turned things round and made a success of my life – well, most of it – but the one thing I've never had is the identity and security that only a mother's love can give.'

'What about your adoptive mother?'

'Well, she was a lovely person, very gentle and kind. She always tried to stand my corner, but her husband was a monstrous brute, who abused me almost daily and completely controlled his wife. She was an old-fashioned wife, who thought that was her lot, but she did her best and I was always very fond of her. I knew she liked me, but I never realised, until years later, that she did love me and I loved her. I always missed her and felt bad about leaving her behind without any contact, but there was no alternative.'

'Yes, that must have been very difficult for you.' He paused. 'I haven't seen your file, so I don't have any idea what's in it, but my role is to ascertain whether you feel ready for anything that you may find out. Do you really want to know the truth, whatever that is?'

For only a moment or two I hesitated.

'Yes, I really do want to know and I'd rather know the worst than not know at all.' I paused. 'I'm sorry I hesitated to answer, but I wanted to make sure for myself first.'

'I'm glad you said that,' he smiled. 'If you had answered without really thinking about it, your answer would not have been so believable, either to me or to you.'

'Yes, I see.'

'Now, because of the nature of this type of meeting, can you tell me what support you would have? Any family or good friends who could come with you? And someone to talk to afterwards?'

'Well, I'd prefer to be on my own in the meeting, but I'm sure I could have a close friend with me, if you think I should.'

'Yes, I do – you might be glad of it. And afterwards?'

'I share a house with a very good friend and he is very supportive.'

'Good.' He paused. 'Do you have any questions, Richard?'

'No, I don't think so.'

'Well, I have just one last question now: are you sure you want to go ahead with seeing all your notes, whatever they say about you?'

Again, I hesitated for a few seconds.

'Well, I've waited a very long time to find out the truth, so I do feel ready to go ahead with it now.'

'In that case, I will ask my colleague to arrange an appointment with you over the phone within two or three days.'

'Thank you,' I said as we shook hands.

'Good luck with everything,' he said with a smile. 'I hope it all goes well for you in the future.'

The day came and I felt as ready as I'd ever be, but naturally apprehensive. I wasn't sure whether the not knowing or the knowing would be worse. A lovely lady social worker met me and introduced herself to Malcolm and me.

'I'm Jenny. Are you coming in with Richard?' she asked him.

'No,' he replied, sitting down again. 'I've just come in case Richard wants some support, but I think he'd rather go in alone.'

They both looked at me.

'Yes, that's right,' I said.

She showed me the way into a small but light meeting room. We sat down across a table from each other and she pulled a folder towards her.

'I gather you've had your counselling session?' she said. 'How did you feel about your discussion? Was there anything you felt unsure about?'

'No. I understand that this can be a sensitive and sometimes difficult situation,' I replied, 'but I've thought about it a lot and I'm happy to go ahead.'

'Good! Well, I was going to ask that question, but you have answered it for me.' She paused. 'I have your adoption file here and the first thing I have to say is that record-keeping was not as good as we would have liked when you were a child. There is some information here for you, probably quite a few things you didn't know, but there may be some gaps where documents are either lost or perhaps were never completed in the first place. Are you ready?'

'Yes.'

'Before I open the file,' she said, pushing a box of tissues across the table towards me (I thought this was odd at the time, but presumed they did it for everybody), 'what I'm going to show you first is a newspaper cutting, which is about you. I'd like you to read it.'

She slowly slid a section of a front page towards me.

This was not what I was expecting. I read the headline:

'BABY LEFT ON CANAL BANK'

'What is this about?' I asked in surprise, thinking she'd picked up the wrong thing.

'It's about you,' she repeated.

'*Me?*'

'Yes, Richard – you were that baby.'

'How do you know?'

'There is more about it in your file, but read that first. It will give you the main facts.'

Already in shock, I read the first paragraph in bold print: it was about a baby being found by a canal one freezing night.

'I can't believe this,' I said, horrified. 'Are you sure it's me?'

'Yes, your notes refer to it, so we are sure it was you. It's a very unusual situation, but we know it was you.'

Baby Left on Canal Bank

MOTHER "AFRAID OF LOSING LODGINGS"

The finding of a newly-born child on the canal side near Gas Street on a foggy night last month led to the appearance of the mother at Birmingham Magistrates' Court today.

Mrs. Lucy Cunningham (aged 30), lodging in Wheeler Street Lozells, was put on probation for two years after she had pleaded guilty to abandoning the child in a manner likely to cause it unnecessary suffering or injury.

She was told by the Stipendiary (Mr. J. F. Milward) that he hoped she realised the gravity of her offence. She might have faced a charge of infanticide, for what she did could have resulted in the child's death.

He advised her that if she again got into difficulties she should be frank with the probation officer, who would help her.

Mr. —— Ritchie, for Mrs. Cunningham, said fear that she would be turned out of her lodgings, plus the fact that the child was born prematurely, caused her to act in an unnatural manner.

Mr. M. P. Pugh, prosecuting, said that just after 9 p.m. on November 17 a postman named Lester, on his way home from work, heard a baby crying. Going down a passage which led from Gas Street to the canal side, he saw a white bundle on the opposite bank and informed the police.

Police-constable Watson found the child wrapped in two evening newspapers bearing that day's date, and a white blanket lying in a small recess near a bridge and close to the water's edge. The baby was taken to the Accident Hospital, where a doctor formed the opinion it was about two hours old. There were no injuries, but exposure had endangered its life, and it was not likely the child would have lived much longer but for the keen observation of Mr. Lester.

The weather at the time was very bad.

Born Suddenly

On the following afternoon the police saw Mrs. Cunningham, who said it was her child and she had left it on the canal bank because she was frightened of being turned out of her lodgings. She added that the baby was born suddenly after she had got home from work.

She wrapped the baby in newspapers and a blanket and walked about with it in her arms until she left it on the canal bank. She felt weak and panicky.

She was taken to hospital, where she remained several days, and the child was now in a Hagley nursery in charge of the children's officer.

Mr. Pugh added that Mrs. Cunningham told the police she was separated from her husband, by whom she had three children, and had had a girl by another man who was also the father of the baby. He helped to support the child.

Detective-constable Bagnall said it would appear that Mrs. Cunningham was likely to be told to leave her lodgings if another child came along.

Mr. Ritchie said it was a tragic case of a woman who left her husband when she became infatuated with another man. He did not live with her but helped her when he could and she had to work as a power press operator to keep herself.

She was devoted to both children and hardly knew what she was doing at the time.

Numb with shock, I tried to read on, but found myself unable to take it in. As I sat in that stuffy room with the sunlight streaming in, my eyes filled with tears, blurring my vision. Within seconds I was sobbing uncontrollably into handfuls of tissues, trying in vain to regain control. The adoption lady sat still and gave me time, then quietly slipped out and fetched Malcolm, who came and put his arm round me, giving me a bit of his strength.

Finally, I was able to compose myself outwardly. The tears dried up a little and I did my best to read the rest of the long piece about my birth mother Lucy Cunningham's trial and conviction for abandoning me that November night. I read the details of the case and extracts of the witness statements from the postman who found me and the policeman who took me to the hospital. There was more about Lucy herself and then about how close to death I had been. She might have been convicted for infanticide, said the judge. Finally, there was a mention of my birth father without his name, saying Lucy had abandoned her three earlier children and husband because she was infatuated by my birth father and had one previous child by him.

My illusions over all those years were shattered. I had always believed she must have been very young, but the newspaper gave her age as 36. I had thought she might have given me away to be looked after because perhaps her family disapproved – I suppose I had put her on a pedestal and now I read that she was anything but an innocent victim.

One thought came into my head: today was my birthday. What kind of a birthday present was this? I looked across at the adoption file and wondered what other awful secrets might lie within.

'Can I see the rest now?' I asked.

'Are you sure?'

'Yes, I'm here now and I need to know.'

'You will be able to sign for your file and take it all away with you today, if you wish, as long as I talk you through some of the main things. Then you can look through the details later.'

'Thank you, please go ahead.'

'Well,' she began, 'there are no more newspaper cuttings in your file, though I believe there were several papers that covered your story at the time, giving more details. However, here are your health records from Field House, which I'm sure you will want to look through at your leisure. Along with these records are some photos of you at various ages, taken by social workers and health visitors.'

She passed over to me a transparent wallet in which there were several photos of me that I had never seen before. Each one brought back a memory – running happily across the Field House Lawn, sitting in a Field House armchair clutching my toy cars, sitting at my desk at the infant school, watering the plants in Pearl's garden, one with neighbouring children and a couple of head shots at different ages. Until now I never knew what I looked like as a small child. For a moment, those photos put a smile on my face.

'Do you know whether my birth mother ever saw these photos of me?'

She hesitated, then said as gently as she could: 'We offered them to her, but she said she didn't want to see them.'

That news stunned me.

'She had carried me inside her for all those months, yet she didn't even have the curiosity to see what I looked like?'

'Yes, that may be the reason or perhaps she feared it would be painful to her to see your face.'

'Hmm, I hadn't thought of that. But it feels like another rejection to me.'

She nodded, but said nothing until I was ready.

'Please carry on.'

'Here is a form signed by the Children's Officer, giving details of your discharge after your abandonment and your treatment at Dudley Road Hospital. There are various other forms and letters here as well, mostly to do with your health in childhood, along with your adoption records. You can look at all that later,' she said, tucking it all back into the folder.

'But there is one other item I would like to take you through, as it covers everything else.' She picked up some

stapled sheets of paper and showed them to me. 'It's the summary of all your adoption records.'

She passed it to me and I put it down to read.

'You will see a section about you at the bottom of page one and how you were found by the canal, suffering from exposure.'

I read that short section, with some alarming details.

Another shock! The sentence that screamed out at me was that Lucy had actually given birth to me on the canal bank and left me there, wrapped in newspaper and a blanket – presumably the one she gave birth on. When I first read that sentence I could scarcely breathe, even more shocked than before: mortified, broken.

I suddenly felt intense shame. This terrible discovery robbed me of my self-esteem, slowly built up over the years since it had been systematically destroyed by Arnold. Now, one old document and all that terrible sense of inadequacy, inferiority and isolation that had lain dormant came back and overwhelmed me.

I made myself read on, taking in what I could. In the 'mother' section, a few more sketchy details were mentioned about Lucy, including a number of addresses, so she clearly moved around quite frequently. It also listed my three abandoned half-siblings from her first marriage. The report went on to summarise more details until right near the end, where it stated the awful fact, the killer blow that, after all, Arnold had been right: my birth father, Harold Wren, was in prison when I was born and didn't know of my existence.

My birth mother had never told him.

I couldn't wait to leave now. My world had been turned upside down in so many ways and I couldn't cope with it – I needed to be alone and hide. I muttered a quick goodbye to the kind social worker, signed for the file and took it away from this stifling place, out into the fresh air. Malcolm drove me home in complete silence – I don't even remember the journey. After that, I buried myself in bed in a tumult of confusion, emotional overload and shock.

That night, sleep evaded me. I couldn't quell the turmoil in my brain. My father had been in prison. My mother had borne me illegitimately and didn't want me, nor even my photos. She could have left me on the doorstep of a police station or a hospital, but no, she deliberately left me there in the cold and darkness, knowing I would almost certainly die.

We had all been brought up at a time where there was a stigma surrounding illegitimacy, not to mention prison.

Malcolm and my other close friends had always been there for me up to now, but wouldn't they shun me when they knew all this?

CHAPTER 24

Closing the Circle

In those first days following the meeting with After Adoption, betrayal was my overriding feeling: betrayal by my own mother. At that point I had no photos of her, so I wrote her name on a piece of paper and, with a large pair of scissors, I cut it up into myriad tiny pieces. That was what I thought of her; it made me feel better.

Malcolm, thank goodness, remained the great friend he had always been and, with my muted blessing, set off a new wave of research at the Birmingham City Library, where for weeks he trawled through their archives almost every day. Painstakingly searching the microfiches, he found various newspaper headlines and articles about me from the day after I was born and rescued, right through until Lucy's trial.

Next, he searched old newspapers for Harold Wren, my father, and found accounts of his trials. It seems he had been in prison on several occasions, spending many years at Her Majesty's Pleasure, for crimes such as large-scale fraud, theft and criminal deception. He was himself a notorious gang leader and was in league with the Kray twins.

Looking at old street maps, Malcolm used the addresses

'HE IS A LOVELY BOUNCING BOY'

New-born baby found wrapped in newspaper

A NEWLY-BORN baby boy, wrapped only in a newspaper, was found under a canal bridge in Gas Street, Birmingham, late last night.

The child had been born only two hours before. During that time he lay on the ground in temperatures of two degrees below freezing.

He was taken to the Accident Hospital in a "very frozen" condition. There he has revived and quickly recovered

she found that some money had been taken out.

Mother of Baby Found Under Bridge Traced

The mother of a newly-born boy who was found under a bridge on the canal side off Gas Street (Broad Street), Birmingham, on Wednesday, has been traced, Birmingham Police stated last night.

The child is in Dudley Road Hospital, where the latest report was: " He is as well as can be expected and there are no obvious signs of ill-effects."

political refugees," he said.

Canal-side Baby: Mother Traced

Birmingham police said today that the mother of the newly-born boy who was found under a bridge on the canal-side off Gas Street (Broad Street), on Wednesday, has now been traced.

The child, who is in Dudley Road Hospital, was today reported to be progressing satisfactorily. He is showing no signs of any ill effects.

given for both my birth parents and found they had lived just two doors away from each other, Lucy the mistress at one house and Harold the lover almost next door, with his long-time wife and five children of theirs. Harold's wife must have known what was going on. Malcolm also traced the other addresses she gave to the police and other officials, at least one of which was fictitious.

I had a lot of thinking time while Malcolm was doing the research. Gradually, with a lot of encouragement from him and other close friends, who all stuck by me, I came out of the depths of my depression and began to live again.

Chatting with them one day, one friend light-heartedly teased me by calling me 'Mr Chips'.

'Why Mr Chips?' I asked her.

'Because you were wrapped in newspaper!'

We all laughed and the nickname has stuck ever since.

After some further sleuthing, Malcolm and his sister-in-law Toni discovered that both my birth parents had died – my mother from an embolism, deep-vein thrombosis and heart disease in 1984 before I'd even started searching, and my father not long after. I had mixed emotions about both these pieces of news. I suppose I was disappointed not to have been able to meet them – I had momentary fantasies of taking my mother flowers and finding out that she was not so bad after all. But it wasn't to be and perhaps that was just as well. Would I have wanted to contact her, only for her to reject me all over again? As for my father, what little I knew about him hadn't endeared him to me. Yes, it was best this way.

Toni and Malcolm carried on with the research – I think it had become addictive for them by now – while I had an operation and recuperated at home. On *Ancestry.co.uk* they found eight half-siblings and three full-blood siblings. Toni now had enough information to draw up my family tree, for the first time. At last I actually had a blood family, an amazing step forward for me.

At this stage, I suddenly had cold feet. I think I feared contacting or meeting any of these people, who had probably had much happier childhoods than mine. What could I say to them? I asked Malcolm and Toni to stop the research right there.

'It's too late now,' said Malcolm, 'we've already found all these names. You can't put them back in the box and pretend they don't exist, you've got to carry on.'

He was right.

Through Toni, I was put in touch with the first blood relative she found. This was Tessa, one of Harold and Lucy's four children together, so in fact we were full siblings. We spoke on the phone and then met, which was a memorable day. When I first saw her walking into the bar, it was a strange feeling – every emotion I had ever known rolled into one. We chatted away with ease and she gave me the first photos I had ever seen of my birth mother and father, as well as my other full sister and brothers. Sadly, she decided not to keep in contact after that because she was upset to find out what our mother had done to me and didn't want to think badly of her. Perhaps that will change over time.

In 2016, I visited the Birmingham home of my half-sister, Sylvia Hudson, and her son, Anthony. Sylvia was the eldest child of my father and his wife Sarah. We got on straight away and became part of each other's lives through our regular contact.

The youngest of the three children from Lucy's marriage that she had abandoned was the next to meet up with me, but this time it was through the auspices of the media. My story had spread and I was interviewed for both BBC and ITV radio and TV programmes. While I was having a live ITV interview, a call was received by the TV crew: a woman called Patricia phoned in to say that she thought she was my half-sister! I knew nothing about her, although her name was on my family tree. The researchers looked into it and found it was true, so they arranged for us to have a reunion in the magnificent Castle Bromwich Hotel with the cameras there, filming us.

Nothing could have prepared me for the emotional roller coaster I was about to experience. It was amazing, that moment we met! I walked through the door and walked towards Patricia, her arms open wide as we embraced for the first time. Both of us just forgot about the cameras and felt an immediate bond. We chatted and got on as if we'd always known each other. There was a genuine connection between us and an outpouring of love that I will cherish for the rest of my life.

Unexpectedly, we shared so much as a result of our mother's abandonment of Patricia and her two older brothers, William (born 1939) and Brian (born 1944). Only a baby when Lucy walked out on them, Patricia alone was put into a children's home for 16 years and was always told that her mother was dead.

'It was a terrible shock when I heard as an adult that she was still alive, but in hospital and wanted to see me before she died,' she told me. She gave a deep sigh. 'I felt betrayed.'

'That's exactly how I felt when I found out about Lucy abandoning me by the canal,' I said.

This meeting with Patricia was a great success. We have so much empathy for each other, through having both been abandoned by Lucy, in different ways, and suffered for it the rest of our lives. These days we are close and have kept in constant contact ever since. We regularly text and meet up for meals with her daughter, Rachel.

* * *

I didn't meet any more of my siblings or half-siblings until, sadly, out of the blue I received an invitation to my half-sister Sylvia's funeral. As the eldest of my birth father Harold and his wife's children, Sylvia was nearly 20 years older than me. I had met her son Anthony, who remembered me and had sent the invitation to me himself.

When I read the invitation I was surprised to see the words 'By invitation only' in bold print. Over the years, I had attended several funerals, but none had been by invitation only, so it immediately put me on edge. But I loved Sylvia and wanted to go, for her sake as well as mine.

I expected to meet some other half-siblings from that side at the funeral, plus perhaps Teresa and my two other full siblings born to Harold and Lucy. I was apprehensive about meeting them, and how they would react to me, so I planned to stay in the background as much as possible, not wanting to cause any upset.

'Guests' were instructed to meet at Sylvia's house in Yard-ley. When I arrived, Anthony greeted me as a member of the family and suggested I sit and chat with others in the front room. I was a bit nervous, talking to total strangers, but that was fine. It was only when Anthony brought Sylvia's tall, slim sisters Rita and Brenda (my older half-sisters) over to meet me that things became uncomfortable. A stern-faced Rita grilled me, asking me who I was and why was I there and why had they never seen or even heard of me before. In fair-ness, it must have been an upsetting situation for them and they knew nothing of what had happened to me. However, gradually, we came to realise we had something important in common: none of us had a good word to say about Harold, their father and mine! Indeed, Brenda, the more friendly sister, told me the story about Sylvia having once stopped him and Lucy happily pushing a pram together past his family's house, flaunting their new baby (my older sister, Veronica), while ignoring his own wife and children, bereft of support.

'Sylvia never forgave him for that,' Rita told me in a loud voice.

The hurt obviously ran deep in this family and I found myself in the peculiar position of apologising for my mother Lucy's unforgivable behaviour. It was obvious from what they said that Lucy was totally infatuated with Harold, who lavishly splashed his illegally gained cash on her to the detriment of his wife and children. They were clearly responsible for a lot of conflict and mistrust.

Suddenly, there was a loud commotion in the front garden, during which two police cars arrived and five officers jumped out to try and gain control of the heated exchange of words and fists. Meanwhile, in the background stood a carriage carrying Sylvia's coffin, ready to be pulled by two white horses adorned with red plumes, waiting patiently in the road.

The words exchanged went along the lines of: 'I'll put a bullet through your head!' The fight, barely controlled by the police, continued loudly and increasingly violently in full view of all the family and friends inside.

I have to admit, I was terrified. As a member of the extended family I felt extremely vulnerable. I recalled the link Malcolm had discovered between Harold and the gangster Krays and sat quietly where I was, trying not to be noticed.

The angry tension inside the house increased and two of the police officers entered to take charge.

'You must all now proceed to the crematorium in convoy and under police escort.'

So that's what we did. This particular funeral procession must have looked quite a sight. I remember thinking I might have had a laugh about it with Sylvia afterwards!

On arrival at the crematorium, there was another police car parked up and everyone's invitations were stringently checked before the police escorted us in. I sat at the back so as not to impose on the immediate family. A piper then preceded Sylvia's coffin and the priest into the chapel. Two of the police officers stayed outside to guard the doors, which were closed and locked. The other officers were guarding exits inside the chapel, while surveying the troublemakers, who looked at each other every now and then, daggers drawn.

When the priest read the eulogy, I was amazed and quite moved to hear my name mentioned, saying how thrilled Sylvia was to meet me and how we'd kept in touch regularly ever since.

At the end we were led out by the piper. It was here in the garden that I stood again with Rita and Brenda, who introduced me to their brother, Dennis. I hoped they had all gained a good impression of me and that we might meet up again one day. After another brief chat, I decided to take my leave, so I said my goodbyes and was pleased that so many of them shook hands with me.

'It wasn't your fault,' said Rita, unexpectedly. 'You were probably best off out of it!'

At this I smiled – little did she know.

That evening, telling Malcolm all about my eventful day, we discussed whether there were any other aspects of my story that I might want us to research.

'Well …'

'I'll go and put the kettle on while you have a think,' said Malcolm. He came back with our tea and biscuits. 'Any ideas?'

'Let's give my family history a rest for now,' I said. 'But there are other people in my story that we haven't focused on at all so far.'

'Anyone in particular?'

'Yes, as Lucy's lawyer said at the trial, it was like a story out of Dickens – "both good and evil played its part".' I paused. 'You found out that the most evil one, Arnold, died in 2004, and then there were the good ones: Pearl died in 1998, six years before Arnold, Uncle Geoff and Auntie Betty in Hampshire have both died, and so have Uncle Jim and Auntie Ethel of the Sunday teas fame. It's too late to meet up with any of them again, but there is one person who stands out for me.' Again, I paused. 'Do you think it might be possible that the postman who found me could still be alive? Other than his witness statement at Lucy's trial, I know nothing else about him. Isn't he the most important person in my story?'

'Yes,' agreed Malcolm. 'There wouldn't be a story at all without him.'

'More than anything, I'd love to find him and thank him for saving my life that night by the canal – I just hope I haven't left it too late.'

'It probably depends on how old he was at the time. Did any of the newspaper cuttings we found give his age?'

'I don't think so, but we could get them all out tomorrow and have a look.'

So that's what we did. Spreading them across the table, we read them through between us.

'Look out for his first name too,' Malcolm suggested. 'We'd have the devil of a job tracking him down with only his surname.'

We studied the small print in silence.

'Here it is!' I leapt up with excitement and read aloud the relevant section: 'A Mr Joseph Lester of 145 Ledsham Street, Ladywood, a postman ...'

'That's brilliant,' grinned Malcolm. 'Not just his full name, but his address too!'

'I don't suppose he'll live there now, but it's a start,' I said.

'Yes. We don't have his age, but we can hope he might still be alive. What do you think?'

'Yes,' I agreed. 'We won't know if we don't try.'

By now, we had a subscription to *Ancestry.co.uk* at home, so Malcolm opened up his laptop while I tidied away the newspaper cuttings. It was surprising the number of Joseph Lesters who had lived in Birmingham, but we found him in the 1950 electoral register, which gave him two middle initials, so we were getting closer. We looked up Ledsham Street and found it was lined with back-to-back houses. I imagined his house and family to have resembled that of Auntie Ethel's and Uncle Jim's – a roaring fire and full of joy. We even went and took a photo of it.

Malcolm was a dab hand at all this research by now and found Joseph's entry in the Post Office Appointments Book, and before that, his World War II service record. Eventually we also discovered his birth, marriage and death dates, which sadly meant he had died.

'Oh, no!' Desperately disappointed, I sat back in my chair. 'I was so much hoping he was still alive – I would have loved to have met him and thanked him, but now it's too late.'

'I know, it's an awful shame.'

'How do you say thank you to someone you will never know or be able to meet?'

That was the dilemma I found myself in.

'That's true,' agreed Malcolm. 'But his wife might still be alive. He might have had children too.'

'Yes?'

'Well, maybe you could meet his descendants. I know it's not quite what you had in mind, but wouldn't that be worth doing?'

'Yes, definitely!'

We soon discovered that Joseph Lester's wife had also died, but they had three sons: Keith, David and John. We focused on Keith first, as he would have been about eight when I was born, so old enough to remember his father's good deed. Toni joined us in our search and helped us to find several Keith Lesters and their addresses, so we sent out letters to them all, to no avail.

Finally, Malcolm did a cross-check, which found me in Bartley Green at the front door of Joseph's son Keith and his wife, Martha. After confirming that this Keith's father was Postman Lester, they welcomed me in. Keith was shocked when I told him the full story.

'I never knew that!' he exclaimed. 'I'm flabbergasted. He never told any of us, I'm sure. But then he often helped people without telling a soul.'

'Do you have any photographs of your father?'

'No, I'm afraid not. But I could ask my brothers – John has all the family photos. I want to tell them both about Dad's good deed anyway. They'll be as amazed as I am to hear your story.'

'That would be great. In the meantime, could you tell me a bit more about your dad?'

I had a cup of coffee and a pleasant hour or so with them, by the end of which we had become firm friends. Keith was going to try and find a photo and we arranged to meet again soon.

'His memory is not as good as it was,' whispered Martha as I left. 'Maybe give him a ring to remind him?'

I did go back and see them once, but by this time Keith had difficulty concentrating for long, so I mostly talked with Martha.

With all the media interest going on, it was some time before I contacted them again. Their phone number didn't work, so I drove over to their house, where I found Martha quite upset.

'Keith's not here,' she said. 'He's in hospital with dementia and going downhill fast.'

'Shall I go and visit him?'

'He won't recognise you and he doesn't talk at all now.' She showed me in and made me a cup of tea. We sat down in her lounge and she told me about the day he was taken to hospital.

'I went in the ambulance with him,' she told me. 'That was the last time he made any sense. Of all things, he was telling the ambulance man about his father saving you as a baby, by the canal, so your story was the last conversation he had.'

I was touched by that and asked her how she was.

'Struggling,' she admitted.

'Do Keith's brothers know? Could they help you?'

'No, I haven't been able to get in touch with them yet.'

'Do you have Keith's mobile phone?'

'Yes,' she said. 'I always keep it charged in case of emergencies.'

She rifled around and found it on a window sill, but when I checked it, there were no numbers stored on it.

'Do you have an address book?' I asked, with my fingers crossed.

'We did have.'

She went off in search of that and returned with a battered red leather book, which I opened on the 'L' page and was relieved to find both the brothers' contact details. Bingo!

'I'll give them a ring, shall I?'

'Oh, could you? And tell them about Keith in hospital.'

'Yes, they might like to visit him. I expect they'd like to come and help you sort things out as well.'

'That would be marvellous.'

When I got home, I recalled Keith telling me that John had the family photos, so I phoned him first and told him all I knew about Keith and about Martha needing help.

'Thanks very much for telling me,' he said. 'I'll drive straight over there and see Martha. Are you a neighbour?'

'No,' I said, 'I'm a friend.' Then I told him about his dad rescuing me as a baby.

John was astounded. 'How wonderful, nobody ever told me about that!' he exclaimed. We talked a bit more and agreed to meet at one of the bars in Birmingham's Gas Street Canal Basin.

Somehow, as soon as he walked in, I knew it was John, tall, broad-shouldered, with a friendly smile. He brought along his wife Joan and a brown envelope containing a photo of his father. I carefully opened the envelope and drew out the photo – it felt so wonderful to be able to look at my hero's face at last. He had a kind, intelligent look about him, smartly dressed and in a hurry.

'He was a shop steward at the Post Office,' said John. 'And he was on his way to the Union's conference at Margate. I'll see if I can find any other pictures of him to send you. I think I have a portrait one of him, about the age he was when he rescued you.'

'Oh, that would be great!'

We talked and talked over our coffees. John was very friendly, interesting and humorous. Then, despite the steady rain, we had a photo taken together, arms round each other, and in the background was the very bridge under which his father had found me more than 60 years ago.

'I can't believe your own mother could be so cruel!' he exclaimed. 'To leave you there, so close to the edge, on such a freezing night, with rats as big as cats prowling in the dark. Thank goodness Dad found you in time!'

We strolled on along the footpath that Joseph trod that night.

I asked after Keith and Martha.

'Yes, thanks so much for letting me know. I went over to see Martha straight away. My other brother, David, visits her as well. He'd love to talk to you too.'

When it was time for them to go, John gave me a big hug and wished me well.

'I am so proud of my father for saving you,' he said. 'He was such a good man, very modest about the things he did. I suppose that's why he never told us. He belonged to a charity that did lots of good work for the needy, so I suppose it was ingrained in him. I'm sure he would have preferred to come home to our warm fireside on that cold night, but I'm so glad he took the trouble to investigate that newspaper parcel that turned out to be you!'

Sadly, Keith passed away soon after, but John and I remain firm friends.

That evening, I phoned David Lester and, as we chatted, I discovered he lived in Droitwich.

'Do you remember the Chateau Impney?' I asked.

'When it was the poshest hotel in the area? Yes, of course. In fact, I remember driving Dad past it to show him one day, in the 1970s.'

'How amazing! That was when I was working there.'

Apart from the night he found me, two hours old and nearly frozen to death, that drive past was the nearest I ever got to meeting my hero – if only I'd known.

These conversations hit me hard and I was filled with conflicting emotions. Suddenly I felt an overwhelming urge in summer 2018 to revisit one of the happiest places of my life: Field House. I had to breathe in those carefree memories one last time. Now a care home for the elderly, I hoped it hadn't changed too much. I found the number and rang straight away. The owner, Geoffrey Butcher, seemed really interested in my childhood memories and invited me to visit.

Driving through the same wrought-iron gates on the drive to Field House, I began a magical journey back into my past. I was relieved to see that the outside of this magnificent house looked exactly the same. On my guided tour around the house and grounds with Geoffrey, I was happy to find the refurbished kitchen and dining room where they had always been, a comfortable residents' lounge in what was once my dormitory, and the walled gardens still in place, with restoration under way in the Japanese garden and the lawns and trees looking just as I remembered them all those years ago.

I stood by my car, listening to the nostalgic sounds of rustling trees and birdsong, and admired for one last time the panoramic views to the distant hills of my memory.

On the drive home, I reflected on what I had made of my life since Field House. In the decade with Arnold and Pearl, I had suffered a lot and have had my ups and downs ever since. In particular, I had trust issues for many lonely years that robbed me of the confidence to form deep friendships or relationships and share my story with anyone. But I am proud that, whatever happened to me, I never copied the bad examples of others' past behaviour towards me.

I feel that I have laid my bad memories to rest in recent years and I believe I have turned into a warm, loving and caring person. I love my life now, with a circle of true friends who have become my chosen family.

While writing this book, there was one last thing I wanted to do. For many years I'd been angry with my birth mother, Lucy; not only because she abandoned me in that terrible way, but because she died quite young, before I could ask her the questions that had dogged my life. Now those questions would always remain. But perhaps there was something I could do to gain a sense of closure.

I didn't know where she was buried, so I rang my half-sister Patricia, who told me that, despite her own abandonment, she had attended Lucy's cremation at Perry Barr Crematorium in Birmingham, where her ashes were buried in the Garden of Remembrance. Now that I knew, I felt overwhelmed by a compulsion to visit the destination of Lucy's final journey.

It was a sunny day in late summer 2018 when Malcolm and I set out towards Perry Barr. I had asked him to drive me there as I knew I would feel emotional. We turned in through the black iron gates right on time and pulled up outside the building to be met by a kindly member of staff.

'I'd like to show you the Book of Remembrance first,' she said, leading the way to where the book had been specially opened at the right page for us.

Malcolm stood back to give me time and peace to look alone at Lucy's entry in the book. To one side was painted a red rose and alongside it four lines of verse and some names that I recognised from our research as her other children – but my name was missing. It felt like another blow, as if I had been purged from her existence.

Through an archway, we walked to some beautifully tended gardens with lawns that have been invisibly partitioned into a grid of burial plots. Our friendly escort took us to the exact place on the lawn under which Lucy's ashes were interred. Here, for my benefit, the staff had placed a decorative marker, giving her name and dates.

I had brought a single-stem white rose with me and I knelt and gently placed it on the spot. She had never wanted to see my photo, but maybe she would now. After attaching one to the marker, I stood up again and looked steadily for several seconds, maybe a whole minute, at the rose, deep in thought. Perhaps I should have wept, but I had shed so many tears down the years, I had none left for Lucy.

Silently, I spoke to her:

'I'm sorry we never met while you were alive. You made your life choices and they didn't include me. But I'm here today to close the circle from where our lives were briefly conjoined. What you did caused a great deal of hurt to me throughout my life, and perhaps it affected you as well. You bore seven children altogether, but there were only six at your funeral – one child was missing.

'My name is Richard. I am the Forgotten Child.'

Acknowledgements

A big thank you to all the following people, who have helped towards this book:

Malcolm Bagley for his unwavering support and his meticulous research.

Toni Downing, for her research expertise and advice.

Craig Stevens, for his help with my research.

Keith Lester, for information about his father, who saved me.

John Lester, for photos of his father and further information.

David Lester, for information about his father.

The management and staff at Field House, Clent, for allowing me to visit.

Ray Bryant for his help and permission to use his photo of the old canal bridge.

The Birmingham Register Office.

The Birmingham Genealogical Research Centre and Library.

The Birmingham After Adoption charity.

Newly discovered half-sisters Sylvia, Patricia and Tessa for photos and information.

Clare Hulton, my literary agent.

Jacquie Buttriss, my ghostwriter and friend.

Finally, a big thank you to my publisher, Vicky Eribo at HarperCollins, for giving me the opportunity to share my story in *The Forgotten Child*.

Members of the press and media, who have helped me along the way:

Josh Layton, *Birmingham Mail* journalist
Georgey Spanswick, BBC Radio
Caroline Martin, BBC Radio
Brett Birks, producer, BBC
Giles Latcham, senior BBC broadcast journalist
Charlotte Cross, ITV News reporter
John Winston, head of ITV drama studios
Kim Willis, *Phoenix* features journalist.

Others:
There have been so many wonderful people who have given me hope and helped me to keep going through my darkest days. I am eternally grateful for their support and friendship.